Perfecting a Piece of the World

Perfecting a Piece of the World

Arthur Imperatore and the
Blue-Collar Aristocrats
of A-P-A

DAVID ROUNDS

 Addison-Wesley Publishing Company

Reading, Massachusetts • Menlo Park, California • New York
Don Mills, Ontario • Wokingham, England • Amsterdam
Bonn • Sydney • Singapore • Tokyo • Madrid • San Juan
Paris • Seoul • Milan • Mexico City • Taipei

Red Sovine's song, "Eighteen Wheels," on page 119, is from the album, The Best of Red Sovine, released on Starday Records, Power Play Music, 1975.

Many of the designations used by manufacturers and sellers to distinguish their products are claimed as trademarks. Where those designations appear in this book and Addison-Wesley was aware of a trademark claim, the designations have been printed in initial capital letters (i.e., Kleenex).

Library of Congress Cataloging-in-Publication Data

Rounds, David, 1942–
    Perfecting a piece of the world : Arthur Imperatore and the
  blue-collar aristocrats of A-P-A / David Rounds.
      p. cm.
  Includes bibliographical references.
  ISBN 0-201-56794-6
  1. Imperatore, Arthur. 2. A-P-A Transport
Corp. 3. Trucking— United States. I. Title.
  HE5623.Z7A187 1993
  388.3'24'06573—dc20   93-18731
                                          CIP

Jacket design by Jean Seal
Text design by Diane Levy
Set in 11-point Palatino by Maple-Vail Composition Services, Binghamton, New York

1 2 3 4 5 6 7 8 9-MA-9796959493
First printing, August 1993

To my friend Tony Riolo, who at his death in 1989 was executive director of the Santa Fe Opera, and who was also a friend of Arthur's, of Armand's, and of A-P-A, this book is dedicated, in affectionate memory.

Contents

1. Arthur's Dissent

Arthur Imperatore, centimillionaire, American entrepreneur, creator of A-P-A Transport Corp. of North Bergen, New Jersey, which for years has been one of the best-run and most profitable trucking companies in the United States, opens the drawer of his Renaissance writing table.

"Read this," he tells me. He hands two stapled pages across the green blotter and the mother-of-pearl inlay. To my left, through a pair of sliding glass doors, a roof-garden fountain is showering a stone maiden in the heavy, sweet, slightly putrescent heat of northeastern New Jersey in midsummer. Just behind Arthur, beyond another pair of glass doors, a narrow balcony overlooks his domain: forty paved acres of the Jersey Meadowlands, across which 300 trucks and tractor-trailers transship four and a half million pounds of freight every twenty-four hours. Arthur's 380,000-square-foot freight dock, one of the half-dozen largest in the country, clanks and rumbles just beneath us. Its vibrations are dampened by the Persian carpet on his office floor.

The photocopied pages Arthur has handed me are a letter written in 1979 by Edward Glynn, S.J., president of Saint Peter's College in Jersey City, thanking Arthur for a tour of the terminal and, indirectly, for A-P-A Transport Corp.'s gift to his college. 'Here is that quote,' Father Glynn wrote to Arthur, 'from the French Jesuit paleontologist Pierre Teilhard de Chardin, that I was prompted to recall by your comment about building and making better that small portion of the world that is around us.'

As I read, Arthur looks across the balcony down to the yard

below. At sixty-seven, his Roman profile is youthful beneath thinning white hair. The aggressive nose rides forth from long, soft, yielding cheeks—the kind of face the Chinese say is full of blessings. His gentle, weary brown eyes are drawn now by the roar outside of a bright yellow Mack tractor, which is shifting an empty trailer between two of the terminal's 192 loading platforms. Behind the tractor (called by truckers a switcher or yard-horse), the trailer is tipped backwards at a fifteen-degree angle for the switching, so that its dolly wheels in front, which are cranked up out of the way for the road, can instead be left dangling now like a kangaroo's forelegs. Arthur's eyes move to a street-sweeper swishing past the main entrance to the administration offices, just below his window. A few minutes earlier, as Arthur and I walked across the yard from his parking space, he had waved and called out to both the switcher and the sweeper. Behind their windshields, both drivers had honked, waved, and grinned. It's not every day that the terminal gets a visit from the chairman, now that he has turned over the running of the company to his stepson, Armand Pohan.

Being by nature, as he says, a take-charge guy, Arthur turns back to me and repossesses Father Glynn's letter. He reads the Teilhard de Chardin quote aloud.

> By his fidelity every man must build—starting with the most natural territory of his own self—a work, an opus, into which something enters from all the elements of the earth.

Arthur looks up and points out the window. "A work," he repeats. "An opus. The guy with the sweeping machine. 'Into which something enters from all the elements of the earth.' What the sweeper is doing is perfecting a piece of the world. He's making it cleaner. He's doing it with his machinery, y'know, with his body, with his mind, his eyes, his hands and so on, and the tool."

Arthur glances down at the letter and continues: " 'Into which something enters from all the elements of the earth. He makes his own soul throughout all his earthly days.' That's metaphysical," Arthur interrupts himself, "but I believe in that. I believe a human mind is of such complexity, such elasticity, that there is such a thing as a soul. *'And at the same time, he collaborates in another work, another opus, which infinitely transcends, while at the same time it narrowly determines, the perspective of his individual achievement: the completing of the world.'* "

Rather tenderly, Arthur places the letter back in his drawer. "So that's what I see in working people, like the sweeper outside, that they need security, but their security is not limited to physical survival. It's a spiritual survival. I've seen in people a quest for immortality—I don't know how to use the words. I mean this may sound like it's total bullshit, but it isn't: I truly believe what I learned early in the game, that men, working people, need to have a bigger purpose in life. They have to feel that they're not only being fed with worldly goods, with food, means to create shelter, all the rest of it—a house, a good car, and so on. They have to be fulfilled. This is where I believe this country lost." The loss he speaks of is the decline of American manufacturing culture.

Arthur lays his hands on the blotter. They're still heavy workingman's hands, though they emerge from the beige sleeves of a three-piece tailor-made suit. He has stated his faith in the honor of work and the nobility of working people a thousand times before, in harangues to the workers themselves on the freight-dock floor, in speeches at business school commencements, in negotiations across the table from the high brass of the International Brotherhood of Teamsters, and in lectures to senators and congressmen at committee hearings. As he speaks now, his conviction deepens the two vertical frown-lines that climb halfway up his forehead. But for the frown and a deep parenthesis around his loose-lipped mouth, his face is tanned and clear.

"In this country," he tells me, "we treat working people in a way like chattels. Most businesses do. They don't really value. They say they do, but they don't. To make a broad statement like that is not right either, but certainly in the big companies, I don't believe they ever, ever recognize that they have employees who have a stake, who live and breathe and eat and have sex and live lives that are potentially distinguished, if not heroic." He gestures with a nod of his head toward the windows and the stifling afternoon. "Take this very day. A man is on a production line in Metuchen, New Jersey, working for the Ford Motor Company at the Lincoln-Mercury plant. Is the plant air-conditioned? No, it's not. Is it hot? Some parts of it are hot as hell, some of them are just impossible in terms of a ninety-degree day and this kind of New York humidity. Now, people accept that as part of their role in life. They're working people. But I remember the old expression when we first started in the trucking business in 1947: 'A strong back and a weak mind.' Well, show me somebody who has a weak mind. I'm telling you that I have met almost nobody among our employees who has a weak mind, or if not a weak mind intellectually, a weak mind spiritually. They need more out of life than just to be a body."

I have to remind myself that this man is not a union leader still inspired by the old labor socialism, but the founder and owner of an extraordinarily successful middle-sized corporation. For thirty years, his A-P-A Transport Corp. has flourished at a level of productivity and profit that is legendary throughout the transportation industry. In the two decades before trucking deregulation in 1980, A-P-A was approximately one hundredth in size among trucking companies, and yet year after year earned over twenty cents on the dollar, more than any competitor, and far more than most. Trucking has always been a risky and precarious business. Now, twelve years after deregulation, as the most brutal shakeout in the history of any American industry continues unabated, A-P-A is much larger and still making money, though not as easily. With $140 million in annual revenues, it remains one of the five major regional trucklines left in the Northeast. It's the only large truckline still based entirely in the New York area, which has long been a truckers' nemesis, in part for its horrific traffic congestion, in part for the corruption in its transportation unions. Yet this is the man who says—when he's asked, as he often is, how his success might be translated into reforms of American industry in general—that the secret is to "call working people to their highest purpose" by pushing them hard and treating them right.

Arthur's ability to win hard work and loyalty in a notoriously hostile labor market has long baffled his competitors, who can't match A-P-A's productivity even when they're based in uncongested, nonunion states like Tennessee and Arkansas. Arthur Bunte, president of Trucking Management, Inc., a consortium that negotiates agreements with the Teamsters for most of the large unionized trucklines, told me when I called him to ask about A-P-A, "People in other trucking companies say what Arthur's done with productivity can't be done. What they mean is, they can't do it in their companies. The ironic thing is that Arthur and Armand [Arthur's stepson] have done it in New Jersey, which is even tougher yet. People think A-P-A must have some deal with the union. But there isn't any deal." On the contrary, in an industry where lax work practices and sweetheart deals have been commonplace, A-P-A stands out for long days, strict rules, high expectations, and swift discipline. "People say I was a slave-driver," Arthur says of his years as CEO before Armand took over. "Well, I was." As for the Mafia and its influence on the Teamsters, as well as on local government in New Jersey and on many of his now-defunct rival trucklines, Arthur says scornfully, "I've never given them a fucking dime." And everyone agrees that a boy-scout integrity, a nitpicking insistence on honesty, is a hallmark of his company.

When they scratch their heads about Arthur's success, nothing mystifies other truckers more than his grand gestures of display and largesse. It's not in the ordinary way of things for a middle-sized truckline to moor a 142-foot yacht on the Hudson River and to hang French Impressionist originals on the cabin walls. Customers and employees are squired upriver on it. Arthur's princely office in the North Bergen terminal nearly rivals the yacht: building and decorating it cost him over $200,000 in the mid-1970's. Its sixteen-foot, hand-carved conference table in gold leaf and green leather, its gilt, muraled, silk-draped walls, its marble fireplace between *trompe-l'oeil* mirrors that double the length of the long room, all designedly call to mind the libraries of Florentine palazzi.

But Arthur hasn't spent the envied profits only on himself. He likes best to show visitors the health club across the lane from the dock. The swimming pool, basketball court, tennis courts, weight room, kitchen, and lounge, free to all employees, have cost him over a million. There are other gestures besides buildings.

The company spends $200,000 a year on college scholarships for employees' children. A zealous equipment-maintenance program, by far exceeding federal standards and normal industry practice, not only reduces company expenses for breakdowns but eases the truckdrivers' fear on the road. In many trucklines, the drivers know perfectly well that the boss is too cheap to keep the trucks safe. The man who deplores the lack of air-conditioning in the Ford Metuchen plant was one of the first in his industry to have heaters installed on his freight docks, where the men suffer not so much from daytime heat as from winds sweeping through the open doors on winter nights. And there is the obsessive cleanliness of the place. Arthur has generaled a lifelong jihad against litter. He tells visitors that to allow a terminal to double as a junkyard, as many truck terminals and railyards do, makes a statement of contempt for the people who work there. One of the company's senior drivers, Ronnie Parham, told me Arthur scolded an executive visiting from another company for stamping out a cigarette on the asphalt of the North Bergen yard. "He made the guy pick it up right there in front of everybody."

"Really?" I asked Ronnie. "Did you see this yourself?"

"No, but it was all over the terminal inside of an hour."

Finally, one can hardly visit A-P-A for an hour without hearing about the truly eccentric million-dollar company outings— 1,800 employees, with spouses, flown to San Juan for the weekend, or fêted on a three-day cruise on the *QEII*. "I don't know if it would justify the expense to do that sort of thing," muses William Clifford, who, as president of St. Johnsbury Trucking Co., A-P-A's archrival, otherwise admires Arthur and A-P-A as "the forerunner and leader in establishing productivity standards and maintaining them very strongly."

Arthur's gestures toward redistribution of wealth, like a goldgiving Norse chieftain's, seem natural to him. He leans forward over his writing table and asks me now, "What makes a businessman? Is it greed, is it ego?" and he answers, "It's very complicated, y'know? There's greed, insecurity, all the rest . . . but I believe that to be a good businessman, you really have to be willing to give, give to the world, give to an industry, give to the working people, give to your customers." As for his employees, they know perfectly well how rich Arthur has become as a result of their joint labors—it would never occur to Arthur to hide it—but that does not stop them from regarding him with a varying mixture of ironic or indulgent affection, grudging or transparent gratitude, modest or devoted loyalty, and unanimous admiration. Most of his employees call him "Arthur." The entire company is on a first-name basis. Somehow, in the midst of a very clear hierarchy, a sense of social equality pervades human relationships at A-P-A from top to bottom. At this company, group solidarity has cooled the class war between management and labor, white collar and blue, which simmers or rages in almost every American workplace.

"What should Ford be doing at the Metuchen plant?" I ask Arthur now.

"I don't know," he says. "But it would start from the top." Arthur looks at his hands. "I'll tell you insights I got, David, on a trip west with Helen and Arthur Jr., maybe sixteen, seventeen, eighteen years ago. We had a motorhome." Like so many of his employees, Arthur explains best in terms of a story. "I remember going to the Gary Works—I forget whether it was Bethlehem Steel or U.S. Steel. It was then the newest steel mill in the country. The United States was losing market share in the world steel market, and the Japanese were coming up. We had a special tour arranged through the mill, since I'd just started negotiating my first labor agreement as part of the national negotiating committee, and I knew this guy who was very well-connected out there labor-wise. So we go all through this plant.

"Now, maybe this bespeaks my naiveté, but you see this massive works that dwarfs men, overwhelms people in terms of scale and magnitude. I go in and talk to a working man. I say to him, 'How do you make this steel?' I say, 'It's done by computer, right?' Because this was the latest technology. And he says, 'No. No. A man has to make the decision. *He* has to cook the steel. You need judgment, even with the computers.'

"Now, what does that tell you, all along the way? Of course, that's just one part of the process; but it's the very creation of the product. And if you've got someone in Pittsburgh or Bethlehem who doesn't give a damn for that character, for his talent

. . . now, it's interesting." Arthur is speaking slowly, guiding me with rhetorical questions, pointing at his meanings gently with the index and middle fingers of his right hand, in a pedagogical manner which, as a high school teacher, I recognize well. "It's interesting. Back then, the mid-seventies, we had rust on our trucks that caused rotting of the steel. It was not only rust. It was rotting. You could almost see it, within six months to a year to a year and a half, you had pieces of truck bodies rusting away." His voice rises. "Holes. *Big* holes. I had a big fight, y'know, with the Mack Truck company, about the steel they were using then. So you investigate it. And you wonder. Is the guy in the steel works cooking the steel right? Is he rewarded enough? Are his employers making use of the creative talents of all their people? Or is this another example of a company completely out of control with their working people, with no mutual respect, no concern about it, no loyalty, zero? I can't say, but look at the record. What does it tell me? The insight that I got at the steel works was that there was a *man*"—Arthur pounds his fist on the blotter—"who *counted*. And *this* is where we fail. I just read a story on Goodyear Tire. Do you know that in the city of Akron there are almost no tires being made now? Akron, Ohio. That was the tire manufacturing center of the world, twenty, twenty-five years ago. Why did they lose out? They lost out with their people. They lost the battle for the people's minds."

In a decade of hand-wringing over American industrial decline, much has been made of the contrast between the hierarchical structure of American corporations and the more horizontal structure of Japanese industry. In this country, the argument goes, management and labor are engaged in battle and have little knowledge and no understanding of each other. In Japan, by contrast, management and labor are bound by cultural homogeneity and organizational loyalties. Prompted by books about typical corporate cultures in both countries, and guided by the management consultants who write the books, American corporations have struggled recently to cut against the vertical grain. They have adopted such worker-management forums as quality circles and have even taken union representatives onto their boards. They have orchestrated visits to factory floors to suggest to the men in the three-piece suits what working in summer feels like without air-conditioning. Studying the Japanese model is valuable. But Arthur's A-P-A belongs to an entirely different and older tradition, not of reform, but rather of dissent. His precedents lie elsewhere than Japan—although he respects the Japanese model and will cite it in his speeches. But his historical forbears are instead the benevolent industrial patriarchies established in Great Britain and New England at the very beginning of the industrial revolution.

How an industrial corporation should be run, and for whose benefit, was not a foregone conclusion when factories with spinning machines, powered first by water and then by steam, began to populate British streamsides during the last quarter of the eighteenth century. At the time, the chief precedent for the structure of large, productive enterprises was the feudal hierarchy of the manor farm, in which the workers—tenant farmers and village artisans—had a considerable stake and considerable rights. The loss of their rights and their stake, and the degradation of their working and living conditions in the new industrial towns, concentrated enormous power and wealth in the hands of the new class of mill owners. Most members of the mill-owning class embraced their new superiority as their natural due, a reward for their risk and acumen. Their contempt for the poor who were making them rich was no less dismissive than that of their aristocratic contemporaries in France. But a few dissented. Mercantile splendor financed by six-year-olds who worked eighty hours a week among unshielded gears was not a splendor that fit comfortably into these few dissenting mill owners' concept of an honorable life. They took it upon themselves to approximate, in their factory towns, the stable and decent community of a well-run manor farm.

The most celebrated and most remarkable of these industrial moralists was Robert Owen. Born in 1771, a Welsh saddler's son, studious, magnetic, ambitious, and brilliant, Owen at nineteen was already the superintendent of a Manchester cotton-spinning mill. In 1800, at twenty-nine, he was the managing partner in the purchase of a much larger spinning mill in New Lanark, Scotland, a day's ride by coach from Glasgow. With the purchase, he and his partners inherited a workforce of 1,600 mill families and of 500 pauper children rented from nearby workhouses. During the next few years, Owen turned New Lanark into a model company town and his mill into a model factory. He paved the town streets, instituted regular garbage collection, installed public bath houses, and, further, required all inhabitants to bathe weekly. At the company store, a new industrial institution whose usual purpose was to cheat a captive clientele, he insisted that only decent goods be sold, and at cost. He forbade child labor below the age of ten, reduced the older children's workday from thirteen hours to ten and three quarters, and established schools, including the first infant schools—kindergartens—in Britain. He outlawed corporal punishment not only in the schools and at the mill, but in the workers' homes. By day on the mill floor, a corps of supervisors urged productivity; by night, watchmen patrolled the town against drunkenness. Throughout the American cotton embargo during the War of 1812, Owen carried all his idled workers at full pay. And for himself and his partners—here is the point—he made an enormous fortune.

In its mature years, Owen's mill was famous throughout Europe. A visitors' list kept between 1815 and 1825 mentions royalty, social reformers, society ladies, and industrialists, and it totals over twenty thousand names. All those muddy treks through the Scottish hills could not have been made merely because Owen was helping his workers. Other reformers were also trying to help the new industrial poor. Charity is inspiring, and is enjoined upon us by all the wise; but there is nothing new in it. The visitors came to New Lanark above all to verify for themselves the astonishing and clearly paradoxical report that Owen was helping his workers *and getting rich doing it*. Preposterously, Owen insisted that he was making money not despite his concern for his workers but because of it. He could easily have said, "The Judeo-Christian code is good business, provided the spirit is genuine"—except that he was a Deist. The saying is Arthur Imperatore's.

Some of Owen's visitors believed his assertion that industrial justice would make industries succeed. Among the convinced was a Bostonian, Francis Cabot Lowell, to whom New Lanark's principles seemed consonant with the new American ideal of individual dignity. To some extent, he followed Owen's precepts in the establishment of the Massachusetts mill town that bears his name. But most of Owen's visitors were skeptical. In fact, his own partners were sometimes his most vigorous opponents, especially when his worker-improvement projects required a major expense. To his protestation that workers' dignity was the foundation of their productivity, and that workers' productivity was the foundation of owners' profit, his partners replied that if less money were spent on charity, more would be retained as earnings. During the twenty-five years that he ran the New Lanark mill, Owen was forced to buy out his partners and replace them with new ones three successive times, in order to get his way. He finally sold out altogether and went to America.

His partners' skepticism belonged to their age, and it belongs to ours. The majority of corporate managers today still think it obvious that a penny spent on labor is a penny lost. Arthur's largesse is considered as eccentric and profitless as Owen's was. Modern industrial society continues to be guided by a philosophical map that was drawn in the first half-century of the industrial revolution. According to the map, the new social and moral order was to take one of two roads. One would lead to a renewed and barbarized feudalism, with industrial barons like Owen's competitors and slum-dwelling serfs like the pauper children Owen's predecessors rented from the workhouse. The other road would lead, through a sort of urbanized peasants' revolt, to the radical social leveling of communism. Both capitalists and communists agreed on the map. At one pole was exploitation of the many by the few, with each individual competing against his fellows for personal profit. At the other pole was an extreme collectivism, with all individualist striving submerged into the state. Both socialists and capitalists agreed with Owen's partners that profit and exploitation were necessarily joined. The answer for socialists was to abolish profit and property, and so put an end to exploitation, while laissez-faire capitalists countered with an individualism, equally extreme, that would justify exploitation. The mill owners' philosophical apologists were the Social Darwinists, who argued that social law should be based on natural law, and according to the natural law of evolution, the fittest should survive (by the fittest they meant those who managed to make the most money). Thus, the Social Darwinists opposed charity and factory reform, on the grounds that to feed and educate working-class children would be to unnaturally abet the survival of the unfit.

Faced with the divergence of two roads, and caught between their uneasy conscience and their devotion to property, middle-class reformers laid down a third road, meant to lead somewhere between the two poles. But they never held the map to be invalid. The majority of the British reformers and the American Progressives and New Dealers were not dissenters, but mitigators. They labored to control the excesses of exploitation, in order to preserve profit. With gradual and partial success, by moral restraint, governmental regulation, and a mild redistribution of wealth through taxation, the reformers sought to soften the effects of capitalist greed and to earn it the softer name of profit motive.

Today, with the abandonment of European communism, and the gradual merging of national economies into the global marketplace, the long-cherished philosophical map of industrialism can at last be recognized as obsolete, and a new map can be drawn. The 1980s witnessed a revival of old class battles, with labor militants in the socialist tradition marching in retreat, while privatizers and deregulators, who are the eventual successors to the Social Darwinists, pressed their momentary advantage over the reformers; but the 1990s have revealed these wars—like so many others—to be anachronisms. In a world economy, the old animosities are distractions. The new century will reward the pursuit of alternatives.

In the search for new patterns, it is helpful to bring to light not only the discoveries made by other cultures, such as Japan's, but also our own traditions of dissent. Robert Owen was not alone in his alternative, in his insistence on human dignity and the flourishing of working people as the surest source of profit.

During his lifetime, other dissenters labored independently of him, and his ideas continue to appear on the fringes and in pockets of industrial society among people who may never have heard of him. Certainly Arthur Imperatore developed his alternative on his own, through trial and error, in the heat of his effort to build a well-ordered company in the midst of a chaotic industry. He was not, at first, the determined idealist that Owen was, and in the beginning he sought to cut away the thickets of class struggle simply because they were interfering with the flow of freight. He found, as a mere practical matter, that men, when treated as men instead of chattels, worked better, and that increases in labor productivity outweighed increases in labor costs. The ideal of a corporation as a moral community, and the discovery, in Teilhard de Chardin, of his own insights into the spiritual nature of work, came later. It was only gradually that he realized that his success was really a moral success, because the foundation of his wealth—mutual support, strict honesty, and devotion to craft—was a moral foundation.

In one of our interviews during the summers of 1990 and 1991, Arthur explained his use of worker-performance standards with his characteristic wedding of the language of morality and the language of the balance sheet—a marriage, he believes, that should take place in the thinking of every corporate manager. Performance standards, he explained to me, are "an operational road map that you can use daily. You can tell who was on the payroll and what they were doing, whether or not they were necessary to have been put on the payroll, whether you're getting your money's worth. That's only one aspect, the economic aspect. I believe there's an emotional side to it. When people are accountable and they know they're being watched and they know that you know that, then they're not lost. They're not just part of a big group of people; and that builds morale. When people know that they're being structured and being directed, being looked to for high purpose, they bring it out of themselves willingly, without even knowing it. I'm a great believer that people don't know how smart they are. I believe that strongly. They don't know how versatile they are. To tap that is, I think, one of our company's great gifts."

I first knew Arthur some thirty years ago. He was the stepfather of a college friend, and later, also, a summer employer when I loaded freight at night at the North Bergen terminal. I did not recognize him then as a dissenter. I saw him, rather, as the embodiment of another, equally unusual type, one that everyone has heard of and that I was now meeting in the flesh: the flamboyant American entrepreneur. He was the self-taught immigrant's son who grew up poor, a tough-spoken guy who had started a trucking company with his four brothers, a multimillionaire with a street-schooled eloquence and a riveting gaze. Just as the lionizing books about entrepreneurs said worshipfully of their subjects, Arthur was self-dramatizing, brilliant, uninhibited, and shrewd, a magnetic presence that filled the room.

But my picture of Arthur was later altered by the painting in of a second figure: Armand Pohan, Arthur's stepson and my friend from college days. Armand was a lawyer and musician whose subtle intelligence and devotion to truth had always held my deep respect. Suddenly, at the age of thirty-two, he abandoned a legal career that was clearly headed toward the judicial bench, and he disappeared into his stepfather's trucking firm. I couldn't see why he had done it. He was ambitious, but for self-worth, not for money—which, at any rate, he would someday inherit. If not by birth, then by training and predilection, he belonged, I thought, with the reformers, not the capitalists. He was an excellent chessplayer, but it seemed to me that he had made the wrong move.

Then I myself became a dissenter: I joined a Buddhist monastery in California as a lay worker. I was drawn to a monastic community not only by religious vocation but by an intensifying distaste for that career of separate, individualist, money-driven striving which is the ordinary pattern of a modern life. I wanted to participate in a communal striving for goals that inspired me. During my years at the monastery, as a schoolteacher, publicist, editor of translations, and administrator, I began to recognize, beyond the particularities of the ancient lifestyle of the Buddhist monk, a commonality between my group and many others that were neither Buddhist nor even religious. America has always been a haven and a breeding ground for groups of people who have worked closely together, in accordance with clear rules, toward what seemed to them a higher common purpose. In the 1970s we called such groups "intentional communities." Granted, they were so diverse in style and intent—hippie communes and political cells, artistic ensembles and progressive schools, community-action groups and settlement houses new and old, recent monastic imports and such venerable religious fixtures as the Amish and the Trappists—that none of them could be expected to agree that all the others were respectable. But all shared a sense of living in accord with an alternative to the plan that most others in society accepted. Above all, we felt we were pulling back from the self-absorbed extreme of individualism that forgets the need for community. Margaret Thatcher later stated this extreme eloquently: "There is no such thing as society." For her and her fellow privatizers, there were only individuals and families. We disagreed. We wanted to define ourselves as individual humans, certainly, but to seek the definition through the opus of building a community. People on the outside said we were escapists; still, we believed ourselves to be serving society indirectly, by our embodiment of an alternative.

Eventually I left the monastery to return to an individual career in journalism and public-school teaching. I still live near the monastery and maintain ties as I continue to search for a sustainable balance between the demands of home and the demands of work, between loyalty to self and loyalty to community. After my move, I saw more of my friend Armand, and his own move to A-P-A began to make better sense to me. He too had adopted a community and had been seeking the same balance. The difference between our choices intrigued me. Obviously, A-P-A was secular, designed for the delivery of a service in return for wages and profit. In even greater contrast, considering the absolute relentlessness of monastic life, everybody at Arthur's truckline went home at the end of their shift, and the whole place shut down on weekends. The demands of individuals and families were manifestly a much stronger presence at A-P-A than at my monastery, where community was dominant. Nevertheless, I knew that when Arthur spoke of his truckline, he spoke of a moral community. When he proclaimed that by striving to fulfill the higher purpose of community work, the worker himself is fulfilled, he was talking about the power that emerges when the balance is found.

I decided to try to understand the opus that Arthur had created and that Armand was still building in that freight yard of theirs on the borders of the Jersey Swamp. I set myself the task of learning about the trucking business. It was odd to think of finding communitarians among truckdrivers, whose folk image is of the anarchic nomad barreling sleepless across the desert. But then, Arthur blurred the image of the entrepreneur, and as for Armand, who ever heard of a trucking boss playing Schubert and Chopin? It was at least plausible that their company was as distinctive as they were as individuals, and that a profit-making corporation could indeed take the form of an intentional community—governed by clear rules, devoted to a common purpose, and driven by zeal to demonstrate the value of its choices.

Certainly, Arthur sees himself as a dissenter, and he believes his dissent is instructive, as he made clear when I first spoke to him about my interest in writing about A-P-A. He can dazzle with talk of rebuilding American industry on an ethical foundation, and the enthusiasm of his spoken paragraphs, delivered in the splendor of the Florentine office while his freight dock pounds beneath the carpet, has energized the pens of many a journalist for the business press. But it's not only Arthur who speaks in this vein, as I gradually discovered during interviews between 1990 and 1992 with about seventy of his employees at North Bergen and four other A-P-A terminals. With varying degrees of commitment, almost all saw themselves as members of a community apart. Augie Pagnozzi, A-P-A's chief time-study man, expressed it to me this way one morning: "We joke about the fence around the property. It keeps the rest of the world out. There's A-P-A over here"—Augie pushed the air down toward the right side of his desk with both hands—then dismissed the air on his left: "and the rest of the world is over there."

To reach through the isolation of the fence, A-P-A, like other communities, extends a missionary arm. Arthur says he's "teaching, always teaching." Besides giving interviews and traveling on the lecture circuit, members of communities teach in another way: they're always taking visitors around on tours. It used to be one of my jobs at the monastery. Outsiders are curious, and they half suspect that communities are onto something that is missing in their world, where there are only individuals and families. At A-P-A, one of Augie Pagnozzi's roles has been to show visitors around the North Bergen terminal. They're mostly transportation executives who want to find out just how A-P-A inspires truckdrivers to work so productively and, above all, to make Arthur's company so much money.

But Augie is resigned to the same incredulous puzzlement that greeted Robert Owen's visitors to New Lanark. "We had Germans here recently, with translators," Augie told me. "They come from Japan, too. I showed the Germans our systems for enforcing productivity standards, but you could see from their faces that they didn't believe me."

Andy Park, A-P-A's vice-president for operations, similarly recalled meeting peers at professional gatherings during his time as a terminal manager in New England. "People wouldn't believe that our level of productivity was possible," Andy told me. " 'You can't get that amount of work out of men,' they'd say. When I got Augie's predecessor up to Boston to talk to them about our systems, some people walked out. They thought it was bullshit. Most management people just don't understand how much work you can get out of men, because they don't understand the workingman."

They don't understand him because they can't get down to his level, and they can't get there because they believe that the direction they need to move is "down." Andy Park said, "At the truckline where I worked before, and at other places, they may talk about being conciliatory to the men, but you never see them talking with drivers in the drivers' room." You don't ask a chattel what it's thinking.

To managers of a corporation that is an intentional community, however, the drivers' room, or the factory floor, is not a foreign place. For Andy Park and his colleagues, allegiance to their community is stronger than the call to class battle. During my visits to A-P-A, as I spoke with managers, supervisors, sales-people, and clerks, as I watched men load freight on the dock at night, and as I rode with truckdrivers over the interstates and on their delivery routes to factories and warehouses, I wanted to learn not only about their work but also about their dissent. I was curious to see what guidance their community might have to offer our industrial economy as, still distracted by hostilities between white collar and blue, we approach the threshold of the twenty-first century.

2. One-Shot Tony

Tony DeRosa is winding his twenty-three-foot straight-body truck through the labyrinths of streets that twist among the old red-brick buildings of the American Can Company, beside the Passaic River. He has a shipment to deliver, but not to American Can; what's filling half his truck is 1,263 pounds of clothing in seventy-three cartons for a job-lot warehouser called Automatic Operations. Like so many of the nineteenth-century mills along the lowland rivers of the Northeast, American Can itself is long departed. Its handsome Victorian shell is tenanted now by a shifting population of warehouses, sweatshops, and offices.

Tony has found his way into the labyrinth before. He's been delivering and picking up freight for A-P-A Transport Corp. in Passaic and Bergen Counties in northern New Jersey for ten years. Most of A-P-A's "city drivers" on "pedal runs"—pickup-and-delivery routes—drive the same truck along the same route every day. Tony, though, is dispatcher Pete Leota's back-up man, the guy who can drive any straight truck in the yard and who knows half the runs on Pete's dispatch-board. "You can put Tony on a new run and after two days he knows the run like the back of his hand," Pete has told me. Tony is the first of a half-dozen A-P-A drivers I'll be riding with, in New Jersey, Connecticut, Massachusetts, New Hampshire, and Maine.

Down a lane ahead looms an enormous old yellow-brick smokestack. Tony swings into the lane and glances at the one slot remaining for his truck among several straight trucks and sixty-foot-long tractor-trailer rigs backed up to a loading dock a hundred feet from the stack. This is Automatic Operations. Tony turns away from the dock and steers the truck toward the brick wall opposite, his eyes shifting from one side mirror to the other. He has to keep in mind what truckers call "off-tracking": the back wheels make a wider sweep than the front wheels on a turn—two feet wider on a truck the length of Tony's. His Mack cab is flat-faced, like a city bus, so he can bring the truck up to a few inches from the wall. He leans over the broad circle of his steering wheel, which is set parallel to the floor, hefts it about several turns, jiggles the gearshift into reverse, and backs up. The work of backing, if done right, is done now. The rest is easy. As the truck glides across the lane and down a chute formed by two trailers twice the length of his truck, Tony lifts his hands off the wheel, in order to nail down his reputation for one-shot backing in. "When they used to give me trainees and I'd teach them how to back," he says, "I'd tell them, 'You position the truck for backing and turn the wheel once.' Did you notice how I'm not turning the wheel now? See? It's backing itself up. And it'll be perfect, too." True to his word, the rear bumper thumps against the dock. First stop.

Concrete steps lead to a door at one end of the dock. Sumac weeds grow at the dock's base. Above us, delicate cornices worked in wood peer down over romanesque arches and columns worked in brick relief above blackened windows. Tony enters without knocking. Inside is a long, narrow room lit by skylights. Piles of empty wooden pallets and huddles of bulky cartons are scattered among the I-beam columns or are shoved against the faded brick walls. A sign states: "This company reserves the right, from time to time, to search employees and their property in order to prevent theft." Two black forklift men in Irish workingmen's caps are driving slowly about; three white down-men—dockmen who work on foot—are walking here and there. Automatic Operations is unwinding its morning in slow motion, on a screen of heat, dirt, and lassitude.

Along the wall that faces the lane, a half-dozen roll-up doors are open to the backs of trucks and trailers; the rear door of Tony's truck now fills one opening. Without comment, Tony stoops to unlock the padlock to his truck, opens the latch, and raises the door to reveal Automatic Operation's three-foot-cube cartons of clothing piled inside the truck from floor to ceiling. He turns to take down a pallet from a stack on the dock floor and drops it beside his truck. The pallet is made of raw one-by-four pine boards, in a double layer, four feet square. Tony piles eight of the three-foot-cube cartons loosely on the pallet and wheels up a pallet-jack, a device that combines the blades of a forklift with the jack of an auto-mechanic. He glides the blades between the pallet's two layers and pumps the handle to raise the pallet and the cartons. He looks up to ask the black supervisor watching him where to put the freight. The supervisor, whose rank is marked by a clipboard, a tie slumped over his large belly, and a short-sleeved blue dress-shirt, looks around a moment and says he doesn't know.

Tony wheels the cartons against the back wall. As he returns to unload the other cartons, grouping them in turn onto eight other pallets, no one offers to help him, although someone on a receiving dock is generally expected to share the work of unloading with a carrier's driver. Tony's formal responsibility ends when the cartons are piled on the dock. While he works, two management types, white, with bar moustaches, ties skewered by tiepins, and *white* short-sleeved shirts, barge out of an inner room to hustle me off the dock. They don't like my camera. One of the women thumbing stacks of paper in the glassed-in cabin at one end of the dock must have called them.

After a while I ease back onto the dock, unarmed. Still alone, Tony is working quickly, concentrating on the count of the cartons as he unloads. He's dressed for motion on a hot day: a navy-blue sleeveless T-shirt with "Niagara Falls" scripted in white across the chest; faded, slightly holey jeans; and running shoes. He's passed up the voluntary A-P-A uniform, blue slacks and short-sleeve shirt emblazoned with embroidered patches. His thick black moustache and black hair are clipped cleanly in straight lines across his lip, brow, and the nape of his neck; the strength of his Italian nose is softened by a gentleness around his green eyes. At thirty-two, and at mid-height, Tony is a well-built man, but the lines of his muscles lack the sharp hardness of men who work at it. He relies on lifting freight and turning the wheel to keep in shape. At home, he likes to float in his above-ground pool, putter at carpentry, and play with his daughters, aged eight and four.

According to Tony's count, there are actually only seventy-two cartons in the shipment, not seventy-three, as his paperwork maintains. Later he will have to call A-P-A's O. S. & D. Department (Overage, Shortage, and Damage) to report the discrepancy. Meanwhile, the women in the glass cabin keep Tony waiting for another fifteen minutes; they want to compare his paperwork with theirs before signing his receipt. Interstate Commerce Commission rules allow A-P-A's Traffic Department to add a dollar-a-minute surcharge for delay to Automatic Operations' $534 freight bill, but A-P-A won't add it. Since deregulation of the trucking industry, power has shifted entirely to the customers, and they know the trucklines aren't in a position to slap them on the wrist. Tony hasn't complained to anyone on this dock, although the women's bill-thumbing and the dockmen's refusal to help have turned a twenty-minute first stop into forty-five minutes. Tony is already behind schedule. He's not going to break his career record of forty-seven pickups and deliveries in one day; he'll be lucky if he makes thirty. It's too early in the day to get frustrated, though. Back in the truck, he says of relations with the dockmen, the supervisors, the bookkeepers, and the managers—the people who are his customers—"It's a game. You're nice to them, they're nice to you. Some drivers, though, would have been climbing the walls in there."

It's after 9:00 A.M., already hot, humid, and gaseous, a New York area late-June stinker. Tony drives out of the chute between the same two trailers and winds back through the labyrinth towards the listless industrial streets of Passaic. He's actually been up since 5:30. By leaving his house near the Jersey Shore around 6:30 on most days, Tony beats the rush hour on the twelve-lane New Jersey Turnpike and keeps his commute north down to about forty minutes. He reaches A-P-A in North Bergen by 7:15 and usually plays chess with Ron Ackerman in the drivers' room on Ron's handheld minicomputer. (Ron drives a forklift on the dock. A chess player of tournament class, he plays Tony without a queen and beats him anyway.) This morning, though, Tony was busy collecting five dollars a head from other drivers for the benefit of a colleague on disability. He put the touch successfully on almost all of the 120 or so men who were sitting in the drivers' room at long rows of picnic tables, chatting, reading the paper, shouting jokes, drinking coffee. Most have been on disability themselves at one time, or can expect to be; Tony himself lost three months last year with a herniated disc after he slipped on the ice dismounting from his truck. This morning, I was beginning my second day with Tony, and everyone had heard about what I was writing on that clipboard I carry. Friendly and curious, the drivers included me in their jokes. On my first day, Tony had been too shy to introduce me, and no one in the drivers' room had spoken to me.

I myself began the morning in the dispatch room, across the hall from the drivers' room in the operations building, which stands on the opposite side of the North Bergen yard from the dock. "You don't want to get here when I get here. I start at 4:30," Vinny Carnavale had told me after I'd said I wanted to meet him in the dispatch room when he opened up. Vinny, as city operations manager, is chief of the pickup-and-delivery operation at North Bergen. His early start every day is evidenced by the fine wrinkles around the eyes that belong to people who habitually skimp on sleep—a look I recognize well from my years at the monastery. Vinny wears a graying bar-moustache and owlish glasses, and like so many men at A-P-A, he's of middle size and somewhere around forty. He began at A-P-A as a driver, nearly twenty years ago.

When I did arrive this morning, at 6:05 A.M. all four of Vinny's dispatchers were already in the room, although, Vinny told me, they're not officially expected till 7:00. They had come in early to review the morning deliveries assigned to their drivers, to begin planning for afternoon pickups, and to set up their Whitney boards—three-sided metal carrels that wrap around each dispatcher's desk. The carrels display pickup-and-delivery tickets in vertical rows, one row for each driver and his route. Each dispatcher is coxswain for about thirty of North Bergen's city drivers, whose routes are divided roughly into four areas: South and Central Jersey; North Jersey, Manhattan, and Rockland County,

New York; Brooklyn, Queens, and Long Island; and the Bronx, Westchester, and Fairfield County, Connecticut.

Until 7:00 this morning, the room was quiet but for men's voices; the entire terminal is clear of the acoustic litter of canned music. Gradually the drivers' room filled up, while in the hall outside the dispatch room, men were leaning across the transom to go over their drivers' manifests with their dispatchers. A manifest identifies the shipments on a driver's truck by listing the names and addresses of the shipper and the consignee (the consignee is the company to which the freight is to be delivered). A manifest also specifies the weight of each shipment and the number of separate pieces in it. The deliveries are listed in an order determined by the Routing Department the previous evening. Stacked in the same order and bundled with an elastic band are the drivers' "delivery receipts"—five-inch-by-eight-inch tags in duplicate, setting forth more details of the shipment, including A-P-A's freight charges, with space for marking the actual time of delivery and the signatures of the driver and the dockworker or receiving clerk of the consignee.

As the men thumbed through their delivery receipts this morning, one driver came into the dispatch room to phone a consignee for directions. "He doesn't have to do that," commented Vinny Carnavale, whose pride is the *esprit de corps* of the North Bergen city operation he heads. Getting directions is actually the dispatcher's responsibility. "Everybody's involved. Everybody's in charge," Vinny said, as he darted about the room, ducking into his office to talk to a driver or to take a call, then rushing out again. "I try not to be the big boss, although, yes, that's the bottom line." As we spoke, another driver sat down at a free carrel to call a shipper for details about a C.O.D. "He *could* wait till 8:00," Vinny said, approving.

At 8:00, A.M. the horn sounded—the same horn blast that marks, or used to mark, eight, noon, and five in a thousand northeastern mill towns. The drivers streamed out of the drivers' room and into the yard toward their rigs, which were either backed up to the dock or parked in rows in the yard or along the fence. City trailer drivers mounted their tractors and chugged, criss-crossing each other, to hook up to the loaded trailers assigned to them. Diesel engines revved and roared; diesel smoke sketched puffs and trails on the air. Trucks formed a line at the gate. Pete Leota, Tony's dispatcher, crossed the yard with Tony and me and several other drivers, who joined to razz Pete about his Corvette. All the dispatchers were in the yard now, to troubleshoot any problems with loads or equipment, Vinny told me, and to discourage the delays of socializing. Hanging out with coffee before starting work in the morning is a tradition at truck terminals (as it is in many white-collar offices), but at A-P-A it's done before the clock starts.

Tony began driving the Clifton and Passaic run on Monday of this week, when the route's regular driver went on vacation. Tony's truck for the assignment had been a twenty-six-footer with power steering and a six-speed transmission, but today, Friday, that truck was routed to a maintenance bay along the north side of the yard, for a wheel alignment. As a replacement, dispatch saddled Tony with a 1975 twenty-three-foot five-speed without power steering, and with 259,000 miles on the odometer. "I sweat with these old ones," he said this morning as he raised the rear door to check the stacking of the freight. At 8:00 A.M. it was already over eighty degrees outside.

I followed Tony around the truck as he checked the springs, the lights, the wheel rims, the tires. He instructed me in the fundamental components of the vehicle: the chassis below, to which the truck's body is welded; the cab in front, painted bright red, A-P-A's company color; the 185-horsepower Saab-Scania gasoline engine; and behind the cab, the body—the "box"— aluminum-gray, with the red-and-white A-P-A diamond mounted on the side panels. The box stands twelve feet eight inches high and eight feet wide. It can legally hold a maximum of 18,000 pounds (although Tony's freight weighed only 9,357 pounds when he began the route today, according to his manifest; the load was light because half of its bulk consisted of Automatic Operation's clothes). The entire vehicle is called a straight truck—a "straight job"—because, with its box welded to its chassis, it cannot bend the way a detachable trailer bends behind its tractor. Even when fully loaded, Tony said, driving a straight truck is closer to driving a long car than to driving a tractor-trailer, except that he can't see out the back. He's so used to checking the side mirrors on his truck that he uses them on his subcompact Dodge to back into his garage.

To start his run today in Clifton and Passaic, Tony first had to cross a fetid, windy expanse of yellow-green reeds, black, still sloughs, and asphalt: the Jersey Meadowlands. Ten miles long and four miles wide, the Meadowlands meander south along the Hackensack and the Passaic Rivers till the two rivers meet at Newark Bay. The Meadowlands thus divide the Palisades, a heavily settled ridge along the west bank of the Hudson, from the rest of New Jersey. These wetlands used to be called the Jersey Swamp, but the name was sweetened in the early 1970s when developers began loading the mud with sports amphitheaters like the New York Giants' stadium, malls with such names as "Plaza on the Meadows," and warehouses faced with pebbly aggregates and called "distribution centers." This morning, in Tony's truck, as we ducked through an underpass beneath the railroad tracks that skirt the east side of the swamp, we could glimpse the chief traditional use of this landscape in the dirt walls of the roadcut. The dirt consists of garbage—a black compost marbled like a devil's-food cake with white plastic, scrap metal, and tires. About eight percent of the Meadowlands was once devoted to solid-waste landfill. With recent reforms and the spread of malls and townhouses, dumping has almost ceased.

Tony drove us along the swamp's eastern edge, where new warehouses, many for sale in the recession, sprawl among impenetrable stands of six-foot-tall reeds. We turned west on Paterson Plank Road, which is no longer paved with planks, but which still serves as the main swamp crossing from the North Bergen heights to the mid-bog hill of Secaucus. Rising on the elevated State Route 3, we then hurtled over sloughs and ponds, across which electricity pylons stalk like herons. Over the wetlands, the New Jersey Turnpike and the old iron-trussed Pulaski Skyway rise and fall in innumerable bridges, so that their profiles form a series of humps on stumpy legs, like a procession of stegosauruses. Once across the swamp, Tony took us north on Route 21 along the slow, dark Passaic River winding down toward Newark Bay.

We have left Automatic Operations behind, and Tony's next stop is Dubnoff Paints, Inc., in Passaic. He has quart cans of paints for Dubnoff in twelve small boxes, a total of 518 pounds, from a paint factory south of Boston. There is no dock at Dubnoff, and Tony needs two shots among the vehicles in the parking lot as he backs to a point near the rear door of the store. He dismounts, then springs lightly up into the back of his truck, now half-empty after the departure of Automatic Operation's seventy-two cartons of clothes. He carries Dubnoff's boxes of paints, in piles of three, out to the back edge of the truck, and a skinny West Indian stockman in his thirties hurries up to unload. The stockman wears a goatee and also a fierce frown that may explain his premature gray hair. Tony tries a joke about the 518 pounds: "It's Friday. They wanted to make it light for you." When the stockman doesn't answer or even glance at Tony, Tony tries the joke again. Without acknowledgment, the stockman calls out to a partner to bring a handtruck, but the partner, soft in the belly and face, wanders up without one. Now they curse each other in a Caribbean English too voluble for us to catch anything but the expletives. The skinny one signs the delivery receipt, and Tony drives off, chuckling. "They're always yelling at each other. Every time I come here they're yelling at each other. On this job, you meet all shapes and sizes."

Richmond Fabrics is on vacation. That explains why Tony's customer-finding instinct can't find the place. After circumnavigating the block on leafy residential streets, he stops a second time beside a shut chain-link gate between two houses. If the gate had been open, with activity beyond it, Tony would have driven through it the first time around. Now a man and a boy playing ball have appeared in the driveway; the man sees us and makes an "X" with his arms: closed. Tony dismounts to investigate. He's got five eight-foot rolls of knit synthetic cloth ("piece-goods"), weighing 105 pounds each, and if he can't deliver them, he'll have to keep heaving them out of the way of the other freight for the rest of the day. The ballplayer confirms that, like many small factories in the Northeast, Richmond Fabrics is closed for two weeks around the Fourth of July. They forgot to notify A-P-A, which is going a little far, even for a customer. For the two trips needed instead of one, the shipping charge of $117.29 will probably be doubled.

General Hospital in Passaic, the fourth stop, takes five minutes: eight cartons from a medical supplier in New Brunswick, New Jersey, 149 pounds, unloaded right onto a dock in a cellar garage that is A-P-A-clean and cool besides. The hospital is guaranteed overnight service, on the theory that patients might be needing what's in the cartons. Nearby, at AGI Welding Supply ("Specality Gases, Bulk Liquids"), the fifth stop, Tony unloads two skids of hand tools, helmets, and rubber hoses, weighing 1,975 pounds, from an industrial supplier in Allentown, Pennsylvania.

Now Tony skips the two stops listed next on his manifest, because he can't see the freight. It's buried somewhere among the cartons and skids packed into the nose of his truck. (The nose is the front end of a truck body or a trailer; the back end is called the tail.) He'll swing by these stops later. Number six, therefore, is Melco, an equipment supplier in Clifton. Its consignment is a crated motor compressor, 450 pounds, from Rochester, New York, and a condensing unit on a pallet, also 450 pounds, from Philadelphia. Tony backs into Melco's dock, dismounts, raises the door, and heaves aside Richmond Fabric's 105-pound rolls, which are wrapped in thick, oiled brown paper. He slides a heavy, cast-iron dockplate, about four feet square, over the junction between the truck and the dock, and Melco's dockman wheels a handtruck over the dockplate onto the truck. They need the handtruck to move the condenser out from among the other freight before the dockman can drive his forklift onto the truck and slide the blades under the pallet.

The dockman, who is in fact still a boy, chubby with long stringy brown hair, pulls down on the handtruck to lift the condenser so it will be easier for Tony to heft it forward. The counterweight of the condenser on the handtruck lifts the boy off the floor; his baggy jeans flop down over his heels. Tony shifts crate, boy, and handtruck side to side and forward. Now it is free for the forklift. The boy drives his forklift onto the truck, with one hand on the levers, leaning back, affecting a lolling ease.

Unloading the compressor will not be as simple. Its crate extends the full width of the truck; moreover, a large, 200-pound carton is wedged on top of it. With his back to the dock, Tony braces his feet against the freight that is stacked further into the nose of the truck and shoves the compressor and the carton outward inch by inch with his butt. He wrestles the carton halfway off the compressor and tilts it over at an angle to rest on the freight behind, and then, with repeated shoves, inches the compressor around so that it lies lengthways instead of crossways along the truck; meanwhile he returns several times to the carton to ease it to the floor. He takes the handtruck, lifts the compressor's end, and backs up, dragging the compressor toward the dock until it is clear of Richmond's rolls. He is sweating now and breathing heavily. On the dock, the boy watches, lounging back on his forklift, his stomach protruding.

Once Tony has dragged the compressor past the rolls of fabric, he pushes it sideways again so that the forklift blades can reach beneath. But the pallet underneath it has been twisted askew during Tony's exertions. "I can't get my blades in," the dock boy tells him—not complaining, just bored.

"You got snips? metal snips?" Tony asks. With snips, he can cut the compressor loose from the pallet and maybe kick the pallet straight.

"It's attached?" the boy asks—a superfluous question, because flat metal strips always bind a crate to a pallet.

Tony: "Yeah."

"I got no snips." The dock boy flops from his forklift with a heavy sigh and crouches by the blades. He loosens them and moves them wider apart, flops back onto his seat, drives onto the truck, and slides the blades home beneath the compressor.

"You *still* unloading that?" someone calls out. A manager in his thirties, very bald, with moustache, white shirt, no tie, walks up briskly. Immediately he is on the truck, helping Tony jostle the compressor so that it can advance smoothly down the truck as the forklift backs out. The second the compressor's weight passes over the dockplate onto the dock, Tony turns his back on the place.

On the road again, in halting traffic on Main Street, Passaic, Tony stops to wave on ahead a parked car that's been waiting to enter the traffic lane. "Tony," I tell him, "you're a gentleman."

"You wouldn't say that if you heard what I was saying about that guy under my breath."

"You mean the boy on the dock?"

"Yeah. I was going to say something. I almost did. But you can't let it get to you. There's no point in getting yourself all worked up. That was a workout, though."

"Is that usual?"

"No. It's all right. I got dirty, though." He turns up his hands on the wheel to show me: they're black from the oil on the wrapping around Richmond's fabric. "My shirt, too. I hate getting dirty. You try to make a good impression on the customer, you know?"

Embarrassed and rather angry at myself, I apologize for not helping, and explain that my lumbar vertebrae permit me to lift hardly anything.

"No," Tony says firmly. "You're not supposed to. *He* should have helped me."

The seventh stop is Arlington Machine, on yet another back street of Passaic, 409 pounds of machine parts on two small pallets from Binghamton, New York. The delivery is easy: one-shot backing in, unloading by teamwork, a joke ("Is it a lot? If it's too heavy, I won't take it"), a routine signature—the way, Tony says, stops ought to be. Number eight is for the big carton that was sitting on the compressor. It was one of the buried shipments—not literally buried, as it turns out, but unidentifiable, because the compressor had raised the carton to the ceiling, and the address on the top of the carton was too high for Tony to see. He knows now it is consigned to Bellevue Surgical on Main Street, 200 pounds of FAK (freight of all kinds) from a Pennsylvania metal fabricator. But finding Bellevue's storefront on Main is not sufficient. Tony needs to find the street Bellevue backs on, and then he needs to find Bellevue's back. He swings off Main Street and looks down alleys, chooses one, jounces down it at five miles an hour, spots an open loading dock, identifies it mysteriously by no apparent sign. He's smiling again. "See? It's that instinct."

Tony has been driving the alleys and back streets and main streets of North Jersey for ten and a half years. "What keeps you going, Tony?" I ask him. "Does it get old?"

"Old? No."

"Why not?"

He thinks a moment. "Ambition."

"What do you mean?"

His answer surprises me. "Ambition to be happy. I've always been that way since I was little. Easy going. Smiling. I come into work every day smiling and people say it's an act. But it's not. Arthur greets me now: 'Here's the grumpiest guy in the company. He never smiles.' " Tony flashes his trademark.

"How does your answer 'ambition to be happy' fit my question about what keeps driving from getting old?"

"Because I enjoy the work. You're out in the open. You always get to meet new people. You're not stuck in one place."

I suggest: "You're on your own."

"Yeah. I'm looking for the word . . . responsibility. To the customer, and to the company."

Tony is silent for a while, and I offer: "The Chinese have a lot of sayings, and one is—"

Tony interrupts: "Yeah, like on fortune cookies."

"No, that's to sell to Westerners. This one is for themselves: 'The wisdom of the wise boils down to this: to know how to be happy.' "

Tony nods, smiling. On his route, his own happiness is found in a balance between autonomy and responsibility. His first remark on the first day I rode with him, earlier this week, was: "We're driver-salesmen." He explained: "If we see that a shipper uses another carrier instead of A-P-A when it ships to another area, we tell them A-P-A ships to that area too, and then we ask A-P-A to send out a salesman to them." He added, "Some people see drivers as low-life who have driver's mouth." His concern was to let me know immediately that he didn't belong in the picture he expected me to have of the profane and coarse-natured road cowboy. (He said later about profanity, "There's no need for those words. They're not in my vocabulary." He doesn't even say the big "D.") In general, he wanted me to understand that he sees himself as a professional whose loyalty is not primarily horizontal, to his craft union, but vertical, to his company.

"See that black thing?" he said, early on during our first day, and he pointed to a round case mounted below the passenger seat, behind my feet. It ticked. "That's a clock. When they strip the freight tonight, they'll look at the disk that's inside it, and they'll compare the stops with the times I've written down on my manifest."

"Does that bother you?" I asked him.

"No, it doesn't bother me. I guess it does some people."

"They feel like they're being watched?"

"Yeah. But they're not watching you, they're watching your time. Time is how they make money. If I'm delayed, I can't make stops, and then they lose money."

The clock, which is connected to a tachometer, records on a circular disk the speed of Tony's truck, the time he takes at each of his stops, and the time he takes to drive between stops. The disk becomes a portrait of Tony's day. It makes wasting time impossible without having to explain the waste. Tony doesn't take the clock's ticking personally because wasting time irritates him anyway, but the tachometer is nevertheless an incessant reminder to A-P-A drivers that they're expected to work diligently and without unnecessary respite. When I rode with Jimmy Roche, a north-of-Boston driver, on his route through Nashua and Hudson, New Hampshire, he said after a thirteen-minute break at a coffee shop, "I'll tell Gerry (his terminal manager) that you kept me the extra three minutes." He was joking, but only half. Inevitably, the clock under the seat, and the knowledge that anomalies on the disk can result in questions and possibly discipline, instills, in Arthur's phrase, "a clock in the head."

Arthur's antecedent, Robert Owen, invented an antecedent of the truck tachometer for his New Lanark mill. A block of wood, painted black, blue, yellow, and white on its successive sides, was suspended from the ceiling by a wire so that it hung beside each worker's machine. The floor supervisor turned the block to exhibit his judgment of the worker's performance for the previous day: white for excellent, yellow for good, blue for average, black for poor. The judgments were recorded and kept in a file on each worker. Owen compared his system to the Recording Angel, because, he said, it was impartial. It was actually less than that, because the supervisor's choice of colors was inevitably subjective and was liable to the distortions of favoritism—a flaw that still mars evaluation systems in many workplaces today. (Owen himself recognized the flaw and tried to smooth it with a system of appeals, with himself as highest court.)

To charges that the tachometer is intrusive, that it's a ticking echo of Big Brother, Arthur replies that its evaluations are objective, and that in general his systems circumvent the pitfalls of subjectivity and favoritism. He argues in his speeches that the objectively evaluated worker provides his own job security. The driver whose tachometer disk shows productivity is protected by it from arbitrary discipline. Machines, of course, are limited by their own sort of inaccuracies. Tony complains mildly that, in setting standards, the computer's distinctions are never fine enough to take into account variations in routes. Still, I'm willing to believe that a tachometer disk and computerized productivity standards are likely to be more fair than a supervisor's personal preference, although I'm not as comfortable with the tachometer's intrusiveness as Tony seems to be. That it spurs him and his colleagues to work above what Arthur calls "comfort level" I have no doubt. Clocks notwithstanding, it's very clear to A-P-A drivers that they have to work harder than their counterparts in other companies.

They're willing to work harder, in part, because their supervisors and their supervisors' managers also work harder. The dispatchers, for example, daily sit at their boards for ten straight hours, sometimes without a break. They'll eat lunch at their carrels, reluctant to leave their radios even for fifteen minutes once the drivers are on the streets, lest they learn of a call for a pickup too late, after a driver has passed the spot by. In every terminal, in this company that prides itself on a driven atmosphere, the dispatchers stand out as the most driven, the most workaholic,

the company madmen. Yesterday afternoon, I visited Pete Leota—
who as dispatcher for North Jersey is Tony's boss—while he
plotted the graphs of thirty drivers' routes in his head. Most of
the time he sat clamped to the phone, the radio, or both at once,
inquiring, directing, exhorting, berating, praising, crooning
threateningly: "Let's get a move on, c'mon, Harry, it's getting
late. It's three o'clock." (Harry was somewhere in North Jersey.)
"Keep an eye on that Folsom pickup, Harry, they close at 4:00.
They don't want to see you at 4:30, they want to go home. Let's
hurry up."

Harry's protest was an unintelligible squawk on the radio, but
Pete understands radio squawk language. He crooned back,
without missing a beat in what was now the room's heavy-metal
of shouts, bursts of static, and ringing telephones: "Well, instead of talking to me, let's get going, okay?" (Squawk.) "Yeah,
Harry, g'bye."

Pete is sharp-faced, sharp-tongued, and a sharp dresser. Yesterday his fawn-colored slacks still kept their flawless crease eight
hours into his twelve-hour day. His narrow shoes, which sported
tassels on the tongues, were in perfect polish. Drivers say that
during Pete's eight years as a city driver, he'd often wear white,
just to show he could return after ten hours on the street without a smudge. As dispatcher he watches his carrel with the same
zeal as his wardrobe. While riding herd over the radio, he studies the pickup tags on his board, and the pages of street atlases
flip back and forth inside his brain. Suddenly his hands fly out
among the tickets, shuffling drivers' routes and pickup assignments according to locations, load sizes, and closing times. "You're
always fighting the clock," he told me yesterday, "especially because some customers close at 2:00, at 3:00—you're like a baseball manager. You got a strategy, but if you can't make the players
do it. . . . It's a question of motivation."

Pete pushes his players because he's being pushed himself.
Every day, Augie Pagnozzi's Industrial Engineering Department
sends down to City Dispatch a green-and-white computer print-
out listing the previous day's performance of each of the local
drivers on each of the dispatcher's boards. This "Truck Operations Chart," based in part on the drivers' tachometer disks, states

the number of shipments picked up and delivered during the day, the number of pounds of freight handled, the number of miles driven, the number of minutes of delay, all stirred and summarized into a series of averages. Two figures in particular always draw Pete's eye: how many stops his drivers made that day, and the combined average of the number of stops all of them made per hour. For a driver, thirty stops is considered an excellent day's work, although the standard varies among individual routes. "See this guy Wypler?" Pete told me, waving to the vertical row of pickup tags for the Wyckoff route in Bergen County. "He turns in thirty-five stops a day. I've seen him do forty." When Tony drives his usual run, to Fairfield, he'll turn in forty-stop days often. His record of forty-seven is the record for Pete's board. "Tony gives you everything, every day," Pete told me. "The customers love him. He just has a way about him."

As the drivers' supervisor, a dispatcher has his own standard: a daily average of 3.0 stops per driver-hour. Yesterday Vinny Carnavale handed Pete his truck operations chart for the day before with several figures circled and annotated in marking-pen red: for one driver's performance, "GOOD!" and for another's, "WHAT HAPPEN!?" Pete looked it over. His wry assessment somehow sounded wryer in his nasal New Jersey speech: "We had a two point eight yesterday. I didn't do so good. Two drivers had low twos." Pete already knew that one of the driver's delays were beyond his or the driver's control. He confessed that the other driver's low performance was a bit of a surprise, and one of his tasks this morning before the drivers' departure would be to call that driver in to go over his manifest.

"If you don't attack a problem right away, it erodes," Vinny told me this morning. "If you leave it for two months and then confront a man, you're going to have a war on your hands." The same is true of praise. "When they perform, you also have to acknowledge." A worker's effort will gradually soften if the boss doesn't notice it. The man has to hear it. Vinny says, "You have to let him know he's not a machine."

At A-P-A, everything is measured, everything is reported, everything is evaluated, every day. This is the essence of the "systems" that Augie Pagnozzi shows the skeptical visitors who don't believe A-P-A's workforce can be as productive as they've heard it is. The systems' prototype, developed in the early 1960s, was set forth on a fifteen-foot-long flowchart that analyzed the movement of a shipment of freight and its accompanying paperwork into 225 operations, from the initial call by a shipper for a pickup to the invoice mailed after delivery. The flowchart has long since been translated into computer programs. Augie's systems set standards for every one of the company's daily operations. The standards are intended to be high, but not so high that they can't be met through reasonable and diligent effort by most workers, most of the time. The goal is to pose a challenge that will protect workers both from the discouragement that results from being assigned too much and from the laziness that results from being assigned too little. When I visited Augie's office, up a flight of stairs from the dock, he told me, "Other carriers are amazed that we evaluate our drivers every day. But they don't seem to realize that if you give a man a half-a-day's work, he'll take a day to do it. If you give him a full day's work, he'll take a day to do it. The key thing is not to overload him, because then he'll get frustrated and say, 'There's no way I can finish this,' and he'll throw up his hands." Augie's job, therefore, is to know how much time everybody should be taking to do everything, and how much it costs.

Arthur calls the company's system of performance standards "the machine." Augie granted: "It may sound like robotics, tracking everything down to the last minute. But our drivers know they're at the top of their kind, the top five percent or higher. They get respect." From the beginning, Arthur argued that to work men justly and hard was not to exploit them, but to ennoble them. The standards urge them toward that high purpose which is excellence in their craft. Armand, who has been president of A-P-A since 1983, recalled: "What Arthur told employees was, if you're going to work, you should do it the best you can, and see it as an opportunity for self-realization. If you're a driver, you should be the best god-damn driver you can be. Now I don't know if everyone believed that, but Arthur believed it, and that's important. They knew he wasn't full of shit."

The drivers knew, when Arthur harangued them at employees' breakfasts, that in the boss's eyes they were "men who counted"—to use Arthur's words about the man he met in the steel works. He would tell them frankly that "each man is a profit center." Of course, not everyone is interested in being a profit center, and not everyone wants to be called to high purpose if that entails making 3.0 stops an hour on a pickup-and-delivery run in North Jersey. To avoid being saddled with laggards and rebels, therefore, A-P-A has constructed an elaborate process of defensive hiring. To be hired as probationary employees, applicants are interviewd by three separate people at the job site, and to become permanent employees—after the thirty probationary days specified in the Teamsters contract—the workers are interviewed three more times in North Bergen by senior management, including the president.

The company is not looking for craft experience, since it prefers training workers itself. Rather, it seeks traits of personal character—above all, honesty. Most applicants have already heard that the company keeps five clerks busy scanning local newspapers for people convicted of crimes. Since the 1960s, it has built a computer listing of over 1.5 million names, which it compares with the names on application forms. Pilfering is a problem at many trucklines, but not at A-P-A. After honesty, A-P-A's interviewers look for a certain intensity that finds expression in hard work, a capacity for loyalty that is willing to take direction, and a complementary self-respect and independence that allows a driver to work under no closer supervision than a two-way radio. In short, the company accepts people who see work the way Arthur and his successors see work. Armand told me: "You give a driver a manifest in the morning and say, 'This is the work for today.' One type of person says: 'Yes, I can do this. I can do this challenge.' Another guy questions: 'Who are you to say this? Why did you decide this, and how?' You want the first one, the guy who views it as a challenge. He has an engine inside of him that wants to accomplish something every day."

A-P-A has used tachometers to measure drivers' inner engines since the 1950s, but even in the 1990s, not every truckline makes use of them. This morning, for example, while I waited out my exile from the dock at Automatic Operations, Tony's first stop, I watched another driver relax in the driver's seat of the tractor-trailer rig parked beside Tony's truck. He was reading a newspaper spread out over the wheel. The block letters painted on the side panel of his trailer proclaimed his employer as one of the six large nationwide trucklines. Halfway through Tony's stop, the driver had ambled up the lane, on his return, perhaps, from a coffee shop.

I ask Tony now whether he noticed the other driver. It was clear no dispatcher would badger *him* about delays this morning.

"That guy?" Tony says. He noticed.

"What did you think of him?" I ask.

"I didn't think anything. He's got nothing to do with me."

I press him: "Wouldn't it be nice to take it easy like that, though?"

"I wouldn't do it if I could," Tony says. "I'm not that kind of guy."

Realizing more might be needed, he adds after a moment: "Working for A-P-A, you got security. You know you're going to get paid. A lot of companies are going under, and that guy's the reason, right there." It may not have been the other driver's choice, though, he explains. Some companies will send a driver out on his route just for the pickups, even when there are no deliveries. "He sits around having coffee for an hour till 9:00 A.M., since there are no pickups before then. The company loses a hundred dollars paying for his half-day. In A-P-A they'd send you out to double on another man's route that has too many deliveries. Like today, I've got two thousand five hundred dollars in deliveries—that's revenue, you know?"

Since deregulation in 1980, bankruptcies among trucklines have far exceeded the national average for corporate failures. Month after month, in a steady stream for twelve years, familiar names such as Spector Red Ball, Transcon Lines, Smith's Transfer, and P.I.E. (Pacific Intermountain Express) have disappeared from the highways. Employment by trucklines continues to fall, above all unionized employment: drivers, dockworkers, mechanics, and other trucking workers organized by the Teamsters numbered 300,000 in 1980 and 140,000 in 1992. That A-P-A has not only survived but gained strength is a spur for Tony and his colleagues to maintain the momentum of hard work. The clockwork in the head is powered above all by the drive to hold onto a good job.

A-P-A's health is not only a reassurance, but also a point of pride. Tony tells me now: "I got a friend who drives for ABF (Arkansas Best Freight, the fifth-largest nationwide truckline). I used to eat lunch with him and another driver at an air-conditioned mall when I was on another run. He told me I was working at the best company around. He said, 'You know you're going to get paid every Thursday. You come in, you know you're going to get work.' He kept saying, 'A-P-A's the best company around.' He was sincere, too. And ABF's a good company. I said, 'If you feel that way, why don't you come work for us?'— 'Nah,' he said. 'I don't want to make that many stops.' "

Both of these men have a stake—one that eroded during the 1980s, as has the stake of most middle-income and also lower-income workers—but a stake that remains substantial. Like many craft unionists, Tony is, financially, a member of the middle class. He's a suburban family man with a new subdivision house and a two-car garage. His next-door neighbor is a Filipino-American, Jersey-City-born like himself, now a vice-president at a Wall Street bank. Tony's yearly income, at $15.91 an hour, with seven to ten hours' overtime a week, will approach $43,000 in 1991—as much as or more than the earnings of many white-collar professionals. But Tony's financial stake is augmented by another investment: a conviction that his team is the top team, that his unit is the crack unit. "We're the best," people at A-P-A, both workers and management, say of their company, not as an aggressive claim, but as a confident statement of faith. They work long hours willingly both to prosper in a hostile business environment and to maintain their estimation of who they are.

A-P-A offers a further reason not to mind the clock under the passenger seat: the company promotes virtually all its managers from the ranks of drivers, dockmen, clerks, and street-level salespeople. During my first weeks at A-P-A, as I've moved from interview to interview and worksite to worksite, I've heard repeatedly: "I grew up here," and, "I guess you could say I'm a child of A-P-A," and, "People who come here young decide to stay for the rest of their lives." The line workers know that, if the clock in the head ticks well, they have the choice either of remaining in place or of rising into management—an incentive that is by no means open to line workers in many American corporations. Even in the traditionally rough, intensely blue-collar industry of trucking, the officer corps of most trucklines—terminal managers and central-office administrators—are usually recruited as management from colleges and business schools or are absorbed horizontally from management in other companies. The noncommissioned ranks of dispatcher and dock supervisor are as high as drivers and dockworkers in most companies can expect to be promoted. Such limits to promotion impose an in-house class system.

At A-P-A, dispatch or dock supervision is not a steel ceiling. Instead, it is a step toward terminal management. (In 1992, A-P-A promoted Pete Leota into management training at the company's Long Island terminal, with an eye to moving him eventually to a terminal of his own.) With the exception of a few people entering from trucklines that A-P-A has acquired, nearly all of the company's 190 managers, from dispatcher and dock supervisor to Arthur himself, began in the company in their teens or twenties as line workers, even when they applied for a management job. There are no MBAs at A-P-A at all. Joe Whelan, the personnel director, recalled that when he applied as a management trainee, Arthur told him his training would be a year driving a straight truck.

Even this early in my acquaintance with A-P-A, I can discern some of the results of a consistent practice of internal promotion. Pete, Vinny, and their bosses know what they can ask Tony to do, and how much, because they have done it themselves. Their judgments are not based on theory learned in business school, but on practical experience. The result is that Tony can respect them as insiders in his craft. He doesn't see them as the men in suits parading down the shop floor and scattering orders about performing some task he's quite certain they themselves don't know how to perform. He can feel that he is a professional among other professionals in part because his bosses are, in terms of skill and training, colleagues who have gone into management, rather than managers who have been brought in to control him.

As all techies know, it's demeaning and infuriating to be directed in one's craft by an outsider, and in American corporations it's commonplace for craft and technical workers, and also professional workers, to consider their managers to be idiots. Managers argue in response that it's their job to manage, not to understand the crafts and professions they're managing. To their workers, that argument is absurd. This is one of the gulfs of disagreement in the American corporate class system. At A-P-A, I hear mild resentment among some drivers and dockmen who, unlike Tony, feel they are being asked to work too hard, but I haven't heard anyone say his boss doesn't know what he's talking about. Jack Poor, who began on the dock at A-P-A's second largest terminal, in Canton, Massachusetts, south of Boston, and who is now the terminal's manager, told me last week when I visited there: "The driver's going to tell me how it was on the street, because he knows I've been there." The skeptical visitors Augie Pagnozzi takes around on tour are not likely to have Jack's advantage.

Another result of a practice of internal promotion is a stable workforce. Line workers who can expect to be promoted are likely to stay; managers who came up from the ranks have too deep roots to want to leave. Turnover, especially of drivers, is a major difficulty in the American trucking industry. It's not unusual for trucklines to suffer a hundred-percent turnover rate among drivers—an entirely new workforce, on the average, every year. When I asked Joe Whelan, the personnel director, what A-P-A's turnover rate is, he said he didn't know. It's so close to zero that he's never needed to measure it. Tony, who was hired in 1980, is seventy-sixth out of 133 on the North Bergen city drivers' seniority list. Raw recruits, the majority in some trucklines, are a rarity here. Tony belongs to a corps of veterans who have figured out how to do what they are doing.

I remember Armand's comment about Tony: "He's not just easygoing. He's ambitious." I ask Tony now: "You ever think of moving up in the company?"

"Yeah. Not dispatcher, though. Too much pressure. And I couldn't yell at people. Routing. That would really be interesting. And my wife doesn't want me driving into my forties."

Like other drivers who know a number of routes, Tony already moonlights several evenings a month in the Routing Department, on the second floor of the operations building. There, the next day's delivery receipts are sorted and ordered, according to the location of the consignees, the hours their docks are open, and the capacity of the trucks and trailers. The stops are then listed in order on the manifests that guide the drivers in the morning. Rather than depending on a computer program, the routing relies on a human mastery of the New York–New Jersey-area maps that paper the routing room's walls, and here Tony can apply his own experience.

"What about driving into your forties?" I ask. "You might hurt your back?"

"You can get hurt anywhere. But I needed my ten years to qualify for the union retirement. If I'd have gone into management and out of the union sooner than ten years, I'd lose all that."

The appeal of promotion is balanced by an alternative vision. "If I stay in the Teamsters, I can retire at forty-six—that'll make twenty-five years—at a thirteen-thousand-dollar-a-year pension, and work part-time in landscaping. I've always wanted to do that. And my wife could keep working. Now I do a little carpentry, a little electricity. I built the deck around our pool."

I can't think that he's overreaching when he thinks of promotion; he must be aware that Pete Leota counts on him, and it is not for nothing that Armand and Joe Whelan chose him when I asked them to find a driver willing to take me along on his route. Still, Tony was genuinely surprised later on in the summer, though I was not, when A-P-A named him "Employee of the Month." In a ceremony in the drivers' room, Armand gave him a $250 gift certificate toward a weekend holiday, and Tony, his wife Diane, and their two girls will be squired on a four-hour outing on Arthur's yacht.

The ambition behind the gentlemanly smile, and the drive for the elegant route inside the man who would move the compressor himself rather than demand help from the lazy dock boy: the picture fits Tony's childhood and youth. He was a patrol guard captain in school, an altar boy in church. There was no one his age on his block in Jersey City, so he hung around with his older brother's friends, and they picked on him. He pitched for the local Little League, for which his father was a coach; for the Senior League, he played on the all-star team in the old Roosevelt Stadium in Jersey City. He didn't get involved in high school sports. "I was a woman's man in high school. Went ice-skating. Hung around on the corner." By sophomore year he was going with Diane, now his wife; they went to paired Catholic schools. Even now he's shy at neighborhood parties, and often will talk with the women rather than the men, Diane told me when I visited their home.

Diane's the one who gets upset in the family. "I'm loud. I'm the screamer, not really the screamer, but I'm loud." Dark-complexioned, with fashionable, tightly wound curls she doesn't have to pay the beautician for, Diane stayed home until Christine and Nicole were old enough for school. Now she gets out of the house on weekend mornings to type physician's notes from a dictaphone. On weekdays, she transcribes the notes at home. "Some of the words she types are thirty letters long," Tony tells me. "I ask her, 'How do you know how to spell all those words?' " Saturdays and Sundays, Tony stays home with his daughters. "Friends say, 'You gotta go for the son,' and I say"—as he relates this, he pushes his flat hand down toward the 478-cubic-inch engine between us in the truck—" 'No. That's it.' "

After high school, he and Diane waited four years before they married, in order to "have a little more money and go places." Tony went to work operating heavy equipment for the Jersey City Parks Department. "We worked 8:00 to 4:00. It was nice. At 9:00 you go to your first job, you have coffee, you start at 9:30;

at 11:15 you break to wash before lunch. At 1:00, 1:15 you start again, at 2:30 it's coffee break again, by 3:30 you're going back to wash before quitting at 4:00. It was nice. Two and a half, three hours of work a day. In winter they'd call you at 2:00 A.M. for snow removal. Sometimes you'd work forty-eight hours straight on a weekend, all overtime. They'd give you a place to sleep."

It was nice, but the engine inside him was on idle. What Tony calls "the politics" finally made him quit. "People would get jobs depending what regime came in. I knew a supervisor who was demoted to laborer when a new regime came in. The regime before, he'd been made a supervisor. I took the Civil Service exam so I could get free of that. They asked me to put up signs for a political campaign. I told them, 'No, that's not me. You can't touch me, I'm Civil Service.' They said, 'We'll give you harder jobs.' I said, 'That's okay by me, I gotta work, right? But you can't touch me past 4:00 P.M.' "

After leaving Jersey City, Tony drove a road tractor for a year, pulling trailers to Connecticut for a former baseball coach who'd started a truckline. He was fearful that it wouldn't last, and his brother-in-law, a vocational-education teacher who was moonlighting then on the A-P-A dock, suggested he try A-P-A if he wanted a good job. Tony asked A-P-A for dock work, but they were only hiring local drivers. He was interviewed by Burt Trebour, then personnel director and now vice-president for labor and administration; Burt hired him the next day. "I was really surprised," Tony tells me. "I couldn't believe it, because everybody said it was so hard to get in."

After the thirty-day probationary period came his interview with Arthur in the Florentine office (it was 1980, Arthur's last full-time year in the company).

"The interview was crazy," Tony recalls. "Arthur said, 'You're the only green-eyed Italian I ever saw.' Then he asked me: 'Where's your wife work?'

" 'Jewish Hospital in Jersey City.'

" 'What's her number there?'

"I gave him the number, thinking, 'What's this guy want her number for?' He called her and put her on the speaker phone and said to her, 'How does he treat you?' and 'You think I ought to hire him?' I was sitting there thinking, 'I hope she's going to say the right thing.' 'Well,' Arthur said on the phone, 'I guess I'll hire him.' That's how I learned I was going to work for A-P-A."

"At first I thought it was a joke," Diane told me later when I asked her about Arthur's call, "because a lot of our friends and relatives knew Tony was going for the interview. Then afterwards I realized—he had it on the speaker phone—I was anxious, but I was honest. I answered his questions honestly. I thought it was great that he was even interested that Tony had a wife and a home life."

When I told Armand about Arthur's call, he laughed and said, "That was standard. I've never had the nerve to do that. Arthur would usually decide on a guy after one look. Then he'd continue with the interview. Ask outrageous questions, put the guy off balance. Like: 'We don't want any more Italians around here.' "

As for Tony, Arthur told him afterwards what had made him decide: "He said I was the only guy who put on his application that I wanted to work for A-P-A to protect my family. Get good benefits for my family. That's why he hired me." At the time, Tony and Diane were twenty-two.

⁕⁕⁕⁕⁕⁕⁕⁕⁕⁕⁕⁕

Telemeasurements, an electronics store near Bellevue Surgical, is consigned 639 pounds of blank cassette tapes in twenty-eight cartons from Sony's warehouse, further south near Princeton in Middlesex County. The stop is later than ninth on Tony's manifest, but he stops there anyway. "I'm moving things around a bit. These two were on the way." (We'd passed Telemeasurements before reaching Automatic Operations.) "The routers should have *started* me here." Tony chafes at the limits to his autonomy: he's a driver who knows the territory better than the Routing Department, but he can rearrange his route only slightly, among neighboring stops, because the freight is stacked in the truck according to the sequence of the planned route. Telemeasurement's cassettes were buried far back behind Automatic

Operation's clothes and Richmond's rolls, so it would have been pointless to stop there before. He can't make the whole route perfect, and it bugs him.

Last night, on the dock, Tony's freight was loaded onto his truck in the reverse order of his route, once that was determined by the routers. The dockman loaded the freight for Tony's last stop first, into the nose; then the shipment for the second-to-last stop was loaded behind it, until, sequentially, the freight for the first stop, Automatic Operations, was stacked last, into the tail. This "sequential loading" limits Tony's revisions and his improvisatory latitude, since freight in the tail must come off first, and freight in the nose, like Telemeasurement's tapes, must wait. Sequential loading also requires more time and thought on the dock. But it allows Tony to make more stops in a day and drive fewer miles doing it than if his route were not unfolding in logical order. (Tony is only grousing because the logic is imperfect.)

Many trucklines don't load sequentially, but instead "progressively"; that is, freight is loaded onto trucks in the order that it arrives on the dock, without thought to arrangement for an orderly delivery route. As a result, the driver has to zigzag randomly the next day as the freight is revealed in his truck. He may cross town and then return to a place he's already been to more than once. "What comes in they throw on, so you have to go back and forth and pick around among the freight," according to Jimmy Roche, the north-of-Boston driver, who's worked under both systems. "With A-P-A," he said, "there's one or two more stops, but it's easier."

Also, without a routing plan, two and even more trucks may end up loaded with freight for the same consignee on the same day, costing the truckline fuel and time. Further, progressive loading makes performance standards hard to enforce. It's probably what freed the driver for the national truckline to lounge in his tractor while he parked at the dock at Automatic Operations this morning. His dispatcher couldn't know precisely where he should be driving or what point he should have reached on his route by what time, because he wouldn't know what freight was loaded where on the truck. "The big nationals concentrate on the long haul and don't try to control their pickup-and-delivery costs," one trucking executive told me. "If they did, they'd make a lot more money."

It's past noon, and we are in Clifton now, a greener, wealthier, newer town than Passaic, its neighbor to the east, although not new enough for its factories to live in industrial parks with lawns and flowerbeds, as they do farther south around Princeton. The tenth stop is Givaudan Corporation, where a chemical sweetness weighs on the summer heat. This is a newer factory, built of white concrete rather than red brick. It fills the skyline with cylindrical tanks and cookers, overhead gossamers of gangways and pipes, chainlink-fenced yards stacked with bright blue drums, plain rectangular buildings with windows in regimented rows. Givaudan makes artificial fragrances. For them Tony has a two-foot-high crated black gadget that wears a red cap; it has the look of a robot from *Star Wars*. In the back of his truck Tony turns the crate over. "I don't know what it is, but it's been upside down." We read the label: a fluid-control valve from a machinist in Fairfield, New Jersey. Tony grumbles about the fragrance factory. "They kept me waiting for a pickup for half an hour here on Wednesday and then told me there was no freight."

As we're leaving, Pete Leota calls in, for only the second time this morning (the first was to ask Tony directions for another driver): "Tony, ten-oh-five?" 1005 is the truck number. "Where are you, Tony?"

"Givaudan. I'm not clean down to there, though. I'm bouncing." He means he's been skipping back and forth among stops listed on his manifest, in order to smooth the route.

"Bouncing?" Pete squawks, in a purely pro-forma outrage. "I hope you're bouncing back. How many you got left?"

Tony (in mild reproof): "Five."

Stop number eleven is a single fifty-three-pound carton for W. W. Grainger, an industrial supplier; next is a 173-pound skid of liquid chemicals in three drums for Bronze and Granite Memorials, a carver of headstones. Bronze and Granite is stationed at the ready across the boulevard from the grassy hillsides of King Solomon Memorial Park Burial Estates. Tony backs into a driveway lined with headstones waiting in rows; they are blank except for a Star of David at the top. It's lunch hour, and no one can be found in the black and grimy garage. The lady in the office, thin, red-haired, in her fifties, frets about the men of the place: "They're never here when you need them." She calls Tony "hon." She can't find snips, so Tony works one of the drums free of its binding to the pallet, lifts it down, then hefts the other two together with the pallet onto the driveway. He says Richmond's fabric rolls are getting to be a pain. We stop for lunch at a faded shopping center, in a parking lot landscaped with trash.

At lunch (frozen yoghurt and a Coca-Cola), Tony sits in the truck, folds the *Newark Star-Ledger* in octavo, and picks the horses for today's races at the Meadowlands Raceway. He rarely bets money, just tests his knowledge. He compares yesterday's winners with yesterday's guesses, which were more right than not, and he totals his fictive winnings: $258. A thirty-five-minute lunch is enough for him today; it's Friday and hot, and he's restless to get through his manifest. Because the contract with the Teamsters specifies an unpaid hour's lunch break, Tony will donate the other twenty-five minutes of labor to the company. (On other days, he'll take a Coke-break in the afternoon, to finish out the time.) Before swinging back onto the road, he calls Pete on a payphone for the names and addresses of the pickups Pete has assigned him for the afternoon. The routing of the pickups Pete leaves to Tony.

There are three more deliveries: a 265-pound drum of pigments to International Dyestuffs, a seventy-four-pound box of fire-brick shapes to Joseph Majka and Sons, a heating-oil distributor, and four cartons of telephone equipment weighing 500 pounds, manufactured by RCA in Lewiston, Maine. RCA has sent the equipment from Maine through the A-P-A system to the RCA warehouse in Clifton, rented from Howe Richardson, a manufacturer of scales. Though the A-P-A routing office scheduled the RCA delivery for much earlier, Tony has postponed it till now, setting the cartons to one side of the truck, because he knew he'd have to stop by both RCA and Howe Richardson in the early afternoon anyway. Both are "dailies": that is, they expect A-P-A to stop every day for pickups unless notified otherwise. RCA has freight for him, but Howe Richardson has nothing, though the dock supervisor forgot to notify A-P-A. "Tell them how I saved time by waiting on a delivery till I came for the pickup," Tony suggests, glancing at my notes on my clipboard. "See?" The smile. "I gave you a pointer on your work."

As he drives, I scan the landscape from the high vantage of the truck. These counties of northeastern New Jersey are among the most densely populated in the country, but the density is horizontal rather than vertical. High-rises are few, but every inch is built. Factories and refineries of every vintage and style alternate with a thousand neighborhoods, their narrow lots crammed with one-, two-, and three-family wooden houses and four-, five-, and six-story brick apartment buildings. The wooden houses are clapboard-faced and often flat-roofed, with stairs leading up to the second-floor entrance: the old New York *stoep* dating from Dutch colonial times. A steel awning reaches over the elevated front door; underneath the steps, a lower stairway parallel to the building branches downward to the basement apartment. The commercial avenues are a visual cacophony of fire escapes scrambling down the faces of the brick apartment houses, from which storefront signs thrust out like schoolgirls' tongues over the sidewalk. Young women with tall hairdos push strollers on their shopping rounds; old men wearing fedoras lean back from the sidewalk in folding chairs. Above their heads, the signs are a lexicon of American ethnography. I culled this list from a few blocks of Central Avenue in Jersey City: Klotzer's Greeting Cards, Don and Rosita Dance Studio, Mack-Contee Funeral Home (police cars parked outside), Brothers Restaurant, Grimms Chiropractic, Lam's Garden, Macabee's Work and Sports Wear, Hauptmann Carpets, Leonard K. Franko, Attorney at Law.

Now several hundred Catholic-school children fill the sidewalk. The girls wear blue blazers, white shirts buttoned to the throat, gray pleated skirts, blue kneesocks; the boys' uniforms are blue blazers, white shirts, blue ties, blue slacks, dress shoes. Teachers move among them, harassed and cheerful, as teachers usually are; policemen, also in blue, stern and pacific, stand one to a corner as the children cross. At an intersection, the children march past a fire station, a century old, its facade three romanesque arches in bicolored brickwork, beige and rust-orange. All three doorways are open, and in the shadow a fireman sits on the bumper of his American LaFrance, his chin in his hand as he contemplates the afternoon.

On a corner nearby, we pass the parish church, built in the same bicolored brickwork. The darker brick outlines the Gothic window-arches. One tall spire has stepped forward of the facade, a shorter spire has retreated beside the transept. Bright in the sun, white crosses ride aloft, one to a spire. Along the sidewalk, a waist-high iron fence skirts the church garden, and at the corner, withdrawn only a few feet from the sidewalk, attended by boxwoods, a white stone statue of the Virgin stands, her draped mantle sheltering her head in the Italian style, her raised hand blessing the neighborhood.

In the wet, riotous summer of the American Northeast, nature is irrepressible, and North Jersey's relentless urbanism is softened. The brick-reds and browns, the black pavements and eye-baffling confusion of fences, poles, traffic lights, and signs, are half-curtained by a sprawling green that presses and spills and bursts out everywhere through the cracks in the all-surrouding urban wall. Maples, elms, grasses, sumac, squared patches of rose bushes by the front stoop, wildflowers climbing the overpass, bright weeds eagerly clogging the gutter: one can see why William Carlos Williams, whose Paterson is the next town north, held faith with North Jersey in his search for beauty in miniature. Only in the most unmitigated slums, such as the Passaic neighborhood Tony threaded us through this morning, has nature been snuffed out entirely by the weight of brick and tar, by peeling billboards and blowing trash, by neglect and despair.

For three more hours, Tony circles and zigzags through Clifton and Passaic to make his pickups: four boxed rolls of cloth from Model Textiles, a third-floor sweatshop in another complex of recycled red-brick mills; two 182-pound rolls of shrinkwrapping film from Sommers Plastics for an off-shore factory in Puerto Rico; ten cartons of books from Sherbourne Distributing Co., a book jobber, for a bookstore south of Buffalo; ten boxes of medical instruments from Pfizer Corporation for Passaic General Hospital, and another nineteen boxes for a hospital in Annapolis; back to W. W. Grainger, a daily, but they're not ready yet; over to Rycoline Products, but their single-space dock is occupied. At each pickup, Tony collects, checks over, and signs the bill of lading, thus beginning the paper trail that accompanies each shipment of freight, just as, this morning, he ended the trail upon delivery with the signing of the delivery receipt. Once he's signed the bill of lading, A-P-A is responsible for the full value of the goods as long as the shipment is in the truckline's hands.

As I study his bills, Tony inches us down a narrow, steep lane that descends the bank of the Passaic River to the water's edge, where Woodlee Furniture still stands. It's a doughty old red-brick parallelogram, built in sharp angles to fit against the riverbank. Woodlee has, as the bill of lading identifies them, a "buffet," a "cream-oyster desk," and an "oval extension dining room table," to be shipped to furniture stores in Massachusetts and Montreal. While we wait on the floor of the lofty, resonating factory for a stockman to find the furniture, we watch a Puerto Rican woman with a high-teased hairdo show off her baby to her fellow workers.

Tony is hot, tired, and dirty. "I've never been so dirty. They should give you a day off when it gets above ninety." Now Pete is on the radio: Howe Richardson has called to say they have a pickup after all, so he'll have to cross town yet again. Tony's irritated. His pattern making is violated, his aesthetic sense outraged. "There go all my plans again."

Back on the streets, Tony bears down, although he keeps to the speed limits. There's an intersection he needs to reach before 4:00 P.M., when left turns become illegal. "After 4:00, you have to go all the way around." We're there at 3:55.

"If you'd made it by 4:03, would you have turned?"

"No. There's always cops here. It's not worth it." Tony has been stopped only once, during his second year at A-P-A. "The cop said I'd run a red light, but it was yellow. 'All right,' I said, 'when's the court date?' The cop tore it up."

He has never been ticketed, and he's never been in an accident since he began at A-P-A. He recites for me in happy detail the series of badges, savings bonds, plaques, and silver belt buckles (with a diamond stud added at the final level) that A-P-A awards for every accumulated five years of driving without an accident. The culmination at twenty years is a $5,000 bond and an extra week's vacation. Tony's flawless record doesn't tempt him to tackle a tractor-trailer rig, although "road drivers" who haul trailers from terminal to terminal over the interstates earn more than he does. He finds highway driving dull, and after a jack-knife in a Connecticut snowstorm on his first driving job, he doesn't relish the danger. Besides, to switch to road driving would mean a switch to another seniority list, and Tony would lose his right to choose his vacation in summer, when his daughters are home. (This summer, he'll take two weeks in July on the Jersey Shore—"the arcade, the boardwalk, the whole bit"— and a week in August in the mountains.)

The safety awards, the employee-of-the-month awards, the scholarships, the free health club, the overnight Christmas bashes at hotels or resorts, and the five-year-anniversary extravaganzas are gestures, rather than substance. In a company that paid poorly, or where morale was low, they would be sops, cheap substitutes for real rewards. In a company where the basics are secure, however, the gestures are genuinely extras, and they are received in the spirit they are given, as expressions of downward loyalty from management and specifically from Arthur, as tokens of what Arthur is not too shy to call gratitude for the upward loyalty of his employees. "Tell him about the trips," Diane said to Tony when I visited them at their house on the Jersey Shore. (She had of course accompanied him.) Tony obliged with a summary of the company's fortieth anniversary weekend: "A barbecue on the beach in Puerto Rico for eighteen hundred people, are you kidding?" He added: "Nobody else would do this. It makes me want to work harder for him and do the best I could. Even if he didn't, I'd still work hard for him."

"Not a lot of us are willing to commit revenues like that with no immediate return on production," Lance Primis, president of *The New York Times* Company, told me in a telephone interview. An A-P-A subsidiary delivers the *Times* in Westchester and Long Island, and Primis, who would like to see better employee relations in the newspaper business, is an admiring student of Arthur's ideas. He said of Arthur's gold-giving gestures, "You hear people say that what A-P-A does in this area is jelly-headed.

'Where's the return?' they say. The return is an excellent business."

Such gestures are indeed motivators, but they cannot be made merely in calculated expectation of a return. They are necessarily extravagant, because if they were cost-effective they would no longer be gifts, and their effect would be lost. "A business man has to give," Arthur says; but not everyone is capable of setting aside the emotional and monetary balance sheet.

Back at Howe Richardson, Tony eases his way down a lane that skirts a chainlink fence beside a trash-clogged slough. From a decaying railspur, sumac sprouts. Before bothering to back in, Tony parks and walks up the steps to the dock to jaw with the supervisor, who is tall, bald, and wall-eyed. Tony stalks back down again, disgusted. "He says they don't have anything. He gave it away. He didn't want to tell me, but I saw it on his bills. He's only got one eye, so when he's looking at you he's not really looking at you. He had two bills to ABF and one for A-P-A and he had A-P-A crossed out and ABF written in." Tony calls Pete on the radio. "I'm out at Howe Richardson? He gave it away."

Pete protests: "He said he had 900 pounds!"

Now Tony hauls us back to Rycoline Products, where the dock is free, to pick up a 412-pound drum of flammable compound cleaning liquid, and then to W. W. Grainger for the third time today, to pick up motor parts, pulleys, and a dockplate for local stores. At the last stop, Atlantic Chemical, the pickup is not ready. It's 5:12. Tony parks in the driveway in the shade of a maple tree, and he calls in to Pete, "Ten-oh-five, ten-oh-five," saying to me, "I'm hoping he won't give me any more work. I'm tired."

Pete is on the radio now. Tony tells him: "Atlantic won't be ready till Monday."

Pete springs the good news. "Have a good weekend."

Tony grins. "Only four more days."

"Four more days till what?"

"The big vay-kay."

Pete affects surprise and concern. "Oh. We didn't tell you about the schedule change yet?" Then, with envious disgust: "Four more days."

It's been a difficult day: a net of only twenty-five stops in eight hours, not counting false alarms. Still, at 3.1, he's beaten Pete's standard of 3.0 stops an hour. Tony drives us back to port. I read over my notes to him, as I did during our first day out, after I'd noticed him glancing at my clipboard. Tony nods, smiles, approves. "I'm living the day a second time." He takes us back along Route 21, this time southward, following the current of the black Passaic, then across the swamp on Route 3, down onto Paterson Plank Road and north on West Side Avenue, under the railroad at 85th Street and onto the spur of 88th Street that ends at the A-P-A gates. To a security man at the guard shack he hands over his manifest, his signed delivery receipts, and the sheaf of bills of lading from the pickups. The paperwork will be rolled inside a cylinder and sucked by pneumatic tube across the lot to the Billing Department for translation onto the main computer. The bills will be microfilmed and stored.

Tony backs into the dock, where the freight he picked up will be unloaded by night dockmen whose shift will begin at 7:00 P.M. He walks across the yard and into the operations building, stops at the dispatchers' window, punches out, turns in his keys. He'll cool down with a Coke in the air-conditioned drivers' room for half an hour, then drive the Turnpike home in his Dodge, his right arm draped across the back of the passenger seat, his speed steady in the truck lanes, where the traffic is lighter. "I'm gonna go home and get in the pool and lie on the raft and look up at the sky. Last week I fell asleep in the pool. My wife says, 'What do you want to do, you want to drown?' I tell her, 'I'll wake up when I hit the water.' She says, 'How do you know that?' "

3. The Night Dock

At twenty minutes to midnight, A-P-A's North Bergen terminal glares with banks of spotlights. Low buildings, some shut down and dark for the night, some with doors open and windows blazing, stand scattered about the forty-acre lot. Tractors parked without trailers line the chainlink perimeter fence; rows of trailers, immobile without tractors, crowd the center of the yard. Beyond the trailers lies the centerpiece of the terminal and of the company: the North Bergen dock, a single cinder-block building that stretches south to north for not quite a fifth of a mile.

As I arrive at the terminal gate, two tractor-trailers loaded for the long haul, one departing, one arriving, have stopped on either side of the guard shack. The inbound driver is leaning out of his window to hand his manifest to a security man. The guard walks back behind the trailers to break a numbered seal on the lock of the trailer entering and to snap shut the seal on the lock of the trailer departing. Seeing security's wave in their mirrors, the inbound driver chugs into the yard, while the outbound driver roars up the steep slope of 88th Street to the long stoplight at Tonnelle Avenue, which is the old U.S. Route 1. His left turn heads him north to the George Washington Bridge, toward another A-P-A terminal in New England, New York State, or Canada. A right turn would have sent him along the edge of the swamp to the New Jersey Turnpike and then south toward a terminal in Maryland or Virginia, or else west to Pennsylvania or Ohio.

Inside the terminal, I park between two tractors near the operations building. I can see that City Dispatch downstairs is dark, while the empty drivers' room is open and half-lit for late arrivals. The night billing office is alight on the second floor. The tractors parked around the outside of the building are Fords and Macks, built in the "cab-over" style, with flat faces and drooping eyes. Their cabs are mounted over their engines—thus the name "cab-over,"—in order to reduce the overall length of the rig. For A-P-A they haul city trailers on daytime pickup-and-delivery runs; therefore, all rest idle in the yard tonight.

Long-snouted "conventional" tractors are parked nearby, behind the ten-bay maintenance building. They haul the largest and heaviest loads—ocean-going containers bound to and from the Ports of Newark and Elizabeth, for example, and trailerfuls of televisions from Sony's warehouse in Cranbury, and miscellaneous freight routed over the interstates to one of A-P-A's thirty-one branch terminals. The engines of conventional tractors ride foward in front of their cab, making that blunt, square, grilled truck's muzzle of film and story. Above and behind the engine, the rectangular windshield, angled forward at the divide in the middle, bestows on the tractor a severe, rather scholarly look about the eyes. The brow sweeps upward into the roof fairing, which on the highway deflects the headwinds over the top of the trailer. Behind the cab, extending over the drive-axles like a low-slung canine back, the black tractor chassis crouches naked, until it slides under a trailer.

Leaving the gate and the operations building behind me, I cross the yard between trailers parked in their rows. These gray, rectangular boxes, built of aluminum panels, are the standard-issue vessel of the motor freight industry. Truckers call them "dry vans." A-P-A's vans measure eight and a half feet wide, nine feet high, and forty-three or forty-five feet long (the more common fifty-three-footers are not permitted in some northeastern states). The vans stand roughly four feet off the ground; thus their roofs are raised to around thirteen feet off the pavement. They ride on two four-wheel trailer-axles linked in tandem near the tail. Interspersed among them on the yard stand the much shorter "pup" trailers, twenty-eight feet long. Pups are hauled over the road as "doubles," one behind the other, each riding on a single trailer axle. Vans and pups alike are sometimes called "semis," because, with axles only at the rear, they are only half-competent for the road. When they are parked alone, semi-trailers are supported near the nose by two rectangular steel posts, with flat splayed feet like an elephant's. The posts are still called dolly wheels, although the wheeled design has largely been abandoned. After a driver has hooked his tractor to a trailer, he cranks up the dolly wheels about a foot clear of the road.

Ahead, beyond the rows of trailers, stands the dock. Eighty-four doors line up one beside another along its east side, which faces back across the yard towards 88th Street and the North Bergen heights. The doors are elevated four feet above the asphalt to receive the open straight trucks and trailers when they're backed in. On the other side of the building, another eighty-four doors face the rail line and the swamp, and a further twenty-four doors face north, for a total of 192, which Sal Passante, the gray-haired, cigar-chomping terminal manager, says are still too few. Above the doors, on a high overhang, each door is labeled by a number painted in fluorescent yellow on a square red background. At the south end of the building, the corporate offices rise alongside the dock and reach partway over the roof, like wisteria on a trellis.

Most of the doors in the dock are plugged now with backed-in tractorless trailers or straight trucks. A few unoccupied doors are open rectangles of yellow light that fling the din of the dock out into the night. By now I've become accustomed, when I cross the yard, to walking among configurations of trailers that may suddenly shift as one is pulled away, and to venturing across lanes down which yard-jockey Kenny Di Grazia, waving, with fey grin behind grizzled beard, suddenly charges in his yard-horse, which is a single-seat cab-over tractor. Kenny and the other yard-jockeys roar about the lot the entire day or night, hooking to or dropping trailers, backing them into doors in the dock ("making a hit"), and hauling them away to be parked again once they've been stripped of their freight and reloaded. Kenny is here at this moment, hooking to a trailer at 29 Door and pulling away, opening a rectangle of light like a magic lantern's eye.

Beside every fifth or sixth dock door, a four-rung ladder is bolted to the concrete wall, not unlike a swimming-pool ladder. If the door is open, one can climb up from the asphalt yard to the floor of the dock as a swimmer emerges from the water. Tonight nearly every door is plugged in the central section of the dock, so I walk up the concrete receiving ramp beside 57 Door. I enter a brightly illuminated cavern, a cacophony of lights and shapes, of colors and clatter.

Four lanes of traffic sweep around the inner perimeter of the building. Across the wide outer lane beside the doors, men are hurriedly pushing carts among piles of crates and cartons of every shape and size. Forklift trucks, painted bright yellow and called "hilos" (high-lows) on this dock, whiz backwards or forwards, silent on battery power, bearing crates, drums, pipes, or skids on naked steel blades that jut forward low to the ground. (Skids are pallets to which freight has been bound by steel straps or by plastic shrinkwrapping.) As I cross the outer traffic lane warily, a couple of men nod to me. This is my second night on the dock.

The middle two lanes of traffic are a rush hour of orange freight-carts inching and jerking along a pair of concentric draglines. The carts, caged on three sides, six feet long and high and three feet wide, carry as much as 800 pounds of freight in loose cartons or small crates. The dragline they travel is a double steel rail open in the center, with a motorized cable circulating beneath. Much of the din on the dock is the crash of the carts as, propelled by the dragline, they lurch into motion, and often butt the carts ahead. Besides, boomboxes, hung from the posts between doors where dockmen are loading or stripping, battle with the carts and with neighboring boomboxes for the mastery of the air.

Looking down the traffic lanes to my right, I can just make out the row of doors in the north wall. To my left, the south wall is too distant to discern. The entire length of the dock is 983 feet, the width 385. The roof is raised to twenty feet by rows of I-beams, but there are no interior walls; the dock is a single room. The outside walls consist simply of the doors, the posts between them, and space enough above the doors for them to be raised straight up on their runners to the ceiling. The floor is concrete.

Above my head are a confusion of beams, rafters, ducts, pneumatic tubes, and banks of blinding fluorescent lights hanging from wires.

Having stepped through brief openings in the lines of cart traffic, I cross yet another, narrower lane for movement of pedestrians and hilos, and then enter the inner section of the dock. Here bulk and solidity dominate, instead of motion. In a succession of areas called "bays," freight is "staged" (parked ready for sequential loading), either as cartons piled into carts, or as skids and crates stacked by hilos. Narrow lanes lead between temporary high-rises of twentieth-century artifacts: photocopiers, fabrics, machinery, spools of cable, cigarettes, pharmaceuticals, valves, gauges, computers, air conditioners, candy bars. Six large bays fill much of the center of the dock, each representing a pickup-and-delivery division of the New York–New Jersey metropolitan area. Another bay holds C.O.D. freight, which is delivered only by appointment; yet another, international and Puerto Rico freight, which is headed for the ocean piers. Signs in block letters proclaiming each area hang on wires from the ceiling and swing in the night wind that sweeps through the open doors from the Meadowlands.

To each of the bays, the inner of the two draglines throws out spurs. Carts are continually turning off the line with a jerk and arriving, and "bay men" pull the carts off the spur and line them up in rows. This staging of freight permits the logical ordering of sequential loading. Most or all of the pieces of a load to be delivered must be gathered before they can be stacked into a truck or trailer in the reverse order of a driver's route. If A-P-A practiced progressive loading instead, and piled its stripped freight directly onto delivery trucks in the order it arrived on the dock, bays and their bay men would be unnecessary.

Between two freight bays not far from the north end of the dock, a three-story "docktower" rises to the ceiling. It is shaped like those squared-off guard towers in the corner of wooden palisades that one sees in drawings of colonial defense-works. Its function, however, is modern: that of the captain's bridge on the plain of an aircraft carrier. The second floor, all blazing windows, is the command center here. (The third floor is the employees' lunchroom; the first floor is a men's room. There is no women's room on the dock, because there are no women on it. Trucking—above all dockwork when it requires heavy loading—remains largely a male domain.)

I climb iron stairs along the outside of the tower. Inside, Mike Trebour, tower dispatcher, recognizably vice-president for labor Burt Trebour's son, with the same large, square, generous face, sits at the corner desk, which is a tilted board. He's busy speaking in numbers to a hand-held two-way radio; it connects him to the yard-jockeys, so that he can direct the flow of straight trucks and trailers in and out of doors. ("Kenny, swing two-eight-three-four into one-oh-nine door.") He also mans the terminal's night switchboard and maintains the close-out board, not in fact a board but a square yard of printed chart on which Mike notes, in old-fashioned pencil, all the outbound trailers that have been loaded during his watch. His shift runs from 1 P.M. to 12 A.M. "I see my wife for lunch," he says of his hours.

Along the south wall of the docktower runs a simple, shallow, built-in desk shared by the dock supervisors—ten men by night, five by day. Their names, laser-printed, are mounted under tape over their spaces: Larry Crawford, Nick Falgiano, Kevork Kharmandarian (lead supervisor at night), Bob Lawlor, Ed McElwee, Joe Ocello, Andy Ott, Mike Riley, Red Ryan, Charlie Trentacosti, Jim Vanzella, Steve Vegliante, Ray Younghans, Rich Yurcisin, and Denis Zanetti. Beyond their shared counter, five four-inch-wide pipes flow together down from the ceiling and end in a row of steel boxes with glass doors. These are the pneumatic tubes and their receiving bins. Into the bins, rolls of paperwork, packed into cylindrical steel-and-plastic envelopes, every so often land with a thump, arriving from a supervisor's station on the dock floor or from the Billing Department in the operations building across the yard. When Mike opens a door to retrieve a pneumatic envelope, the air in the system rushes mysteriously. Across from the tubes is a desk with a photocopier of the ancient type that unexpectedly slides its lid across the surface, pinching slower fingers. Next to that is a microwave riding on a half-refrigerator, behind which stands a cubbyhole office shared by Brian Nallen, day operations manger, and Sam Chominsky, night operations manager. On their open door is thumbtacked an aging poster displaying the national flag with the motto: "We support our troops in the Persian Gulf," and, below, "Proudly distributed by Fischer Printing Co., Union City, NJ."

Mike takes up the microphone that stands on his desk, and he booms across the dock: "All right, fellas, lunchtime. Let's go to lunch." It's midnight, and the night crew has been working for five hours. To stop the dragline, Mike reaches up to punch one of two red buttons mounted in a gray circuit-board above his head. The carts below utter a final series of clanks and crashes, and are still.

Sam Chominsky is climbing the stairs. He is trim and muscular, about six feet tall, just over forty, with a small, sharp face, a thin black moustache, and intense dark eyes, which are friendly but too serious to smile on the job. With the day brass gone, he's in charge of this place. He's been walking the dock to see how things stand just before lunch hour. Sam's job is to ensure that the freight on the trucks is stripped and reloaded with the least amount of error and with the most efficient use of manpower. Most important is that the city trucks and trailers be loaded and ready to go out for deliveries to New York and New Jersey when Tony and his fellow city drivers arrive at 8:00 A.M. Meanwhile, Sam must advance the flow of freight in and out of trailers that have arrived "inbound" from A-P-A's branch terminals or that are headed "outbound" to them. With this inter-terminal traffic, there isn't the same pressure to finish, because inbound and outbound trailers arrive around the clock, and the work continues through Brian Nallen's day-shift.

On an average night, Sam tells me, sixty straight trucks will be stripped of local pickups and loaded with local deliveries. Eighty-five to ninety local trailers will be stripped and fifty local trailers loaded. More trailers are stripped than loaded because more freight is picked up in the New York–New Jersey area than is delivered back to it. The surplus goes outbound to other terminals. "City trailer drivers will come back full early in the day and then take out an empty," Sam explains. "E.I. duPont in Clifton will quickly fill two or three trailers with skids a day; so, three strips, one load." Meanwhile, about sixty trailerloads arrive over the road from other terminals during an average twenty-four hours, and about a hundred depart, forty on the day-shift, and sixty at night. Altogether, an average of 5,100 separate shipments, 3,500 by night and 1,800 by day, move across the dock in twenty-four hours.

By 7:00 P.M., when the night-shift begins, Sam has to decide how many men to hire. He uses a core of sixty-five "regulars" from the seniority list, but often that isn't enough. He can supplement the veteran force with "casuals"—part-time people who show up in the hope of work, but without a guarantee of it. They may be policemen, firemen, or warehousemen on their nights off, or men who have been laid off by other truckers or by factories or warehouses, and who are looking to make the list at A-P-A. (My three weeks on the dock in 1971 were "casual.") If a regular is on vacation, a casual will fill his place. Tonight Sam hired sixty-eight men, and the group includes fourteen casuals, a very high proportion, because it's the second Monday in July, and eleven regulars are on vacation. Joe Whalen at Personnel made telephone calls this afternoon to ask casuals to come in. This night crew will be supplemented by the fifteen regulars on the 1:00-A.M.-to-10:00-A.M. shift. During the 7:00-A.M.-to-4:00-P.M. day shift, thirty-six regulars move freight for Brian Nallen.

The number of pickups made by city drivers during the day is Sam's rough basis for deciding the night's level of manning. "If dispatch tells me 1,600, 1,800, 2,000 bills" ("bills," short for bills of lading, is the monosyllabic equivalent of "shipment"), "then I know if it's going to be light or heavy," he tells me. The volume of pickups can't predict the work precisely, though. An average shipment at this terminal weighs 900 pounds, but averages are merely statistics, and weight can be deceptive. A veteran dockman can usually strip six or seven trailers a night, handling an average of twenty-four shipments an hour, or, measured otherwise, an average of 9,000 to 10,000 pounds an hour. But last night, Sam says, a trailer came in from Georgia "packed from nose to tail" with lighting fixtures, which are featherweight but awkward and delicate. "They all needed to be walked on a flatbed cart. It was a twelve-hour stripping job. The other extreme is a

hilo man taking forty-five minutes to strip a trailer that's all skids,"
though altogether they may weigh 35,000 pounds.

There's also no telling what "foreign" trailers—belonging to
other companies—are going to arrive bearing "distribution freight"
for A-P-A to sort and deliver. As many as a dozen such trailers
may arrive during the night. For example, as Sam and I talk—
while applying ourselves to coffee and muffins retrieved from a
lunch-truck that parks in the yard at midnight—a driver arrives
at the door to the tower, wondering whether he's in the right
place. Even without the bewildered look that says he's never
seen a terminal of such vastness before, it's plain he's not an
A-P-A driver from the soft belly that flops over the jeans, which
flop over the cowboy boots. Mike says of him pityingly: "He's
from out West." (To Mike, that suffices to explain the man's be-
wilderment.) The Westerner is a longhaul trucker who's moved
an entire trailerload of electrical equipment cross-country for
W. W. Grainger, the industrial supplier that Tony picked up
for in Clifton. Most of his load is headed directly for the Clifton
warehouse, but Grainger sent him a curveball by asking him to
drop three skids here with A-P-A. Such a small shipment
won't affect Sam's plans, but a second lunch-hour arrival is more
substantial: yet another trailerload of electrical supplies for A-P-
A to deliver. This second driver, from Milwaukee Electric Tool
Corp., has been here before. He drops the trailer on the lot,
drops his paperwork with Mike, and heads back to his tractor,
which he'll drive to a motel. He'll return for his emptied trailer
in the morning.

Tonight is unusual, even beyond the usual variables. In the
first place it's a Monday, and distribution freight brought by foreign trailers has piled up over the weekend. (The North Bergen
dock is shut down from sometime Saturday morning till 1:00 A.M.
Monday morning.) Independent longhaul truckers, who often
move this freight under contract, like to get to New York on the
weekend so that they can sleep before seeking a new load on
Monday, when they're most in demand. On the Saturday just
passed, independent truckers dropped three trailerloads of Sharp
computers, televisions, and copying machines, which they'd
brought across the country from the Port of Los Angeles. There

are also Saturday pickups to strip. An A-P-A driver went to Sony's warehouse in Cranbury three times on Saturday to hook up to trailers full of stereos. (These were "spot boxes"; A-P-A leaves the empty trailers at the warehouse, and Sony's dockworkers load them.)

Further, the volume of freight increases at the end of the month, and also at the end of the fiscal year, when managers want their docks cleared for inventory. Thus the end of June and the beginning of July are especially heavy weeks of the summer, which, for truckers, is otherwise slow. In 1991, however, the national economy has picked up in late spring and early summer (only to fall flat again in the normally much heavier fall, as it later turns out). Finally, July Fourth has fallen this year on a Thursday, so that last week, after closing for the holiday, A-P-A ran only a skeleton crew on the dock on Friday, and now, on the following Monday night, even after the work of the small Sunday night shift and of the Monday day crew, the dock is still bursting with last week's freight. So much volume is slowing the work down, especially since more than a fifth of the crew tonight are casuals, who don't move as fast as regular men. Sam is behind schedule. He's hoping the fifteen-man 1:00 A.M. crew will feel especially vigorous tonight.

The 1:00 A.M. crew works alone Sunday night, then supplements the second half of the night-shift and the first half of the day-shift Mondays through Thursdays. It's not properly a graveyard shift by itself, because at North Bergen, A-P-A really runs only two basic dock shifts: 7:00 A.M. to nearly 7:00 P.M., and 7:00 P.M. to nearly 7:00 A.M. Most dockmen expect at least two hours overtime daily, for which they're paid time-and-a-half wages. When the freight is light, in summer and also in January, the dock may be silent for about four hours out of the twenty-four: for an hour at dawn and again at dusk between the shifts, and at the two lunch periods at midnight and noon. When the volume of freight is heavy, as it is tonight, the shifts blend into each other and the dragline stops only for lunch.

The night-dock operation at North Bergen was not always so complex, nor its manager's responsibilities so intricate. When Arthur and his brothers first built this dock—it opened in 1951,

with 7,500 square feet, in what is now the southwest corner—
it was a "city operation" only. The men stripped freight that
A-P-A trucks had picked up in New York or New Jersey and
loaded the freight into A-P-A trucks that would deliver it back
to New York or New Jersey. A-P-A Transport was then a "local
trucker," of which every middle-sized city in the United States
has at least one. A local trucker will move freight only back and
forth across town, or between nearby towns. He may handle
freight headed to or coming from more distant points, but only
if another trucker that travels more distant routes brings the freight
in or takes it away. His own trucks won't leave the local area.

In 1958, when A-P-A opened its second terminal, in Reading,
Pennsylvania, it immediately entered a more outward circle of
the business: it became a "regional" truckline. Since then it has
opened thirty more branch terminals, as far west as Cincinnati,
as far south as Richmond, as far east and north as Halifax and
Montreal. Thus its region has expanded to include the entire
Northeast of both the United States and Canada. The company
also "interlines" with other regional trucklines in the South,
Southwest, the Midwest, and the Northern Plains. Under an interline arrangement, A-P-A may send a trailerful of pickups from
New England to Minneapolis for its associate truckline to deliver
in Minnesota and Wisconsin; the associate will refill the trailer
with pickups in its own region and send the freight east for
A-P-A to deliver in New England. The revenues are shared. With
its regional partners, A-P-A's reach in effect is national.

The eight cartons of medical equipment that Tony delivered to
General Hospital in Passaic on Friday morning were local freight.
A-P-A's driver on the New Brunswick, New Jersey run picked
the cartons from the shipper on Thursday afternoon. They were
stripped from his truck onto the dock Thursday night and loaded
onto Tony's truck before 8:00 A.M. on Friday for him to deliver
before 10:00 A.M. A-P-A could have handled that freight in 1951.
The compressor that Tony sweated inch by inch off his truck for
Melco in Clifton, however, was regional freight. It had been picked
up in Rochester, New York, on Thursday afternoon by a city
driver based in A-P-A's branch terminal in Syracuse. Thursday
evening a hilo man on the Syracuse dock stripped it from the

Rochester truck and stacked it on a trailer he was loading outbound for North Bergen. In the middle of the night, an over-the-road driver hooked his road tractor to the trailer and "made the linehaul," as truckers call it: he hauled the freight down the shortest line (in time) between two terminals—in this case, the New York Thruway. Arriving at North Bergen, at 4:00 A.M. perhaps, the Syracuse trailer was stripped of its contents, the compressor was staged in the North Jersey bay, and a hilo man squeezed it into Tony's truck for delivery Friday morning. The compressor, then, was overnight freight, requiring one linehaul and dock-handling at two terminals.

Some freight takes two days, two linehauls, and three handlings at three terminals. A skid of wooden clothes pegs, say, may be headed from a wood-turning mill in Bridgton, Maine to a warehouser of building materials in Newport News, Virginia. The pegs will be packed loose in a dozen large bags of white plastic cloth, and the bags strapped to a pallet. On Wednesday afternoon, the clothes pegs will be collected by a "pedal driver"—a stop-and-start pickup-and-delivery driver—based at A-P-A's southern Maine terminal at Scarborough. (Mainers, determinedly rural even in downtown Portland, disdain to speak of "city drivers.") On Wednesday night, at the Scarborough terminal, the skid of pegs will be stripped and then loaded onto one of Scarborough's two trailers designated for the nightly eight-hour linehaul down the New England turnpikes to North Bergen.

On Thursday morning, a North Bergen hilo man will strip the skid of clothes pegs from the Scarborough trailer and bring it across the dock to a jutting extension of the building, called by the men who work there the "east tit." (It's asymetrically balanced on the other side of the dock by a "west tit.") Signs announce "RICHMOND" over two doors in the east tit; if there's a trailer backed in, waiting to be loaded for the Richmond terminal, the hilo man will load the clothes pegs onto it. Sometime that same day, a road driver will hook to the Richmond trailer and make the eight-hour run down I-95 to Virginia—one of the most desirable of A-P-A's linehauls in winter because it's the least subject to snow, and a plum for A-P-A's senior drivers, just as the Syracuse and Buffalo runs are the winter banes of the younger men. Early Friday morning, the skid of pegs will be stripped once again, staged on the Richmond dock, then loaded for the last time onto a city trailer, and at 8:00 A.M., about forty hours after the pickup in Bridgton, Maine, the pegs head out for delivery in Newport News, the southernmost of A-P-A's pedal runs.

The reason for the gigantism of the North Bergen dock is its dual role of city operation for the largest local freight market in the country and of "break-bulk" operation for a large regional carrier. The term "break-bulk" arises because, as in the case of the putative clothes pegs, not just the pegs but the entire bulk of the trailerload arriving at North Bergen from Maine must be broken up on the dock and redistributed. The clothes pegs from Bridgton will go to Richmond, but the trailer will have, perhaps, also carried four skids of shoes from Lewiston, Maine, consigned to a shoestore in Scranton; thirty drums of carageenan (processed seaweed) shipped from Rockland, Maine, to a speciality ice-cream maker in Annapolis; a fifty-pound carton of golf tees from a wood turner in Guilford consigned to a sporting goods warehouser in Milwaukee; and ten skids of cardboard inner-sole liners from a Rumford paper mill headed to an offshore shoe factory in Puerto Rico. The shoes will go by hilo across the dock to the Scranton door, the carageenan and the golf tees will move in carts on the dragline to the Baltimore and the Chicago doors, while the cardboard shoeliners will be left in the trailer, which itself will now be routed to the Port of Elizabeth. All night long, nearly everything on every truck and trailer in every door must be stripped, sorted, carted or forklifted, staged, moved again, and reloaded.

In the necessity for break-bulk and hubs lies the complexity both of trucklines like A-P-A and of airlines. No single one of the shipments will fill the trailer, just as no single passenger can fill the airplane. Flying from Providence to Omaha, you find yourself first in Kennedy Airport in New York, next in O'Hare in Chicago, and only then in Omaha, going no more directly than a skid of clothes pegs. The lady by the window has come from Burlington through Kennedy and will trudge through O'Hare on her way to Des Moines, and the family across the aisle with the squalling infant has come from Heidelberg through Frankfurt bound for a holiday in Aspen through O'Hare and then Denver, having linked up in O'Hare, they hope, with Grossmama flying in from Milwaukee. It would be easier on everyone, including the airline, if everyone on the plane were headed from Providence to Omaha with you. Then the plane could fly direct and skip the hubs.

It's the same with trucking. The skid of clothes pegs needs transshipment through the North Bergen hub because the building-materials supplier in Newport News doesn't need an entire trailerload of clothes pegs. But he might well order a trailerload of doors. If he does, then the similarity with hub-and-spoke air travel disappears. The trucker's job has suddenly become simple. To move a single shipment of doors that fills a trailer, a trucker doesn't need a break-bulk operation: he doesn't need a terminal at all. He doesn't need an office or a salesperson or a dockman with a forklift or a secretary with a computer. He doesn't even need a trailer, which could belong to the lumber mill that cut the doors or to the building-materials warehouser that ordered them or to a trailer-leasing company. All the equipment he needs to own is a tractor—unless the bank owns it—and a telephone. He can park the tractor in his driveway in South Portland. He learns about the doors by telephone from a freight broker in Boston. He drives his tractor up the Maine Turnpike and State Route 4 to the lumber mill. He hooks up to the trailer, which is already loaded, probably overloaded, with the doors, and drives down the interstates to Newport News for sixteen hours straight (after ten hours that's illegal, but he's unlikely to be caught). He drops the trailer at the building-materials supplier, calls Boston to reserve another job (which may take him home to Maine or may take him to Montana), parks his tractor in a truckstop, and flops in the sleeper-berth behind the cab.

This trucker is the independent owner-operator, called by other truckers (with the ancient contempt of settled peoples for nomads) a "gypsy." He is the one who is obscured by the popular stereotype: the big beard, the bleary eyes, the beer belly, and the bigotry, the road cowboy romanticized by country singers. His sector of the trucking business is called "truckload" hauling because he moves a single shipment from one source to one destination, and because his shipment fills the trailer, so that no intermediate handling is required. Truckload operators (TLs, as truckers abbreviate them) may haul raw materials headed for refiners, or refined materials headed for component manufacturers, or components headed for assembly plants, or finished goods headed for warehousers, or job lots headed for retailers: the gamut of commerce from extraction to consumption. Anything that will fit reasonably into a trailer will do, provided—and this is the fundamental, though seemingly simple condition—that there's no second shipment in the load.

But if the doormaker in Maine sees that his shipment of doors, like the shipment of clothes pegs, is not going to fill a trailer, then he won't call the freight broker in Boston for a truckload hauler. He needs a very different kind of transportation: a "less-than-truckload carrier"—an LTL, as truckers say. He has to call someone who is willing to carry his doors packed together with other goods belonging to other shippers, and who has a terminal where the freight can be sorted and reloaded. If the freight is to travel to another city or state, then he needs a regional less-than-truckload carrier like A-P-A with a system of terminals that includes at least one hub. He's going to pay perhaps three times as much per door in shipping costs than if he had a full trailerload, because he's asking for complexity. Logistically, his doors are no different than the passenger who wants to fly from Providence to Omaha.

The trucker whom the doormaker now calls—a less-than-truckload carrier—needs city drivers for pickup and delivery and over-the-road drivers for linehauls; he needs dockworkers, branch terminals, and hubs; he needs a logistics strategy for sorting and routing freight and a data processing system that keeps track not just of trailers but of every carton, skid, crate, and bundle of pipe that enters his system. Above all, the less-than-truckload carrier needs a skilled and honest workforce that can move and handle freight without misplacing it, damaging it, or stealing it. In other words, he needs money, teamwork, and brains. The less-than-truckload carrier dismisses mere truckload work as a no-brainer, and he'll snort that anyone who can drive a truck and make a down payment on a used tractor can go into business as a truckload operator. In fact, during the boom of the 1980s, tens of thousands of truckers did so. In 1991 there were almost 48,000 common carriers registered with the Interstate Commerce Commision, perhaps ninety-eight percent of them owners of a single tractor.

The simplicity of truckload work attracts undercapitalized enterprise, and many owner-operators have started out driving "fender-flappers": "junk" trucks bought third-hand, at a million miles, from a leaser who himself bought it second-hand at half-a-million miles from a truckline. Many of these independent truckers are bankrupt within a year or two. But if his tractor is new, and if he drives long hours—perhaps with his wife as a partner to spell him and make the long hours both legal and bearable—the owner-operator may earn enough surplus to buy a second tractor. He'll employ a second driver, and now he has two loads on the road instead of one. Some truckload operators grew large in the eighties, employing hundreds of their own nonunion drivers and contracting other loads to hundreds of owner-operators.

Thus the transportation industry may be divided into overlapping categories. One pair of categories divides passengers from freight. Another concerns transportation "mode," as people in the industry call it: air, ocean, lake and inland waterway, pipeline, rail, and highway. Yet a third category represents the size of the shipment, and this is the consideration that determines the complexity of the task. Pipelines, ocean-going tankers, lake and river barges, railroad hoppers and tankcars, and lastly truckload trailers move goods in bulk: oil, coal, chemicals, steel, grain, lumber, gravel, automobiles. But once a ship carries not oil but containers, the train not coal but a variety of boxcars, the airplane not troops but business travelers and tourists, the trailer not a truckload but a mixed assemblage of freight with differing destinations, then complexity enters. The freight and passengers must be unloaded, sorted, and reboarded. An ocean pier is required with cranes and stevedores, or a railroad switching yard or an airport hub, or a less-than-truckload terminal with a night dock.

The complexity is not merely logistical, but social. Movement of bulk goods is centrifugal, propelling the freight-moving man outward into a loner's life of purposive wandering: into the life of the sailor, the bargeman, the longhaul trucker, the cowboy on the cattle drive. But in the less-than-bulk movement of freight, the centrifuge of trade is balanced by the centripetal pull toward the hub. The smaller the shipment of freight, the greater the need for transshipment, and the more complex the teamwork and the logistics. In the hub, the team player is honored and the loner is a misfit. In this context, Arthur's goal of establishing a community in the wilderness of the trucking industry seems not at all anomalous, but, instead, appropriate. It is no accident that the smallest of all shipments—letters and parcels—require the largest teams and the greatest concentration, so that in this country, parcel and letter delivery is dominated by three organizations: Federal Express, United Parcel Service, and the United States Postal Service. The latter two are the largest corporations in the American transportation business.

At 1:00 A.M., Jamie Gutierrez, who has spelled Mike Trebour in the tower, announces over the microphone, "Lunchtime's over, fellas. Back to work." Jamie punches the red button that starts the dragline, and a warning siren slides five times up and down a diminished fifth in a strident wail. The carts suddenly butt and jostle with a crash. At the base of the tower stairs, the 1:00 A.M. crew is lounging, sitting on skids or leaning against crate highrises, awaiting assignments from Sam Chominsky. Among them is John Occhiogrosso, whom I watched for several hours last night as he loaded break-bulk freight into outbound trailers on the east side of the dock. I'd linked up with John more or less by chance, on a briefly considered recommendation by one of the dock supervisors. He agreed to continue the interview tonight.

Loading outbound is John Occhiogrosso's usual and preferred task, and he's a senior man, but Sam uses his authority now to direct John elsewhere. The night operation is behind schedule, and Sam needs strippers. He sends John over to the Central Jersey area on the west side of the dock to strip a city trailer which, on most nights, would have already been unloaded before John's shift had begun.

John stands an inch below six feet and is just forty. He has a strong nose, heavy-lidded eyes, thick chestnut-brown hair, and a full brown beard. Tonight he's wearing a turquoise tee-shirt, jeans, and running shoes. As I follow him across the dock, he walks fast, carrying his 200 pounds lightly. He looks back and forth to keep watch for moving carts and hilos, meanwhile in-structing me with his head turned toward me so that I can hear him over the din. He already knows from last night that I want to hear all the details and understand everything, and his expo-sitions are patient and thorough, humorously self-deprecatory, frank, and sardonic. In explaining why he's not entirely happy with having to strip tonight, instead of loading as he prefers, he begins with the negative, the reason against his preference. "Loading is harder work than stripping, because you're putting freight up, not taking it down. Loading bothers some people's shoulders, but it's never hurt me. A lot of guys would think me crazy for saying this, but I like loading because I like to keep moving. Stripping is tedious, a lot of reading and counting, and a lot of waiting around for hilos to come and take the skids. When you're loading outbound, you're in charge of several doors for several terminals and you've got several trailers to load, so you can work while you're waiting for a hilo. Also, after mid-night the local operation is under more pressure, so the out-bound area is left alone, especially if you're a good worker. You have more independence."

We stop before the trailer he's been assigned to strip. It's backed in and open to the dock, and a goose-necked spotlight mounted on the wall of the dock glares at the freight. For John it's a dis-heartening scene. As far back as we can see towards the nose of the trailer, small loose cartons are stacked in rows that rise nearly to the ceiling. The effect is that of a series of very sloppily built brick walls standing one behind the other. The nearest two walls of cartons have spilled partly to the floor in transit, since they weren't packed in tight all the way to the tail.

Normally, each shipment—each group of cartons headed from one place to another—is loaded together in a trailer. Here, though, as John says with grim understatement, "Some of this may be mixed up." He'll have to identify and sort every one of the cartons, and they all look more or less the same, because they all come from one company, Ortho Pharmaceutical Corporation, of Somerset, New Jersey. Each carton is printed thickly over in blue with package-labeling. General appearance won't help; he'll have to locate the name and address of the consignees, which will be stated in small black capitals printed anywhere on the carton where there's space among the advertising.

John hands me his strip manifest, which is computer-printed on three sheets of stiff paper. Each sheet is divided into eight cards, separated by perforated edges. The sheets are backed by carbons that aren't perforated. The cards are "strip tickets," and they guide the stripper's work. Each strip ticket represents a shipment on the trailer and states the shipment's essentials: the names and addresses of the shipper and of the consignee; the number of pieces in the shipment (most of the pieces are loose cartons, in this case); the combined weight of the pieces in each shipment; and, finally, the number of the dragline spur to which the shipment is to be routed when assembled and piled on a cart. The ticket is to be torn off, stuffed in a little cup mounted on an upper corner of the cart, and sent on with the shipment. The carbon backing is to be checked off shipment by shipment and submitted to the dock supervisor when the trailer is clean.

Tonight John's strip manifest consists of twenty-two tickets on three sheets, representing twenty-two shipments in 1,405 pieces, weighing an aggregate of 8,985 pounds (cartons of drugs are light). Seventeen of the shipments are the cartons from Ortho Pharmaceutical, comprising 1,398 of the pieces. The other five shipments are from Merck and Co., another New Jersey pharmaceutical manufacturer. Four of the five Merck shipments consist of a single piece each—undoubtedly skids. They're out of sight behind the walls of cartons and must have been loaded in the nose.

As I read, John squats and begins sorting the Ortho Pharmaceutical cartons strewn on the floor. Some are addressed to an outlet of an Eastern drugstore chain, in Rome, New York; these are all, according to the blue advertising, athlete's foot powder.

Other cartons on the floor, containing foot powder, dermatological ointments, and vaginal creams, are consigned to a drugstore in Melbourne, Florida. John has dragged two carts into the trailer, so that, he says, he doesn't go crazy. However, though he's searched not only on the floor but along the top row of the first wall, he can only find forty of the forty-eight cartons for Rome and only ninety-five of the 100 for Melbourne. There's no point in tearing down the walls to search; he'll have to put the two carts aside until the missing cartons surface. "Maybe the driver threw the last few over the top," John surmises—a thoughtless deed if it was done, certain to draw down a dockman's reserve of patience. Deadpan, John offers a possible excerpt from the driver's stream of thoughts when he let fly the athlete's foot powder cartons far into the nose: " 'This is for that guy who loaded my truck this morning' "—and presumably loaded it badly. "It's the same," John adds, "as when they back in and pump the accelerator an extra time to fill the dock with exhaust and send dockmen scattering to the bathroom."

In describing this sparring between driver and dockman, John's tone is cheerful. He's enjoying the satisfaction of the pessimist— he would say realist—who sees proof everywhere of his dim view of human striving. But I'm wondering whether a factional rivalry between drivers and dockmen, even a somewhat friendly one carried out in a spirit of practical joking, is compromising A-P-A's solidarity and diligence. Drivers who pick up and load what dockmen strip, and dockmen who stack on the truck what drivers then take off for delivery, are setting the conditions for each other's work. If each is undermining the other, carelessly breaking up shipments by throwing into the nose cartons that belong in the tail, Augie's systems are corroded. I'll have to find out who loaded this trailer.

The next group of cartons John encounters are labeled "vaginal suppositories and Ortho-Novum norethindronel ethinyl estradiol, clinical package, not for retail": a twenty-piece shipment for a public health agency in Akron, Ohio. "Twenty should be easier," John says, stooping to sort, and searching along the top row of the first wall in the loose masonry. "But, of course, it's not complete. Now the fear is I've put some of it in *there*," he says grimly, nodding to the Melbourne cart with the ninety-five.

Still, there's hope: he's now got his first completion: eighteen cartons to a family planning clinic in Baltimore. He stacks them neatly on a cart, tears off the strip ticket, curls it, and stuffs it into the cup on the cart. Three sides of the cart are wire cage; across the open fourth side John stretches an elasticized "bungee cord" to keep Ortho's Baltimore cartons from being jostled to the floor when the cart is butted on the dragline. Beneath the cart's front bumper lies a strip of steel with ten numbered holes in it, and John lowers three "probes"—magnetized steel pins that hang by a chain from the bumper—into the 5, 1, and 3 holes, for spur 513. That's the spur that bends off the outbound dragline toward the three Baltimore doors in the north wall of the dock. At the junction of the spur with the line, the probes will pass over a magnetized plate. The plate at the Baltimore spur is magnetized to match the configuration of the probes set at 5, 1, and 3. When the match is made, an electric circuit will close, a flange will swing aside to open the spur, and the cart, obedient as a trotting sheep, will shunt aside toward the Baltimore door.

Now John is tearing down the carton walls. According to his strip manifest, there should be twenty-two cartons of Erycette topical solution for a pharmaceutical wholesaler in North Amityville, on Long Island. But, though he kneels on a half-disassembled wall and reaches over the top to read addresses, he can only find eighteen. "They really did a good job here," he observes with cheerful sarcasm. He finds all twenty cartons of Ortho-Novum—"Here's one that's complete"—for a wholesaler in Portland, Maine, and all thirty-four—"This is a good one"—of Retin-A cream to a drugstore in Pawtucket, Rhode Island. "Nice thing about this truck: everything's light." He puts the Pawtucket ticket in the cup of the wrong cart, the incomplete North Amityville cart, and is about to pull *that* onto the line when I stop him.

"I've got to help you," I say, "since I'm distracting you."

"I get confused very easily," he says graciously. He sends off the Pawtucket ticket with the Pawtucket cart and then immediately finds two more Pawtucket cartons; he'd counted thirty-two and thought that was right, but it's really thirty-four. He sends the two off in their own cart, with a note on scratch paper, "With 34 lot," stuffed into the cup. "This is definitely typical of me. You're looking at so many boxes."

He presses on. Of seventeen cartons of vaginal cream consigned to a pharmacy in Harrisburg, Pennsylvania, he finds twelve; of sixty-five cartons of the same for a pharmacy in Cheektowaga, New York, near Buffalo, he finds fifty-two. "OK, we'll put that on the side." By now he has pulled six carts into the trailer, and they stand along the walls in various stages of completion. "This isn't so bad. Some of them come in so bad you can't even get it done in eight hours. It could have been loaded better." He completes a shipment of eighteen cartons headed for Laconia, New Hampshire, and sends that off; then is stymied by forty-seven for Stamford, Connecticut. He's kneeling and looking over the top. "Stamford, Harrisburg, we've got everything up here. This has to be deliberate. See, there's supposed to be nine pieces to Lindenhurst, and they're not together. It couldn't have been too much trouble to keep that together. But then," he philosophizes, "the driver may have suffered from poor loading. Maybe someone put two skids on top of one another, but the place he was at didn't have a hilo. But then, management wants you to cube out." (To "cube out" is to fill the trailer from floor to ceiling and from nose to tail.) John concludes: "Everybody's to blame all down the line."

Now he completes the Lindenhurst (on Long Island), then the Harrisburg, and next the Rome, which he began the trailer with. He wedges them tight into their carts, "since carts get bumped to start, and it doesn't always spur off, so it can go around several times." Meanwhile, I find seven of the Cheektowaga, making sixty-four of sixty-five. "Good," John says. "I got to find one more, if I counted right. Right, Burt?" Burt, wearing polo shirt and shorts, a "casual" part-timer at work stripping the next trailer, has been glancing in occasionally at the spectacle of his neighbor narrating a stripping job and a writer scribbling it furiously down on a clipboard. Burt places hand on chest, pledge-allegiance position, and says piously, "I never make mistakes."

Half the succession of walls of cartons are down, and John has reached a second Baltimore shipment, of 113 pieces. "When you see a lot of boxes, you may want to skid it for the driver, so he doesn't have to handle it," John instructs me. The 113 cartons weigh 903 pounds. "If a shipment's over 800 pounds, you can skid it." To skid a shipment is to pile its various pieces onto a pallet and tie them down, to simplify handling by the driver. Sometimes the opposite—breaking a skid of cartons down—makes it possible to fill odd spaces on a truck. Large skids, though, are normally kept intact. John says, "If a skid is over 800 pounds, you're not supposed to break it down. The other day a supervisor was in a bad mood and told a platform man"—a dockman—"to break down a thousand-pound skid. They don't get along. Some people get the reputation of not being a good worker, or not working at all, and supervisors give it to them."

While zestfully offering this further example of ill-feeling, John has grouped the larger Baltimore cartons to one side on the floor and has stacked the smaller ones in a cart. "I'll show you how to block a skid." He pulls an empty pallet onto the trailer from a stack nearby. On it John lays out ten of the rectangular cartons, setting out first a row of three along their long axis, then next to them a row of four set along their short axis, then next to that another row of three the long way. He lays a second tier in the same pattern, but starts the pattern from an adjacent side of the skid, so that the patterns cross at ninety-degree angles. Thus all the cartons' edges overlap one another, and the pile is stable. This is blocking. He makes the pile six tiers high, a total of sixty cartons altogether. He marks one on the top with a pencil; "60/113 + 1 cart, 513"—the Baltimore spur. He'll send the strip ticket with the cart, which is not yet complete.

As John wraps a length of twine around the skid, Chris Kocaj, cigarette dangling, spies business as he cruises by on his hilo. He swings his machine about in that wide, drifting turn forklifts make, because the toy-sized wheels that do the turning are in the back, while the large drive-wheels are in front, just behind the load. Chris clanks over the dockplate and thumps onto the trailer, which reverberates nicely (no doubt an empty trailer is a fine place to sing). The trailer dips from the hilo's weight. Chris slides the blades underneath the block of cartons, between the pallet's two layers of boards. He yanks at the black knobs in front of his steering wheel, thus raising the blades and the skid with them. The blades rise along an upright frame, called the boom, which is mounted on the front of the hilo. A-P-A's hilo booms can raise freight six feet; in warehouses, where goods are piled on steel shelves that rise to high ceilings, booms can raise freight twelve or fifteen feet, and the forklifts must be much heavier for counterbalance.

As Chris backs out of the trailer with the skid, John follows, still tying the twine. He asks Chris about the illness that kept Chris out for five weeks, and then Chris chats with the curious Burt about baseball. Meanwhile John returns to attack a thirty-six-piece shipment to Butler, Pennsylvania, but stops instantly when Jamie bawls from the tower: "Coffee time." The dragline jerks into silence. It's 3:30 A.M. John's been piling and counting Ortho's cartons for two and a half hours. "That went fast," he says. "See you in ten minutes." To Burt he adds, as they walk off to the ramp at 57 Door, where the lunch-truck parks: "That's all we do here, coffee and lunch. I don't know how this guy makes money." He means Arthur.

The 7:00 P.M. shift is on coffee-break, too, although technically they have only another half-hour of work before their eight-hour shift is over at 4 A.M. But they rarely finish by then. Sam Chominsky charges by, still worried. "It's a tough night," he tells me. "Lots of work left over from the holiday. We'll be on till 7:30"—a close half-hour before the 8:00 A.M. deadline, when the city drivers arrive.

John clearly wanted a coffee break from narration as well as from counting, so I've stayed in the trailer. I'm still getting used to thinking of it as a stationary workplace, rather than a vehicle. It's a long, narrow, windowless room, glaringly lit, and stacked with the inanimate things that modern humans have learned to desire. The walls are thinly whitewashed plywood slabs; the floor is of hardwood strips, much scarred; the ceiling is of naked aluminum, slightly bowed upwards to the center, its width traversed by a succession of ribs.

This room, and rooms nearly identical, have been John's workplace for fifteen years. In a company bristling with the vigor of twelve-hour days, he's a leader in stamina. Besides his normal shift Sunday night through Thursday night, from 1:00 A.M. to 12:00 noon or to 1:00 or 2:00 in the afternoon, he also works as a casual for the 7:00 P.M. shift Friday—a six-day week that is very often as much as seventy-two hours. Last night, when I watched him load outbound, he told me that he also drives a paper route for the *Bergen County Record.* He delivers papers for five hours on Tuesday and Thursday afternoons, for an hour on Friday night during lunch break, and for four hours on Saturday. "My wife Karen and I never argue," he told me last night, "but we argue about how much sleep I get. If I get six hours, I'm okay. If I'm sleepy, it's all right if I keep moving."

Just as Jamie booms, "All right, fellas, coffee time's over," John steps back into the trailer. The siren wails, the carts crash. I ask John again about his sleep patterns. Now that I myself am working for the second night in a row, I'm beginning to sense that sleeping by day and working by night may involve more than a simple reversal of schedule. I'm told that day-sleepers, for one thing, sleep less. "It's easy to get to sleep, but you wake up," John confirms. Yesterday, which was Monday, he worked till 12:30 P.M.—"two-and-a-half hours overtime, not too bad. I went to bed at 3:00, got up at 8:30, got the kids to bed. I was going to go out running, but I had to pick up another platform man, so I didn't. I slept another half-hour." That made six. "Today I have five hours of paper route, plus I may have to substitute in a church softball game this evening. No sleep won't do. Got to keep Mommy happy. She says, 'What am I going to do when you're gone?' I say, 'You'll have more money, with the Teamster policy and social security.' She doesn't want to hear that."

As we talk, he's dismantling the last few walls of Ortho's cartons. He's sorting and assembling the remaining shipments, each in a cart, without trying to complete them. The carts that he has dragged in nearly fill the trailer. He's looking for thirty-four cartons for Rochester, twenty-four for Miami, 250 for Victor, New York, and 385 for South Hackensack, New Jersey. He drags in two skids and blocks them with cartons for the big Victor and South Hackensack lots. He chants tens and pencils subtotals onto cartons as he talks. "Night work is preferable because of the money: there's more hours. I chose to have five kids. The first one's in college. We like a few nice things: cable TV, two cars, vacations in Florida. The kids go to a Christian school in Hackensack, where my wife teaches music."

"What keeps you going all these hours?"

I asked Tony the same question, and John's answer is like Tony's answer—"Ambition to be happy"—and yet different.

"God gives me the strength to do it all. I guess for some people it's a heavy workload, and it is. I want to provide for my family, I want to pay the tuition bills. It's the grace of God and the desire to have a good life. We earn good money. I work long hours, but I don't have an education. I made that choice not to do well in school. Where else could I earn sixteen dollars an hour? I'm grateful for the work." From his long hours on the dock, John is making over $57,000 a year, not counting fully paid health insurance and retirement benefits, nor the earnings from the *Bergen County Record.*

Last night he told me he "was married at nineteen, went to A-P-A at twenty-five, was saved at twenty-six. Being born again changed me. Before, I had a gambling problem and didn't come home after work. I went to the track with the guys. I'm not the same person now."

He mentioned his religious conversion naturally, as a matter of ordinary fact. Tonight I ask him: "Tell me more about being saved."

The journey began in Queens, where his grandfather had started a bakery. His father and his four uncles inherited it. During his high school summers in North Bergen, to which his own family had moved, John commuted to Queens to work in the bakery. After graduation from North Bergen High in 1968 (he'd flunked out of Catholic school in the ninth grade), he went to work selling Electrolux vacuum cleaners. "It didn't work out. I'm not a salesman." He worked next as a coffee dumper for Savarin Coffee, on Broad Avenue in Palisades Park, which is two towns south of the George Washington Bridge. "That was a good job. A hilo brought you 150-pound coffee bags, you'd slide them off with a hook, open them, dump them in a chute according to the blend they wanted. The chute went to the roaster. The plant's still there. It's owned by Tetley Tea now. An easy job, five hours of work a day total, lots of free time." Meanwhile, he'd married Karen. She'd grown up in Fairview, the town just north of North Bergen. She'd been among a group of friends John used to go bowling with in grammar school.

After a year at Savarin, John's family asked him to work at the bakery. He stayed five years, until he walked out after a fight with the uncle who was in charge. "I was bad then. Gambling, putting my hand in the till." He'd begun gambling at fourteen; there was an Off Track Betting office next to the bakery. "With the OTB, you have to have money to bet. But the last two years, it was sports, too. There you get into debt, and I did. I didn't care a lot about my family. I'd go to Roosevelt Raceway for the last race, a forty-five-minute drive at night before work." He was also smoking marijuana. Meanwhile, he was going to a Baptist Church with Karen, who was raised a Protestant and who was the church's organist. "For five years I'd been hearing the word. But I couldn't give up my desires."

"This was June of 1976. I had a friend in church who worked at A-P-A. He got me started as a temporary for a month; then on July Fourth weekend, I began as a casual, four days a week. After fourteen days, I made the list." There were other changes and pressures. His first daughter and second child, Kristin, now sixteen, was an infant then, and his eldest son, John Jr., now nineteen, had just spent seven weeks in the hospital with a streptococcal infection that had moved to his chest. "They had to operate on him in New York to remove the fluid from his lungs."

The conversion came in church, in January, 1977. "Communion was coming up. I'd always thought that I had to give up my desires before accepting God, but I finally realized that it works the other way. I accepted that God could do it for me. I'd hit bottom. Now, over the next twelve weeks, I gave up the habits. The desire just wasn't there. My wife was happy. Everybody in church had been praying for me, but she thought I'd never be saved."

"Do you have doubts?" I ask him.

"The doubts do come," he says. But the experience of release from his addiction has been too strong for him to forget. "It had to be an outside power."

John's story reminds me of Martin Luther's story—a founding paradigm. Like John, Luther sought release from desires, habits, and doubts that separated him from peace of mind, a peace that Luther had entered his Catholic monastery to find. But, like John, he couldn't find it. Luther could have said what John just said: that he'd always thought he had to give up his desires first, before he could feel he was acceptable to God. That conviction conformed to the Catholic teaching that through prayer, penance, and other good works, as well as through faith, release from sin is gradually achieved. But Luther felt he had failed, and he gave up trying. He generalized his failure, concluding that the human sins of pride and selfishness made trivial anyone's attempt to earn divine favor. Good works were after all useless in the quest for Heaven; the only road to grace was surrender in the hope of mercy. Salvation, Luther said, acknowledging that he was adding to scripture, was *sole fide*, by faith alone. In John's words: "I accepted that God could do it for me." This conclusion brought Luther an emotional release powerful enough to sustain him through years of enormous literary labors, together with a successful defiance and partial defeat of the most powerful institution in Europe. John's release from his addiction to gambling and the energy that fires his years of vigor on the dock draw, it seems to me, on a very similar psychological event.

John describes his beliefs: "We're not Baptists necessarily. It could be any Bible-based church that says the Bible is the word of God. It's different from Catholicism, in that there's no intercession except through Christ. And there's the knowledge that because I believe, I will go to Heaven. If you're Catholic, you don't know. It's not because I'm perfect, but because of what Christ did on the cross. He paid for our sins."

There's no preaching in John's tone. He might be explaining how to block a skid. His distinction between Catholicism and Protestantism carries the authority of one who's lived in both traditions. To him, the human drama is a drama of individuals, each separately, and in every act, choosing the doomed human path or the path to grace. He wouldn't agree with Arthur that, in straightening out a trailer load, he's perfecting a piece of the world. The world is forever imperfectible. Arthur likes to say, "God needs help," but that is not a Protestant view. John's dark estimation of human efforts underlies his suspicion concerning the mess in the trailer—that it was caused by a driver's deliberate carelessness—and also his wry judgment of his own worth, in the face of his bosses' confidence and a shower of awards. He told me earlier: "Some people think I don't make mistakes. I was the first-ever employee of the month, the first-ever employee of the year. Why, I surely don't know. It's got to be for hustling and not complaining. It can't be for the counting and the paperwork. I'm no good at the minutiae."

His self-deprecation is not a mere doctrinal stance, however. He has a genuine sense of unworthiness, that of others and his own. It is the essential emotional basis of his faith, as it was of Luther's. I suspect that if he were to believe himself worthy of the recognition he has earned, he would equally have to credit himself with his victory over his addiction. Put otherwise, to develop his pride would mean to take the responsibility of his salvation upon himself and away from his God. Then his conversion would unravel, and his sleeping dogs might again become dangerous.

Later on this morning—to step forward into the future for a moment—I stop by Terminal Manager Sal Passante's office in the operations building. I'm curious about the cause of the jumble in John's trailer. Was it really, I wonder, a half-joking, half-spiteful driver's revenge? Is Arthur's vision of a community, whose members work by the rules purposively and enthusiastically, perhaps half a fantasy? In the operations building, behind stacks of far more time-study print-outs than he could possibly read, Sal sits at his desk, chewing on his unlit cigar. He's a big man, in his fifties, gray-haired and clean-shaven, wearing a short-sleeved white shirt, with tie askew. I ask him about the Ortho Pharmaceutical load. He paws through this morning's print-outs from Augie's systems, then calls in Dave Hillman from the dispatch room down the hall. Dave remembers the trailer. Louis Lessner was the driver, but the trailer was loaded by Ortho.

"What they do is, they put the conveyor belt right onto the trailer and load by commodity," Sal explains. "The driver has to stand there and count." All the skin creams rode in, maybe, then the dermatological salves, then the foot powder, sorted by item, not by destination. "The products came in together. The load isn't organized by shipment. That's why it was all mixed up for us." Ortho wants the A-P-A pickup driver to back into its dock between 2:00 and 2:30 P.M., Dave explains, so the driver has time for only one or two pickups beforehand. Yesterday it was the Merck skids, which Louis loaded into the nose. Then Ortho kept him waiting for four hours, till 6:30, so he couldn't make another pickup before going home. That's why the tail was empty and Ortho's cartons tumbled to the floor.

Far from scoring off a dockman by tossing cartons of foot powder into the nose, Louis counted them as accurately as John did and no doubt reacquainted himself with the boundaries of his own patience. The disruption in the trailer was not personal, but structural: not due to revenge, but to competition between institutions. Ortho could have skidded most of the cartons itself, but it passed the labor-cost of sorting them on to A-P-A. In the past, A-P-A might have added what amounts to a fine to Ortho's freight bill for the delay this afternoon, which must have removed much of A-P-A's profit from the pickup. But no trucker levies such charges these days. Their formal survival in the rate books is a vestige of the palmy days of trucking before deregulation.

As I leave Sal's office, I have no plan to confront John with another account of the mess in the trailer. His sardonic view may have distorted this particular small history, but the same might be said in another case of Tony's smiling optimism, of Pete Leota's exacting aggressiveness on the radio, of Arthur's visionary earnestness. I'm not here to confront and correct these people, according to some standard of my own that I suppose to be superior and objective. I lack the journalist's facile confidence that my standards are something other than, after all, merely another view. My purpose here is to learn these people's views and enter their world. Besides, John Occhiogrosso's pessimism, his assumption that the chaos in the trailer was deliberate, a minor instance of the general depravity of man, after all applies in some degree to what actually happened. Competition is an ascendant god nowadays, but no one would argue that a world in which institutions struggle to pass off costs onto each other is a world in a state of grace.

∙∙∙∙∙∙∙∙∙∙∙∙∙∙∙∙∙∙∙

Back in his trailer, John has been blocking a skid for the 385-piece South Hackensack shipment. "We're getting there," he says. The boxes are small and light, too much so, normally, for stacking on a skid, because the blocking is likely to be unstable. On the other hand, consolidating the boxes on the skid will help out the dockman who will load the cartons and then the driver who will unload them upon delivery. John will have saved them the hassle of stooping and counting, and there will also be less likelihood of error. Therefore he'll stretch the rule against unstable blocking, but, as a precaution, he'll rope down the cartons to the pallet with slip knots. But he's assuming his decision is the wrong one. "Whenever I feel something isn't right and I do it, someone passes by and tells me not to. I have a knack. See? Sammy Chominsky just walked by." He's smiling now. Mastery of Ortho's cartons is within sight. As for Sam, he didn't even glance into John's trailer. He never needs to check on John, who, he tells me later, "always does to the best of his ability and exceeds it."

John crowds 295 of the South Hackensack cartons onto the skid. He sets the carton with the packing slip on top—"the driver might need it"—and on that carton he marks "295/385 + 1 cart." Now the skids of freight from Merck are exposed, with Ortho cartons scattered in among them. We both set to clambering around the skids, picking up cartons and turning up the stamped addresses of the consignee, then retreating back to the parked carts to complete the shipments. Soon all the cartons are off the floor of the trailer and sorted into carts. But some of the counts don't match. South Hackensack's strip ticket calls for 385 pieces, but John has counted 387: the 295 on the skid, and now ninety-two on the cart. John recounts the skid twice. If he's stacked the cartons symmetrically, adhering to his blocking plan, he can calculate their total by multiplying the count along the three sides of the stack. An irregular blocking secretly buries cartons and thus throws off the count. The same is true of cartons packed in carts. Now his recount shows 293 on the South Hackensack skid, not 295 (the top rows are incomplete, thus the odd-numbered total). He checks his slip knots. "Let's see if we can find the rest of the mistakes." Chris Kocaj, the hilo man, who has clanked and thumped into the trailer again to fetch South Hackensack, overhears and raises his eyebrows in mock alarm: "Mistakes!"

With Chris gone, John fetches a pallet-jack to move the 250-piece shipment for Victor, New York, which he's also blocked onto a skid. "They're loading now. I can't wait for another hilo." (It's near morning, and almost all the hilos will be busy loading city trucks.) John's pallet-jack—hilo blades mounted on wheels and a handle to pull them—is motorized by a large battery pack mounted in front of the handle. John pulls the Victor skid off the trailer and continues his recount.

"Let's start with Stamford." He recounts that cart. "Now it's forty-seven. It's right. Let's send it out." As he swings Stamford onto the dragline, the Queens bay man comes looking for three of the Merck skids, which are headed for Elmhurst, Queens. "They're in here," John tells him. "Be out in a minute."

Now he's missing one carton on the Baltimore cart. The skid, which had sixty cartons, is long gone, and the cart has fifty-two, making 112, one short of the 113 total. John explains the possibilities: either he's buried the missing carton on the now-departed skid with an incorrect blocking—"which I don't normally do"—or he sent the missing carton off hours ago with the *other* Baltimore shipment—or, of course, there were really only 112 to begin with, a shipper's shortage, like the absent carton among Tony's delivery of clothes to Automatic Operations. "Some people would have written this up already," John says—would have written up an exception report, on which a shortage of one piece would have been noted; and then the cart would have been sent off incomplete. "But there's a very strong Biblical principle that I made the mistake. I'm a strong believer that I made it, not the shipper." He tears down the Melbourne, Florida cart, which has been waiting incomplete for nearly four hours, and he begins repacking the Melbourne cartons on a new cart. Immediately he finds the one missing carton for the Akron cart, which has also been waiting incomplete. He wedges the Akron carton among its fellows and pulls the cart onto the dragline. Now he's back to repacking Melbourne, and he finds the missing Baltimore, too.

"I was probably talking to you when you loaded that cart," I say.

"No. I would've done it anyway. I'm no good at the minutiae."

Now Melbourne turns out to be right, too, at 100. The sorting of Ortho's cartons is complete, and nothing is missing. "So everything came out right after all, which is usually the case."

He is, in fact, good at the minutiae. He's not just a hustler who doesn't complain; he's conscientious, skillful, replete with strategies, tireless, and thorough. He may doubt the cooperative spirit of some drivers, dockmen, and supervisors, but he himself is the ideal team player, who not only covers his section of the field expertly but takes thought for the men assigned to other positions. He bends the rule to block the skid, an exception a less-confident or less-intelligent worker would not have ventured to make; he's careful to bind the packing slip on top, a detail that may have saved the driver half-an-hour on delivery; he extends the boundaries of patience to recount the cartons, in order to put an end to the disruption of the jumbled trailerload before it can spread. A person of lesser character would have struggled on the job an hour longer and ended by filing half-a-dozen exception reports, resulting in several hours' profitless work for an Overage, Shortage, and Damage clerk, several misdelivered cartons, and, perhaps, a claim filed by Ortho. It speaks well of Sam Chominsky's judgment as a manager that he moved John over to this job.

Virtually all that remains in John's trailer now are the pharmaceuticals from Merck, packed in seven skids. There are four single-skid shipments: 276 pounds for a drugstore in Bohemia, New York; 352 pounds to a pharmaceutical wholesaler in Brooklyn; 252 pounds to a second Brooklyn wholesaler, and 353 pounds to a third. Last are the three skids to a wholesaler in Elmhurst, weighing 1,024 pounds, the shipment that the Queens bay man came looking for. Chris Kocaj arrives now to whisk them off. Each skid is shrinkwrapped: a sheet of black plastic has been wound around it and partly over it. It's considered a single piece of freight, although it's composed of a blocked stack of cartons beneath the wrapping.

Shippers consider shrinkwrapped skids more secure, because they are less vulnerable to damage, loss, and theft. For their part, truckers prefer simple banding to shrinkwrapping, because it's hard to determine the acutal count of cartons under the wrapping. If the shipper's dockman has counted them wrong, the trucker can be blamed for a loss that was not his fault. Further, if the wrapping tears and cartons fall by the wayside, it's very hard to reroute them, because there's no separate paperwork concerning them. For this reason, A-P-A pickup drivers are instructed to sign for receipt of "one SWS (shrinkwrapped skid), *said* to be twenty-one pieces." Then a claim is harder to make when the consignee finds only twenty under the plastic.

Finally, along the side of John's trailer near the nose, there lies an eight-foot-long lighting fixture, one of the truckload of fixtures, the twelve-hour stripping job, that arrived as distribution freight from Georgia on Sunday night. It went out Monday on this trailer to Somerville Electric in Somerville in Central Jersey, but Somerville Electric refused it, and it has come back again. The carton rattles, and one corner is bent and torn. "I have to write this up," John says. On an exception report, a five-by-eight-inch form printed in duplicate, he writes down the names of the shipper and the consignee and adds, "F/NC [freight, no card], damage." He sends the fixture with the report to Overage, Shortage, and Damage at the south end of the dock. "The driver should have called it in. Probably did." No doubt the fixture was broken in the trailer on route. O. S. & D. will call the shipper, and A-P-A will pay the shipper's claim.

The trailer is clean. John gathers up the carbon-backing sheets of his strip manifest to hand in to Denis Zanetti, the supervisor for this area. It's 5:30 A.M. Stepping out of the trailer onto the dock, I notice it's morning outside in the yard. I ask John if he'd been aware of it. "I'm oblivious," he says.

Claims for loss and damage are a sensitive subject among truckers and their customers. (Among railroads, by contrast, the area of weakness is delay.) Trucklines' track records for loss and damage are expressed in their "claims ratios," that is, paid claims for loss and damage as a percent of revenues during a given period. At A-P-A, dock procedures for caution in freight handling are the subject of monthly quality-circle meetings between dockworker representatives and management, and also the subject of frequent Wednesday-at-midnight exhortations from Sam Chominsky. A-P-A increases its risk of claims by seeking what's called "high-value" freight, for which higher freight charges can be levied, but which requires skill, care, and honesty in a trucker's workforce. John's trailerload of drugs is typical of A-P-A's high-value freight, and the North Bergen dock is stacked with similar goods that, for concentration of value and ease of fence, would delight a den of thieves: crates of consumer electronics, drums of chemicals, cartons of tobacco.

The dock is piled also with goods that are vulnerable not to theft but to damage, either because they are fragile or because they are hard to stow and awkward to move: lighting fixtures, electrical conduits, overlong skids of plastic sheeting. Truckers call awkward, irregularly shaped freight "junk" or "garbage freight," but A-P-A does not disdain it. Like high-value freight, moving it pays well. From the company's first years in the late 1940s and early 1950s, A-P-A's strategy has been to secure a share of the freight market by selling the safe handling of vulnerable freight. Many truckers will not seek such freight because they can't trust their management or their labor.

In general, less-than-truckload truckers charge for moving freight according to three factors: the weight of the shipment, the kind of freight it is, and the distance it is to be moved. (Longhaul, less-than-truckload lines—the six remaining national carriers—thus have an advantage in revenues through distance.) As to kind, freight is further grouped under four classifications, called ratings. These are, first, the freight's value; second, its density, which is a factor involving both size and weight; third, the freight's ease of handling on the dock; and, fourth, the freight's "stowability," which is its compatibility with other freight on the trailer or the truck.

A-P-A will charge more to move Ortho's cartons than it does to move similarly light cartons of paper cups, because drugs are of high value. It will charge extra to move small skids of machine parts such as the two Tony delivered to Arlington Machine because, though compact, the machine parts are heavy; and extra, also, for the cartons of clothes he brought to Automatic Operations because, though light, they took up half the truck. Despite the damage to the carton consigned to Somerville Electric, distributing the truckload of lighting fixtures from Georgia will be profitable because freight that is difficult to handle commands a premium to move. Finally, the skids of coiled cable that litter the dock are premium freight because they are awkward to stow: skids of cable are too heavy to put on top of anything and too irregular to put underneath anything, so they end up sitting alone on the floor with a four-foot-square column of unprofitable air reaching to the ceiling. All this is set forth in the *National Master Freight Classification,* a thick book that attempts to place a rating on every object of human wish moved by truck across highways in the United States and Canada. Its author is a committee of truckline representatives (A-P-A's Director of Pricing, Douglas Dick, is a member). The committee meets and writes under an immunity from antitrust laws granted by federal statute.

John's typically high-value stripping job was, in another sense, atypical. In the past, freight that was as light and as small as Ortho's cartons of powders and creams, traveling in shipments as small as the nine cartons to Lindenhurst and the first eighteen to Baltimore, were the norm on the North Bergen dock. But now such freight is the exception. Heavy skids, Merck-style, dominate. In the 1950s, Arthur and his brothers established themselves not only by seeking out high-value freight and awkward "junk" freight but by pursuing small shipments and small cartons. This was a market that few companies wanted, because small shipments and small pieces are fussy to handle and easy to lose, and, being neither heavy nor large, they pay a small return. Inefficient carriers lose money on them. Small shipments strain profit further because they cost more to deliver. A truck filled with thirty small shipments has to make thirty stops; a truck filled with three shipments has to make three. A carrier of small shipments, therefore, needs what truckers call "density": many customers close together, so that, though the driver may make many stops, he doesn't drive many miles between them. From the 1950s through the 1970s, moving small shipments of high value or awkward shape through the New York-New Jersey market became A-P-A's specialty: its niche, as businessmen say. It was the foundation of Arthur's fortune.

All things are impermanent, including market niches. In the 1980s, small shipments began to disappear from less-than-truckload docks. They were taken by the package-delivery lines, above all by United Parcel Service. "Before the early eighties," Armand explained to me, "the Interstate Commerce Commission precluded UPS from moving shipments of more than 100 pounds and from handling pieces weighing more than fifty pounds and measuring more than 108 inches around. The area of small shipments above UPS's limit, which nobody wanted, was where we cleaned up. In 1983, as part of the deregulation of the trucking industry, all restrictions were lifted on UPS. They've now gone up to shipments of 300 pounds and sometimes more, and up to pieces of seventy pounds. That was a substantial part of our market. They can do it cheaper, because of the tremendous density they have." (UPS is unlikely to move much farther towards larger and heavier freight, though, because its freight is moved across its terminals and also in and out of its linehaul trailers on conveyor belts. In its pickup-and-delivery step-vans, the freight is stacked by hand onto shelves. Heavy skids would damage the belts and wouldn't fit on the shelves.)

Since 1983, because of the encroachment of package-delivery lines, the average weight of an A-P-A shipment has gradually moved from less than 600 pounds to more than 900. The average number of local pickups crossing the North Bergen dock at night has dropped from 2,800 to 2,100, while the average total weight per night has grown. "We're moving more weight and less bills," Sal Passante says. Sixty-five percent of A-P-A's shipments now consist of skids. The hilo force on the night dock grew from fourteen to twenty men during 1990 alone, and the hilo men are still too few; John sometimes has to stand and wait for someone to be free to move a skid for him.

The movement to skids and the decline in small shipments was not anticipated when the vast North Bergen dock was built. "It's killing us," Sal says. "The hilos may have to go two or three blocks to stage the freight. The cart system was built for loads of ten or twenty cartons. We used to have that business cornered." Thousand of the carts are lined up in a storage building just north of the dock, and some are being rebuilt as flatbed carts for movement of awkward freight like pipes, conduits, and lighting fixtures. Nowadays, trucklines generally build terminals with city operations and break-bulk operations separate. The terminals may be T-shaped, with break-bulk freight moving across one bar of the T and city freight across the other; sometimes management offices form a third bar to make an I. More often, large less-than-truckload carriers have built their break-bulk and city operations in entirely separate terminals, with the city terminals on the outskirts of metropolitan centers, while the break-bulk terminals are deployed in the countryside, in order, chiefly, to give the truckline more control of its labor. (Rural blue-collar workers are usually isolated. If the dockworkers for a break-bulk operation in a rural area threaten to organize, or if they are already organized and threaten to strike, management can plausibly threaten to close the terminal and move.)

The complexity and the great size of the North Bergen dock brings countervailing benefits, however. If, like most less-than-truckload carriers, A-P-A were to scatter smaller terminals around the metropolitan areas it works in, its freight would cross shorter docks. But each of its linehaul trailers would be driven farther and would be less likely to be filled, because the freight would be distributed among more terminals. The scattered city trucks, also, would each be more lightly loaded and more loosely routed. Half-empty trucks lose money. Fewer hubs (to use the airline analogy) mean fuller planes.

▰▰▰▰▰▰▰▰▰▰▰

At 5:30, without comment, Denis Zanetti, night supervisor for the Westchester area of the dock, hands John a wad of delivery receipts. John's next job, then, will be loading—more to his taste. The delivery receipts identify the freight he is to stack into a city trailer, which he finds backed into 39 Door. It has been routed for morning deliveries in Westchester County, north of New York City. John flips through his board—a shorthand term for a batch of delivery receipts, which are usually kept in sequence by clamping them onto a half-length clipboard. The load is drawn from A-P-A's niches on the industry shelf: tobacco, electrical fixtures, computer parts, loose automobile-muffler pipes, long bundles of metal braces. "Lots of junk," John observes, adding, "I don't know how I'm going to make this load by 8:00 A.M."

The Westchester bay man has penciled spur numbers on the corner of each of John's delivery receipts, to tell him where each shipment has been staged. Normally, the tower supervisor would have radioed the yard-jockey to back the trailer into a door directly opposite the bay. But tonight, there has been so much freight that at 5:30 A.M. Denis still has four straight trucks and three trailers in his area to strip, and he doesn't have any free doors.

John turns his delivery receipts over on a crate in the bay and splays the receipts out in reverse order. Because this is a city delivery run, he needs to load sequentially: last stop first, into the nose. Portchester, on the New York–Connecticut line, is the farthest point on the driver's run. Therefore, John will begin by loading into the nose four separate shipments consigned to Golden Distributors, Ltd., in Portchester: seventy-six cartons of cigars; fifty-one cartons of chewing tobacco; three cartons of Pez candies and thirteen cartons of Napoli chocolate cream-filled wafers, made in Vienna; and sixty-three cartons of Red Man pipe tobacco. The four shipments weigh 5,258 pounds altogether. John finds the tobacco and candy in carts in the Westchester bay and swings the carts onto the dragline, so the line can do the pulling as he walks them. He also snags a day hilo man, Carl Center, and points out to him some other shipments for the load, on skids. Back in the truck, John heaves Golden's tobacco cartons into the nose. He builds the structure up over his head to the trailer's ceiling, counting and grunting as he goes.

Some of the cartons weigh over fifty pounds. I ask him, "How come you don't pick up these cartons with your legs—you know, squatting and your back straight?" and I regale him with an account of a skinny little gray-haired dockman named George, whom I never saw without his fedora hat; when I worked on this dock twenty years ago, he trained me how to lift according to the book.

John, of course, is skeptical of the book. "Two-hundred-pound boxes of bolts, yes. For the lighter ones, there just isn't time. If I squatted for each one, I'd never get the job done."

"You're just built right," I tell him.

John demurs. Instead: "If the Good Lord wants me to take care of my family, he'll have to keep my back safe."

"Lunchtime," Sam calls over the microphone. The dragline doesn't stop, though. This is lunchtime only for John's 1:00 A.M. shift. John heads to 57 Door for a sandwich, and he'll lay out some skids for a nap in a quiet bay, if he can find a quiet bay. That won't be as easy as it usually is: on many days, the night crew would have left by now, after two hours of overtime, and by 6:00 A.M. the dock would be silent. But this morning there's no pause.

I make my way to the docktower. Sam is at his desk in his cubicle upstairs, calling supervisors on the dock phone system, to find out which city trucks and trailers still have to be loaded. Brian Nallen, whose desk this is during the day shift, has just arrived, and at 7:00 he'll be in charge. Sam tells him: "We've still got eleven straight jobs, ten trailers: twenty-one boards total." That city drivers should have to wait past 8:00 A.M. to pull out with their trucks is very unusual, but today Sam estimates that a few drivers will have to wait as late as 9:30, even with Brian's thirty-six-man day crew helping. Normally, the day crew concentrates on working break-bulk—on loading and unloading trailers bound to and from other terminals. Today, Brian could hardly begin break-bulk even if Sam didn't need his help, since the late city trucks are still plugging the outbound doors. Sam complains, "The yard-jockey can't make hits." (He can't back linehaul trailers up to the dock, because no doors are free.) "Road trailers are all over the yard." Sam lists for me again the reasons for the logjam: a long weekend's buildup, no Thursday or Friday night crew because of the Fourth, an unexpectedly heavy July, and the large number of green men on the dock tonight. "You see how it can get," he says.

Dockmen and their supervisors are measured against productivity standards that are the counterpart of the standards by which Tony and the other city drivers and their dispatchers are measured. At the end of each shift on the dock, all the dock supervisors fill out a "supervisors' engineering chart," which lists the names of the workers the supervisor is responsible for and the identifying numbers of the trucks or trailers each worker stripped or loaded, with the total number of shipments in each load, the total weights of each load, and the time each job took. The supervisor is judged according to the average performance of his men, while Sam Chominsky is judged on the performance of the entire night shift, which is what has him worried now. The delays tonight are challenging his reputation. He charges down the stairs to exhort his crew.

Sam's primary tool for achieving productivity is lean manning, but, if it's right, not so lean that the men are rushed, just as dispatchers aim to push drivers hard, but not so hard that they cannot finish. Tonight, Sam manned too lightly. Still, in budgeting work, A-P-A prefers to err on the side of hard, rather than easy. Armand told me: "Arthur is a great believer that the work pushes the man. Give him more, he'll work harder. Parkinson's law says that the work expands to fill the time allotted. The corollary is that if workload increases, you work harder to finish. One evening a couple of summers ago, there was a regional power failure due to overuse of air conditioning. We had no power for two and a half hours. The night men couldn't start work till 9:30 because the billers couldn't produce the bills. The men finished by the same time anyway."

In order to focus the men on their responsibilities, Sam rarely puts two men on a trailer. "They talk," he says. Like drivers, they work alone. "I'm a teacher," he adds, "not a yeller. I come on gently and ask them how they could have done it differently, what they've learned from the mistake. I tell them, 'Your mistakes are my mistakes, since I'm the controlling person around here.' I call them on everything. I can't let them get away with it."

I myself have known this kind of teacher in high schools: strict and fair, intense and honest, soft-spoken and demanding, somewhat humorless, a little plodding, a godsend for students who need direction, encouragement, and the security of clear rules. Like such teachers, Sam relies on exhortation. "The point is to have pride in your freight, pride in your work," he tells me. "You're not just Joe Schmoe. I tell the new men, 'Everything you've heard about A-P-A is true. We're hard, we demand a lot from our men. But there are rewards. You're working for a safe, secure company. You have the recreation center and the trips, which is the company showing its appreciation, and also the opportunity for advancement if you have ambition and drive. Look at me: I started on the dock.' "

He could be an auto-shop teacher in a working-class high school, or, more precisely, a shop-teacher who was once a mechanic, studied nights to be credentialed as a teacher, and has now been promoted to principal. Sam exhorts the supervisors who work for him as he used to exhort his dockworkers when he himself was a supervisor. "I try to communicate to the supervisors the value of efficiency for the whole operation. Even if your own area is moving a bit slower, you want to forge a team to improve efficiency for the whole company." He gives me the example of Canada-bound freight, which, as a marketing strategy, A-P-A promises to deliver overnight. "There's a list, we call it the 'rat sheet,' of Canada freight that didn't go overnight, maybe because the customs paperwork wasn't there, or there wasn't enough room in the box going up there. The supervisors compete not to get on the rat sheet."

He summarizes: "It's team effort and personal pride in the work that make us special and on top in this business. They make this a pleasant place to work. Like John Occhiogrosso, he always does his best. And most of the people in A-P-A do. Why? Personal pride and self-esteem is a big motivation. Competition is part of it. It's from the top. Arthur told me when he interviewed me in 1969, 'You want to work for this company? You're going to bust your balls.' Even though there's been a change of the guard, the atmosphere of dedication continues. We promote competition among the men, we adjust to the mood of the men and exhort them. We don't take any average person. We take the above and beyond people." In the unabashedly religious term A-P-A managers use to describe company loyalists, Sam is a believer.

I leave Sam to his exhortations and his faith, and I head for the lunch truck. I've been standing up now for eight hours straight, talking and scribbling notes, forgetting to sit down, and my back aches and my right hand is cramped, but I don't feel at all tired. I remind myself to sit down on a crate while I eat a hard roll, drink oversweet coffee, and watch the show.

When lunch is over, at 7:00 A.M., John is back, ready with a strategy. He'll ask for his own hilo to speed the loading of the Westchester trailer. As Charlie Trentacosti, one of the day supervisors, scoots by on the little electric go-cart that he fancies— a supervisor's perquisite—John stops him. "I'm not getting this trailer done by 8:00 unless you turn over a hilo to me." A hilo man clanking over the dockplate of the neighboring truck overhears. Jealous of his exclusive rights (which are to sit down on his machine all night and to be paid a twelve-and-a-half-cent-an-hour premium for doing it), the hilo man calls out: "Yeah, bullshit." Denis Zanetti, the Westchester night supervisor, converges on the group. I say to him: "You're still here." Denis nods. "Till the last box is stripped. Twelve hours every day." (He means every night.) Now Carl Center, the day hilo man, returns with some of the next shipments for John's trailer: three twenty-foot-long bundles of copper structural braces, for Pelham Tool Co., in Portchester. He has hoisted the braces crossways six feet up on his hilo blades, cutting a lofty twenty-foot-wide swath as he approaches, while he honks a very goose-like hilo honk. John won't need his own hilo now, since Carl is available.

The group disperses, but not before Carl bumps the rear of Charlie's go-cart and then the flank of another passing hilo, all the while pretending to study his structural braces.

"Watch out!" John calls out, in mock alarm. To me: "He did that on purpose."

Carl lowers the braces to the dock and backs away from them. Then with one blade he picks up one of the three bundles by one end and swivels it around till it points longways at the trailer. With the tip of a blade, he delicately nudges the bundle so that it slides across the dockplate and along the trailer wall. Repeating the process, he nudges in the second bundle along the top of the first and then the third along the top of the second. He clanks onto the trailer, and with the side of one blade bumps the bundles sideways till they lie flush against the trailer wall. "See why I need you, Carl?" John says. "I need the best." To me, he adds, "All of the guys could have done it, but not as quickly."

Soon Carl is back with a fourth, shorter bundle of steel braces, twelve feet long, which he drops onto the other bundles. Then he shoves his blades back underneath the entire pile and coaxes the longer, heavier bundles on the bottom of the pile an inch or two out from the trailer wall. John explains that the crown in the middle of highways tends to tip freight on a trailer's left side (which travels along the crown) in toward the trailer's center. Carl's architecture will stabilize the pile. Now Carl lifts up the top two, lighter bundles while John slips twine beneath them and ties them to one of the bull-rings attached at intervals to the plywood wall. Without comment, Carl dismounts and reties the knot. When Carl remounts and backs out, John reties the knot once again, remarking: "Nice guy, but messy knot."

Carl returns with a final load of electrical equipment for Pelham Tool, this one a shrinkwrapped skid of boxed steel straps, and then, in three more trips, five skids of data processing equipment for a computer store in White Plains. At John's behest Carl ranges the computer parts behind the tobacco boxes, and John piles on top of it all seventeen cartons of plastic dinnerware for Strauss Paper Co., Portchester. The dinnerware is lightweight "top freight," which is desirable because it doesn't take up floor space. For Bruni and Campisi, White Plains, Carl fetches seven air conditioners on four skids while John tips back a crated 300-pound house furnace onto a handtruck and walks it to the trailer. Throughout the fetch and carry, John is planning the load, not only according to sequence but according to weight and balance. The ideal trailer is "cubed out" and "high and tight"—loaded up to the ceiling and out to the tail, and braced so that the freight doesn't shift in transit. The load must also be balanced more or less evenly on either side, so that the trailer doesn't tilt and tip over on a turn. Finally, it must be weighted gradually heavier toward the nose, since if it's heavy on the tail, traction may be lacking on the tractor's drive-wheels beneath the nose, and the trailer may not stop when the driver brakes. The competing needs to cube out, to balance the load, and to load sequentially make perfection in the dockman's art unlikely.

Only four shipments remain for John to bring onto the truck, but it's already past 8:00, and trucks and trailers are pulling away from the dock. Leaving 38 Door, adjacent to John's 39, a straight truck blasts billows of stinking diesel exhaust over Carl and John and me. Its white clouds swirl prettily in bars of sunlight. "There's a theory that diesel fuel is the worst thing for you, as far as breathing it in," John reports cheerfully, as we wave the fumes aside. (According to the Environmental Protection Agency, the theory John cites is correct medical doctrine, which rates diesel exhaust more deadly to inhale than cigarette smoke, because the solid particles in diesel are smaller.)

Now the man who's going to haul this trailer strides up: muscular, mid-thirties, with long, permed gray-and-black curls tumbling to his shoulders, a face with manly actor's planes—a heart-throb. This is Bobby MacDonald, fourteen years at A-P-A, now plying the gentler streets of Westchester after nine years with a straight truck in the South Bronx. He inspects the load, kibbitzes genially: "Make it so I can unload it, fellas. Don't be overzealous. You going to send a hilo so I can get this down?"

John is running out of floor space and is too busy building for repartee. He has Carl stow on the floor a skid of crated black muffler pipes on their way from Walker Manufacturing Co., Harrisonburg, Virginia, to a White Plains muffler shop. Then he lugs in six empty pallets and piles them up beside the mufflers, thus creating a platform across the width of the trailer for a twelve-foot-long skid, also of mufflers. They lie twisted in their crate like a swarm of fat black worms. John lashes three more loose mufflers on top, along with twenty small boxes of lighting fixtures from Lightolier, Inc., Norwich, Connecticut. The fixtures are the only small shipment—A-P-A's old niche—on the entire trailer.

Finally, Carl brings five six-foot-long skids of paper liners for cassette tapes, from a printer in Québec, while John wheels up a cart with 235 cartons of bathroom exhaust fans headed from Cincinnati to Yonkers. Bobby and I help John load the fans into the tail. Bobby, having quizzed me, says that he can see why I'm interested in all this. "Driving," he remarks, "you meet interesting people, you see different industries. You get privy to things that most people wouldn't know."

The job is done, and John is ready to joke again. Carl Center whisks by with a structure of truck tires layered on his blades. He yells: "Anybody know where these are going?" Bobby jumps down to the asphalt. John rolls down the trailer door. "What?" John calls.

"TIRES!"

John: "I'm not tired."

He's been at it nearly seven hours. It's 8:45, and Bobby is the last city driver to leave the dock. Sam was only forty-five minutes behind after all.

While he's been loading, I've asked John what he thinks of Sam's exhortations and zeal. John is skeptical. He likes Sam, who works as hard and is as serious as John is, but he doesn't feel an emotional identification with the company like Sam's or even like Tony's. "Management will never be happy with us, and we'll never be happy with them," he says. "It's the nature of the game. We do what we gotta do, and they do what they gotta do, and somehow it works." The fact that it works is what he's loyal to. That A-P-A is "the best," as Tony's friend who drives for ABF attested and as Sam and many others at A-P-A believe, is not a matter of pride or of faith for John, but rather a practical consideration, a matter of security.

I ask John if it's important to him that A-P-A makes money, and he answers: "It's important to me that I do my job right. If I do, then Arthur makes money. Of course I want A-P-A to stay in business. He can make thirty or forty percent on the dollar, I don't care. It doesn't matter to me. Some guys resent it. In December, he sent out his Christmas greetings on a videotape to everybody in the company—Arthur with his horses on his farm. The next day a lot of the guys were mad about it. Jealous, I guess, is the word."

But John has no sympathy with their jealousy. Inequities of wealth and the class struggle don't interest him. "A-P-A's a solid company. I hear enough crying from my kids. I don't want to hear it on the dock. They cry all the way to the bank. There's security at A-P-A. Our union is weak, and A-P-A is in control. They can harass you on the little stuff. Some guys say you have to work too hard, but . . . like our pension. That's another reason A-P-A is good: the pension is safe. It's not gutted by crooked officials."

John thinks about retiring at fifty, when he'll have twenty-five years as a Teamster on the dock. The current pension schedule, which will probably be raised eventually to conform to higher pensions for Teamster locals in New England and the Midwest, will give him $1,200 a month after twenty-five years of work. "We'll sell the house, make a profit, move south. That's my dream." This is what he appreciates about A-P-A: it fulfills his needs, and, because he does his work well, the company and his position in it are secure. The praise from his bosses is emotionally irrelevant to him, although he appreciates practical extras. He has just received a fifteen-year safety award that earns him a day off and $500 reimbursement of travel expenses. This Thursday he's going to Montreal ("because I heard it's a nice, clean place") for four days with Karen.

"Look at me," Sam Chominsky says, to rally his crew to loyalty. "I started on the dock." The open door to management and to the prestige and income of white-collar, middle-class work is certainly a call to loyalty, a call especially strong to those who, like Sam, have in fact moved through the door. They know perfectly well that few companies open that door wide to their workers, and that even fewer follow A-P-A's deliberate policy of recruiting the officer corps almost exclusively from the ranks. But not everyone is called. John has been offered a supervisory job several times, but he's always declined it. " 'John, you won't have to work,' they say. But," he explains, "it's a question of money." Supervisors are salaried and are not paid overtime, so in the first few years they often make less than the men they supervise. With John's six-day schedule, his pay cut would be substantial.

There's another reason John is still a dockman: he's too diffident to imagine himself as a manager. "I can't see myself standing around watching other guys work." He wants to take care only of himself, and he wants to keep moving. He isn't tempted by a job in which the work is physically easier but emotionally more difficult. His preference for long hours of hard physical work is exactly why he fits at A-P-A. His stance is not unusual. A-P-A executives are constantly on the watch for workers who can be raised to supervisor and for supervisors who can become management; Armand compares the truckline to a professional baseball team that draws on its minor-league farm system to build a strong bench. But often the most able workers do not want promotion. "They have to want the kick of telling other people what to do," Armand says. "They have to give more mental space to the job and take shit from twenty-five people instead of one." And they have to be willing to let go of the security of union membership.

A college degree, in this country, provides the single surest entry to the middle class. Though the A-P-A farm system circumvents this turnstile, many working-class people feel that without a college education, they cannot aspire to middle-class work, even when it is offered to them. Several A-P-A workers have told me that they have declined promotion because their lack of a college degree made them feel unfit for management. That doesn't mean they esteem physical labor more highly than white-collar work. They do not. The old European working-class solidarity that disdains a middle-class identity is not a strong force in the United States, and I have never heard it expressed at A-P-A. These workers may be intimidated by a middle-class education, resentful of the wealth it can lead to, and scornful of the middle class's spurious claim to moral superiority, but they too dream the American dream of entry into the middle class— if not their own entry, then their children's. I hadn't been with John half-an-hour on Sunday night when he remarked, "I wouldn't want my kids doing this." He is not the only one at A-P-A who has told me that.

The answer for these people is to send their children to college. Jim Gillespie, a city trailer driver, has done for his three children what John intends to do for his five. "We've put three kids through college," Jim told me when I rode with him on his run to the Conrail yard in South Kearny. "The youngest is twenty-one now. And my son is doing industrial design. With his new raise, he's making more money than I am." Jim amended: "Don't get me wrong: I'm not jealous. I don't want him to be no truck-driver." He amended again: "Don't get me wrong, I don't mind driving a truck. But you need an education nowadays. This is the best money you could make without an education. We've been able to put them all through."

That Arthur's most important perquisite for employees is his college scholarship program bespeaks his understanding of what is really important to working people. An A-P-A scholarship has paid the entire cost of tuition for the two years John's eldest son has spent at Montclair State. Of the many anti-statist government policies of the last decade, perhaps none will prove more damaging—in this country which has flourished above all through expansion of its middle class—than the precipitous reduction of public support for higher education.

All this is not to say that workers must aspire to management in order to develop a loyalty like Sam Chominsky's. Jim Gillespie is a believer. Curlee Campbell, a high-and-tight artist who loads outbound trailers and volunteers on the terminal's quality circle, is a believer. Curlee, who like Jim is black and approaching fifty, presides over the Canton and Baltimore doors on the north dock. He wears a moustache and goatee that describe a circle around his mouth and a red-and-white A-P-A baseball cap cocked sideways on his head. "I got no complaints," Curlee told me. "They just want a good day's work from you, that's all. When you go home, you're well tired. And love that overtime. That overtime comes in handy. You can't beat this company."

Loyalty comes in various strengths. But it would be a mistake to conclude, it seems to me upon reflection, that because some members of A-P-A, or of any other purposive community, are lukewarm in their faith, the community has therefore failed to jell or is unlikely to survive. On the contrary: it is better that their degrees of loyalty differ, and that enthusiasts like Sam be tempered by skeptics like John. Groups of pure zealots are unpleasant and destructive, and they do not last. The reality of stable, productive groups is that they consist of a variety of individuals who need the group and serve it because it advances their quite various individual aspirations—only one of which is to belong to a group. Ideally, the urge to associate is balanced by the urge to realize the self. When these forces are in equilibrium, a community and its individual members can thrive.

Thus Arthur from the beginning sought to hire people with stable families, on the theory that they would make stable workers. He liked to call applicants' wives during interviews because of his instinct that a bad husband would make a bad driver. Armand—who plays skeptic to Arthur's enthusiast—himself postponed joining the company until he was married, believing that without a family there would be nothing in his life to pull him out of the vortex of the truckline. He argues further that employees are healthiest when their work is balanced not only by family but by what he calls "a second passion"—whether it be a light passion like Tony's carpentry or Pete's wardrobe, or a strong one like John's Bible-based church or Armand's own music.

———————————

Now that Bobby MacDonald has departed for Portchester, Steve Vegliante, a day supervisor, stops by 39 Door to summon John to the North Jersey area. He'll strip an inbound trailer just arrived from the Meriden, Connecticut terminal. He's not going to be loading outbound at all tonight. He shrugs. "It's a night's work. I ought to be done by 12:00, 12:30." He'll need to be, if he's going to deliver papers and substitute in that softball game.

I let him go. I want to visit Curlee Campbell to see how outbound trailers are loaded, and also keep an appointment with Burt Trebour, A-P-A's vice-president for labor. Night has rolled over into day now, and it seems odd that New Jersey has reached Tuesday without Monday having reached, for me, its accustomed conclusion in a night's sleep. The entire night crew has departed, and the dock is far quieter. No one is working in the city bays. Light and cool air from Newark Bay and the Atlantic flow in through doors left open by the departure of city trucks. Last week's humidity has undergone a maritime cleansing, and in the yard the bright morning stimulates and disorients me, since the end of a workday ought properly to be evening.

By noon I've returned to my borrowed apartment in Cliffside Park. In the distance, at the end of an avenue of air between buildings, the sun glitters on the Hudson. There's no question of sleeping. I eat, do laundry, read the paper, make phone calls, pack a carton of books and clothes to send home. Finally, after dozing for three hours, I admit defeat. I head back to the truckline. As I drive south on Palisade Avenue and across North Hudson Park, it's 5:00 P.M.—still full day. I'm reminded of a visit to Iceland in a long-past June, when people were busy in the sunlit streets at midnight as if it were noon. I was told they do their sleeping in the winter there.

Mike Trebour, Burt's son, is at his desk in the docktower. "I can't stay away from this place. I'm obsessed," I tell him.

Mike nods; it's what he expected. "We're all like that. You go home, you talk about it, you think about it. If you care about this place, you do get obsessed."

It occurs to me that the relentlessness of the A-P-A style has roots not only in its group culture but in external conditions. The flow of A-P-A's business never ceases. Night devolves into day, day into night, while the trucks keep arriving, the trailers keep backing in, the skids pile up, the carts spur off. These people *can't* stop. Armand certifies my thought when I see him later. "When I leave here at night, I feel like I'm doing something bad," he says, 'because there's always something going on." The entire less-than-truckload industry is ceaseless from Sunday evening to Saturday afternoon, and the thirty-hour weekend respite merely makes the five-and-a-half-day intensity possible. As for the longhaul truckload business, it doesn't stop at all.

Night work, especially, can set workers apart from other employees in their companies and also from their families—in fact, from their own bodies. "Night dockmen tend to feel more alienated than other groups in the company," Armand tells me later in the evening, "because they're on a different schedule and they feel separated." In general, throughout the modern economy, night workers suffer more from such stress-related illnesses as ulcers and asthma than day workers do, and they are more likely to suffer marital problems. The biological rhythms are disturbed, and the family is either asleep when the night worker is awake, or is awake and demanding when the nightworker comes home exhausted. At A-P-A, night dockmen, night billers, and road drivers who drive linehaul at night rarely sleep more than six hours a day, often in patches, and many skip a day's sleep almost entirely on Saturday, in order to gain family time.

Yet a strong group culture can balance the isolation of night work. For example, the thirty night billers at North Bergen, who create strip manifests, drivers' manifests, and delivery receipts from bills of lading, work a 5:00 P.M. to midnight shift. Most have worked together on the shift for over twenty years. All women in a male-dominated company, they place a high value on their role: "We're the most important part of the operation," their supervisor, Arleen Chwatel, told me. "Everything starts here." They also delight in the independence of their odd hours. "The pressures are less than during the day," one biller said. "You don't have the big bosses hanging around, breathing down your neck. They assume that we're responsible adults up here."

On another evening, in a group interview in the office pool on the second floor of the operations building, I asked the billers: "How has it been to raise a family and have a night job?"

"We don't sleep."

"Three hours a night."

Mary O'Gorman offered: "There's been many a week I didn't see my husband. He leaves Monday morning and I don't see him till Saturday morning. We talk on the phone, but I don't see him. When he sleeps I'm at work, and when he goes out in the morning I'm certainly not getting up. He goes out and when he comes home I'm not there. His supper is there, he heats it up, but I'm not there. We have the family time during the weekends."

"What about the kids?" I asked.

"Well, my son is grown, but the one thing I liked about it, I was there when he came home from school, and if he was sick."

Maureen Campbell, who nurses the computer that prints the manifests, said, "Once, maybe fifteen years ago, I went home one night and I said to my husband, 'Am I tired. I'm not working any more. I'm going to stay home and raise the children.' He said, 'Maureen, I've already raised them.' " (At this the entire billing department collapsed in hilarity.) "He said, 'Why you gonna come home now? I don't need you now.' He said, 'What do I need you for?' He said, 'I did everything already.' "

The billers' distance from their families is balanced by their loyalty to their work community. Arleen Chwatel said: "I've been here thirty years. I started as a baby, as a biller on electric typewriters, 'BC,' before computers. I was only married one year before I came to work here. I left my five-month-old son with my husband. I'm antsy, I got to work. I enjoy it here. It's like a second home to me. It's a very comfortable, homelike atmosphere. Everybody helps everybody out. A sense of humor carries us through when the pressure is on."

The billers were united in disdain for day work.

"I think if I worked days," Mary O'Gorman said, "I'd go home and make supper and go to bed. With night work, you can do your shopping before you go to work, do your cleaning and whatever you want to do, and you still have time for yourself. If you work days, then at night, really, what's left? You come home and you're exhausted and after supper you sit there and you watch television."

"You feel you have more useful time than day people?"

"Definitely."
"Oh, yes."
"Definitely."

꧁꧁꧁꧁꧁꧁꧁꧁꧁

At 5:30 P.M., I walk around the dock again with Brian Nallen, the day operations manager. His appearance is Sam's opposite, day to Sam's night. He's just below middle height, chubby, with a big square smiling face, double chin below, light brown hair above, and steely eyes. "I always wanted management," he tells me. "I went to college, but I dreamed A-P-A." Now nearing forty, he started as an O.S.&D. clerk, following his mother, who worked at A-P-A for twenty years, and his brother, who works for the company's truck-leasing subsidiary. While he recollects, his eyes sweep the outbound areas and dart into trailers, "seeing where things stand for Sammy," just as Sam did for him twelve hours ago. He had thirty-two men today—the four other men on his shift are on vacation—and they stripped and loaded approximately 1,900 bills, he says. "That's high; a busy day today. Steve's still stripping three. I'm looking to shut down the line by 6:00 P.M."

Steve Vegliante, who supervises the North Jersey dock, demurs. "I still got a lot to load, and some stripping. Still got some freight coming in. Be done by 7:00."

"6:30," Brian counters. "Everybody out of here by 6:30."

At my request, Steve and Brian piece together John Occhiogrosso's assignments for the remainder of his shift, after I left the dock. First, Steve says, John stripped half of a trailer of furniture that had arrived from the Meriden, Connecticut terminal on its way to J.C. Penney's New Jersey warehouse. He'd taken the job over from a night-shift man, who'd gone home. "There were some big boxes," Steve says. "He had to walk them to their doors, because otherwise they'd have stuck out from the carts and jammed the line." Next, John stripped a trailerload of large cartons of piece goods from a textile warehouser in Long Island. "It was a tough stripper," Steve says, "a sloppy load, because the shipper loaded it themselves." Last, John began stripping another load from Meriden, ninety-two boxes of novelty products: costumes, make-up, spray cans of sparkle. The 1:00 A.M. crew went home at 1:30 P.M.

I'm wondering about John's newspaper route. "Couldn't he have gone home earlier?" I ask Brian.

The dock policy, Brian answers, is to let ten percent of a crew go after eight hours if they request it, with a limit of two per week per person. "John could've asked, but he didn't. If he would've asked, I would've let him go. The same guys always ask. He never asks." (Later, John tells me he slept four hours, delivered papers for five hours, "came back to A-P-A at midnight, and sacked out for an hour on a couple of skids.")

At 6:00 P.M., Brian shuts down the dragline. From his desk phone in the tower cubicle he calls the three outbound supervisors to tell them that with the dragline stopped, the remaining freight already stacked into carts will have to be moved by hilo, with the loaded carts mounted crosswise on the blades. As the men finish, they punch out at their supervisors' desks. Sam arrives, and at 6:30 the desk in the cubicle is his again. Brian is standing beside it as they confer. The night supervisors are ranged along their long counter in the tower, checking through their manifests. Rolls of strip tickets thump regularly into the bins of the pneumatic system. At the base of the tower, the night crew is assembling, standing around, lolling on freight, talking, smoking. Normally, at 7:00, Sam will emerge and stand on the top stair. Reading from his notes on a clipboard, he'll call out the "shape," the night's hiring list, to the men below. The casuals will find out only then if they'll have work that evening. If the volume of freight is low, even the regulars near the tail of the seniority list may have to go home. "DeBerry," Sam will drone, "go to North Jersey. Tuso, go to Queens."

Tonight, though, Mike booms over the loudspeaker: "At 7:00, everybody report to the cafeteria." The men shuffle up the other staircase that climbs the east side of the tower two flights to the top-floor lunchroom. They're grumbling a little: routine is being violated. They're expecting another lecture from Sam about careful counting and loading, to minimize claims for loss and damage. "Two hours," one man sighs.

It's something else. Armand is there, with his son Andrew, and so is Burt Trebour, vice-president for labor, Andy Park, vice-president for operations, and terminal manager Sal Passante. Andy is the only A-P-A vice-president whom one might peg for a trucker: tall, muscular, blond hair cut very short, hard blue eyes that take a while to smile. Armand looks ten years younger than his forty-six. He has black hair, dark coloring, and large, keen, humorous, hazel eyes that suggest intellect, detachment, and a competitive spirit. His black bangs confer upon him a boyishness which is amended by half-glasses for reading; the glasses rest on his diaphragm at the end of a grandmotherly black ribbon. Andrew, thirteen, standing shyly with his father beside the vending machines, has his father's eyes, his mother's fair hair and coloring, and his father's pianist's hands.

The members of the night crew file in, sit at the picnic benches, plant elbows on table, wait to see what's up. Armand moves to the center. "I began on the dock in 1961," he begins, "so I'm the senior dockman here."

Louis Coppola's voice is heard: "I started in 1958."

Armand laughs, then restarts his introduction. "I realize how hard a job this is. We compete with nonunion workers, who are paid nine or ten dollars an hour, so we need more from you. We *get* more from you. The economy has been bad. You see how few extra men we're hiring."

Now he comes to the point. Bob Marinelli, a fifteen-year member of the crew, is employee of the month. There is applause, yips, hoots, cheers. Bob, in his fifties, in blue tee-shirt with the company's quality circle emblem, stands up shyly. Armand praises him, and Bob replies: "I'm honored. I don't know what to say. There's lots of good men and women in this company." There are handshakes with Sal and the V-Ps. Armand presents the plaque. Bob will get a designated parking space, his picture will go on the wall in the administration building, there'll be a trip up the Hudson with his wife on the company yacht, and a note for $250 reimbursement for entertainment expenses. Armand tells him: "That'll buy you a drink-and-a-half at Arthur's Landing"—Arthur's high-toned, high-priced restaurant on the Hudson waterfront. It's a standard joke; everybody guffaws.

Sam Chominsky watches from the side, beaming. He confesses to me that he stole Armand's thunder: he couldn't resist telling the crew, as soon as he knew it, that the execs had adopted his recommendation that Bob receive the award. "The men cheered," he tells me. "They said it was about time one of us got it." (Actually, Bob is the third of the night crew to get it.) "I'm glad the V-Ps came out," he adds, "so the guys don't think they're the forgotten army."

The men file downstairs for the shape. Management stands around in the lunchroom, chatting, in a happy mood. Their day is done now, and it was a good meeting, a good crew. It's Andrew who breaks the mood; he's tugging on his father's sleeve, reminding him of a certain promise concerning an Arnold Schwarzenegger movie. Sal and Andy tramp down the stairs, then stand with Sam by the dragline to discuss the need for more hilos on the dock. There are twenty-six hilos now, and they're thinking of buying six to ten more to handle the skid freight, so that the platform men like John don't spend dead time waiting.

I sit on a crate of drums and line up figures, which I'll complete and confirm with Sal and his print-outs in the morning. During the last twenty-four hours, from 7:00 P.M. Monday to 7:00 P.M. Tuesday, July 8 and 9, 1991, 115 men on the North Bergen dock stripped eighty-one straight trucks and 199 trailers, including 142 vans and fifty-seven pups. They loaded eighty-six straight trucks and 240 trailers, including 169 vans and seventy-one pups. They stripped 4,524 shipments weighing a total of 4,528,907 pounds and loaded 4,828 shipments totaling 4,221,527 pounds. (There were more shipments loaded than stripped because of the accumulation of already stripped freight on the dock over the holiday weekend.) The night men each handled an average of 11.2 shipments and 16,298 pounds per hour, exceeding their productivity standard by twenty-two percent. The day men handled an average of 12.6 shipments and 11,970 pounds per hour; their standard was exceeded by thirty-two percent. Once again, the work has pushed the men.

I look out an open door. The sun is sinking over the swamp. Even the yellow haze over metropolitan New York can deepen to rose and brighten to golden evening. Denis Zanetti strides past me, his hurry not too great for him to wave and call: "Good morning!" It's 8:15 P.M. I have an interview tomorrow at 9:00 A.M. in *my* morning. In Curlee Campbell's phrase, I'm well tired. I guess I'll sleep.

4. Nomad One

Ronnie Parham, senior over-the-road driver on the North Bergen list, is standing in the middle of the yard beside his new brick-red Mack CH-12 tractor. He's wearing a blue A-P-A baseball cap, with the red company diamond over the visor, and a blue company shirt thickly studded with embroidered patches, but no jacket. The February afternoon air is mild: that wet blend of warm and cold, smelling slightly metallic, which hints of snow. Rough weather is a trucker's bane, but I myself am selfishly intrigued by its possible complications to the ride, now that I'm finally ready for a jolting trip on the interstates in a road tractor.

Ronnie walks forward to meet me. His fifty-seven years show in his posture, which is bent slightly to the right at his waist, but his milk-chocolate brown face is unlined, although there is gray in his pencil moustache. A Roman nose as strong as Arthur's retreats on each side into flared nostrils. He squints in the low winter sun sinking behind me as we shake hands. The words surface in my stream of thoughts: "Oh. Another A-P-A aristocrat." The first thought is the true one, the Chinese say, but I'm not sure what this thought means. What's this about aristocrats?

Ronnie has already hooked up his tractor to the first of two pup trailers that he'll be hauling this afternoon to A-P-A's terminal in Canton, Massachusetts, twenty miles south of Boston. The pups, each twenty-eight feet long, are hauled in tandem as "doubles," the longest combination of trailers legal in New

England. I ask Ronnie what freight is on the first trailer, and he shows me his line-haul manifest. On it, the freight is listed in truncated computerspeak:

Shipper	Consignee	Destination	Pcs	Wt
AIR FORCE	TRANSPORTA	LORING AF ME	1	999
SILVER SECUR	TREND LINE	CHELSEA MA	1	550

and thirteen other shipments, fifteen in all, in 483 pieces weighing a total of 14,904 pounds. Despite my curiosity, I'm not going to learn much more about the freight. As a road driver, Ronnie doesn't need to know what the Air Force is sending to its base in northern Maine to ease the pain of imminent closing, or what Silver Secur has sold to Trend Line to frustrate mall thieves. He isn't going to deliver the freight to the consignees, as Tony did, or even open the trailer door to look at the load. He's just hauling it to the Canton terminal.

Ronnie has scanned his manifest in search of three things only: the identifying number of the pup, the total weight of the freight on it, and any listing of dangerous cargo. He's already matched the number penciled on the manifest, 28128, to the digits painted on an upper corner of the trailer's front panel. "If you move the wrong trailer from one terminal to another, you don't get paid for it," he remarks. "You've made the trip for nothing." Further, with its 14,904-pound load, pup 28128 weighs more than the other pup he's been assigned, 28101, with its 12,550 pounds, and the heavier pup must ride in front. "If the back trailer is more than a thousand pounds heavier than the front trailer," he tells me, "it'll fish-tail. You see it wobbling and you have to pull off to a flat place and rehook. Sometimes yard-jockeys who hook for you in other terminals screw you up."

Ronnie speaks the English of the New York–New Jersey region with an accent of middle strength. His 'r's are more fully eclipsed by the preceding vowels than are Tony's or John's 'r's, but they don't completely disappear as do Pete Leota's. He says New Yawk for New York, foitha for further, and, of cawse, Joisey.

As we talk, Ronnie circles his rig and pulls three diamond-shaped signs out of aluminum frames that are mounted at eye-height on the back and side panels of the trailer. The signs are "HazMat placards"—public warnings that there are hazardous materials among his cargo: flammables, corrosives, poisons, or explosives. He turns the signs around so that the word "DANGEROUS" shows, and he slips them back into the frames. His manifest says that 804 pounds of corrosive cleaning liquid, headed for Hartford, Vermont, are among the load, and also 866 pounds of flammable liquid adhesive, headed for Brattleboro, Vermont. Only these shipments are described in detail on the manifest. Once in a while, the corner of a neighboring skid will breach the walls of a drum full of poison, or a pail of corrosives will swell in the heat of a closed trailer in summer and burst its bung. When there's blue foam boiling out of a drum, it helps to be able to give it a name. On the manifest beside the Hartford and Brattleboro shipments, there's a page number referring to a book that describes initial clean-up procedures—a kind of first-aid manual for chemicals. Ronnie must carry the book in his tractor, on pain of a fine of several hundred dollars if he's stopped on the road without it. All commercial truck drivers now have to pass a national test on the contents of the clean-up manual. "I tell you, you got to be a lawyer out here now, and a scientist and just about everything else to haul a trailer," Ronnie says cheerfully.

Tractors are linked to trailers by the "fifth wheel"—a round, greased, notched plate that rests on the tractor's naked chassis behind the cab, above the drive-axle. The fifth wheel slides back beneath the trailer and engulfs the kingpin, which points down from the trailer's belly like a bull's pizzle. Ronnie hooked his tractor to the front pup trailer before I arrived. Now, to hook the front pup to the back pup, he drags across the yard a freestanding, four-wheeled coupling axle, called a "boggie" (pronounced "bogey"). On top of the axle is mounted a fifth wheel; extending forward from it is a six-foot-long hitch-bar, called a "tongue," which ends in a small horizontal circle. Ronnie eases the tongue up to the back of the front pup until a vertical, circular clasp (the "pindle"), jutting out from underneath the pup, snaps shut over the circle. The linkage is like that of the two circular clasps of a chain necklace, except that, Ronnie says, "an airlock on the tongue is energized and locks onto the pindle so the boggie doesn't flap-flap-flap in transit."

Next, Ronnie climbs into his tractor and drives forward until the tractor, the front pup, and the boggie all stand in a line with the second pup. Then he backs up, and the fifth wheel on the boggie slides with a thump under the back pup, making the back pup jump. Ronnie jerks the entire assembly forward to make sure the kingpin has slid home down the notch in the fifth wheel. Although the notch widens at its opening to no more than ten inches, it is unusual for a driver to miss.

Finally, Ronnie ties all the components of the rig into the compressed-air-braking system by means of two black hoses, which end in clamps called gladhands. A black lightcord, too, snakes across the couplings. Again he circumambulates the rig, checks the tires, the kingpins, the springs, the lights. Stooping, he surveys the ground for oil leaks and the undersides of the pups "to check if anything's hanging off." He eyeballs each of the five axles, all of them single axles, each with four wheels except for the two-wheel steering axle in front. (Tractors used for cross-country hauls or for especially heavy loads, such as freight containers headed for railyards or ocean piers, are fitted with double drive-axles, on eight wheels, called "screws.") Finally, Ronnie winds up the dolly posts of the second pup with cranks that fold out from beneath the trailer on each side. The rig—tractor, lead pup, boggie, and back pup, on eighteen wheels, altogether seventy-four feet long, weighing, with its load, 59,634 pounds—is now complete and ready to roll.

I climb the two-rung ladder by the passenger door, and with the help of the grab-bar, haul myself up and in. Inside, the new Mack, all in black, soothes the eye: molded dashboard, vari-colored lights, deep seats, wide windows, a heater that's already working, but discreetly. Ronnie's citizen-band radio is mounted on the floor by the gearshift, with the microphone dangling from the dash. From an FM radio ensconced in a pocket above his sunvisor, a Baroque concerto floats. Not only the driver's seat, but the entire cab rides on an air cushion. Ronnie warns me to latch my shoulder-belt, because at every bump in the road, "the whole thing leans and tips like you're in a boat."

It's 2:30 P.M. A hidden bell clangs as Ronnie pushes in two large buttons on the dash: a yellow diamond, which releases the emergency brakes on the tractor, and a red octagon, which controls the emergency brakes on the boggie and the pups. Ronnie drives forward to the guard shack, exhibits his two manifests, waits for a security man to wrap seals around the locks on his pups, and then crawls in first gear up the 88th Street hill to the long red light at Tonnelle Avenue. As he waits, he turns off his radio. The caged purr of 300 horsepower is more than the massed horns of Mahler could override, not to speak of Vivaldi. When Ronnie's alone in the truck, he listens with one earphone. (Wearing two earphones while driving any vehicle is illegal.)

"You always listen to classical?" I ask him.

"Talk shows, call-in shows, classical. . . . My kids like rap." Ronnie purses his lips in distaste, then quotes his grown son and daughter: " 'Why do you listen to that old fogey stuff?' I tell 'em, 'Don't put any of that bumpety-bump music on *my* radio.' I like concert music. I don't know any names, but I know the sounds. I can put myself in it and visualize myself in it . . . mountains, the ocean . . . like in a movie."

He swings left onto Tonnelle towards the George Washington Bridge and begins working up through the gears. We have to shout over the engine. Air-suspended or not, the cab vibrates subtly with every piston-thrust, and jerks up, down, forward, back, right, left, and diagonally at every road seam, frost heave, pavement patch, pothole, wheel rut, lane change, down shift, and curve. The troubled waters of my coffee leap out onto my pants. My pen bounces and slides, turning l's into i's and o's into d's. I shove my clipboard back into my satchel. There won't be any stops for me to catch up on my notes, as there were when I rode with Tony. "I'm going to have to use my tape recorder, do you mind?"

"Oh, no."

"Some people mind."

"You can use this one if you want." Ronnie pulls out a microcassette recorder from his breast pocket. When he sees that I'm surprised, he explains that he always carries a tape recorder with him on the road. "You're just going along on the highway, and you're in a sense in open space. You're not associated with anything familiar, and you can get your thoughts together much better. But what I find is that your thoughts are like watching a TV or something. They all pass in front of you, and not much of it registers, at least for myself, unless you have some way of recording it. You can't write it in the tractor, so with me, if something comes up and I have it all worked out, I got all the details and everything, and then it just disappears, it's gone, you can't seem to get that thought again." He records the landscape of his thoughts in the sketchbook of his microcassette. "Like I was going to work on an antenna at home, and I was trying to figure out how I could put these pieces together, and while I was going down the road I had the whole thing in my mind—I could do this, I could do that—because you got nothing else to do than sit here—and I had it all figured out how I wanted to do it. Then when I got home I played the tape and wrote it down, and I was able to put it together."

Ronnie's description of his evanescent stream of thought intrigues me. We speak generally of the stream of consciousness, but it is unusual for people to experience their own thoughts this way, to recognize them as an autonomous, mysterious, ceaseless display that passes of its own accord before the inner eye and ear. It is an insight that arises only during long and focused solitude. But then, solitude is the hallmark of the longhaul truckdriver's life. It is one element of his folk heroism. In fact, the extraordinary isolation of the road driver, and the heroic stature it has conferred upon him, are what has above all made me curious to ride with one.

Intrepid wanderers in film and story are often companioned by heroic steeds, and the American longhaul truckdriver fulfills that story requirement admirably. He masters his behemoth steed from his high-perched saddle, like a dragon-rider in the fantasy novels my high school students read in order to learn, vicariously, how mastery feels. Yet another heroic element of the truckdriver's story is his workplace, the open road. It brings him—at least in the myth-making minds of country singers, and, I would venture to say, in the minds of most Americans—an enviable independence from the constricting routines of mass society. We imagine the loner of the highway free of the alarm clock, the time clock, the office, and the boss, while we are left behind (as Melville's Ishmael observes of the downtown New York crowd he is leaving behind) "pent up in lath and plaster—tied to counters, nailed to benches, clinched to desks." The long-haul truckdriver is our Ishmael of the interstates, flung out by the centrifuge of commerce into the paved wilderness. His sweet-sorrowful partings from his family and his longings for home are the noble themes of country songs:

> *There's raindrops on my windshield*
> *And teardrops on my steerin' wheel*
> *This lonely truck's the only thing I own*
> *And in my heart I'm pinin'*
> *While her old engine's whinin'*
> *Eighteen wheels a-hummin', home sweet home.*

Paying, on behalf of the rest of us, the price of loneliness, he mounts his rig and drives out from under the heavy boot of modern institutions, as he calls out for all of us, "Don't tread on me."

American myth has assigned the role of the defiant loner, with the tough nerves and the soft heart, to other workers also: cowboys, frontier lawmen, private eyes. It is hard not to suspect that the real road driver is no closer to the myth than is the real ranch hand or the real county sheriff or the real private investigator. Further, the loner is the opposite of our other dominant American ideal: the family farm, the idyllic small town, the utopian community, the united nation, the society that lifts individuals up instead of treading on them. It is the notion of community that guides A-P-A. I'm curious to know if the company's road drivers can subscribe to this second ideal, any more than they can conform to the ideal of the loner.

As we jounce across the George Washington Bridge and wait at the toll booth (twenty dollars, four dollars per axle), I ask Ronnie how he landed on the road.

He began at A-P-A in 1962, by chance. "The company I worked for at the time, Hudson Transportation—they used to move newspapers in Hudson County and general freight—was going out of business, and they were in the process of being bought out by A-P-A, because A-P-A wanted the operating rights. So while they were going out of business, I came over to A-P-A to drive temporarily, and a strange thing happened. I had no intention of working for A-P-A, because the way they worked at A-P-A was something altogether different. This company believes in high productivity. They want their money's worth out of the working individual, and I wasn't used to that. I was used to going out and putting in a half-a-day and getting a day's pay for it. And A-P-A's attitude was, you put in a day-and-a-half and you get a day's pay. So I had no intention of working for this company, but a strange thing happened—just luck. I got here and in the process of going from one company to another, A-P-A paid me for four weeks, and the hiring practice then was that if you work for a company for fifteen days, you're on the company list. That was the union regulation. So that's how I got the job. I didn't have to go through the trial period. And it turned out to be a very good thing. I probably would have went to one of the other companies which no longer exists."

For a man who works in isolation, Ronnie is a practiced talker, more fluent than anyone else I've interviewed at A-P-A, except for Armand and Arthur. Like them, Ronnie speaks in paragraphs. He often rushes the words of the last sentence of each paragraph to mark the conclusion. He's relaxed in his driver's armchair, steering mostly with his left hand, gesturing with his right. In order to check on my reception of his ironical wit, he glances swiftly at me now and then with his large, contemplative brown eyes, which dominate his face.

He instructs me: "A-P-A is still in business because their attitude is, get the most you can from the labor for the least you can, in the least amount of time. And it works. It's worth the effort because you're with a stable company—and the security clearance that they require for hiring enables you to get a job anywhere else—but going from what Hudson Transportation was to what A-P-A requires was a *whole* different ball-game."

Ronnie cocks an eye at my tape recorder, which I've been holding out towards him, near the gear shift. "You might check that to see what the level is, to see if you have to get it any closer," he says. I rewind a little of the tape, and there is Ronnie, a faint voice calling beside a roaring surf. I hold the recorder closer.

"If you come out a second time, I'll see if I can parallel two mikes without getting a feedback on them. Maybe if I put on a dropping resister."

I can't resist following up on a remark like that, although I'm still anxious to test Ronnie against the road-cowboy stereotype. "You said before you were working on an antenna?" I ask him.

"Yeah. I'm an amateur radio operator, licensed by the federal government for thirty-five years. Not CB. CB's only supposed to be a two-mile range. Amateur radio is short wave, it goes out possibly 200 miles, except in winter when the band is better, and you can talk to Japan, Europe, South America from the truck. I used to be on nets where you get on at a prescribed time and you talk to different people, usually stateside. Some fellas have schedules set up to talk to people in different countries. They'll contact them at a specific time. It ends up as talking over the back fence. 'How's the wife and the kids, what'd you do this week, what's doing in the area, did you finish painting the house?' and some of these people you never see because they're in other countries. You never know who you're going to get to talk to. In the U.S., any citizen can pass the test and get a license, but in some other countries you can't get a license if you're not a political person. So you might be talking to somebody in one of these countries who's the president or king or something, but they don't say who they are, they just say, 'Hey, my name is Mike or John or Joe,' and you carry on like that."

I have found in my interviews that when people's lives are the subject of conversation, their second passions, in Armand's phrase, surface quickly. In Armand's view, they're needed to counter the intense pull of community. Ronnie's passion for socializing by radio, though, is more suited for alleviating a road driver's solitude than for ensuring independence from a group. I ask, "Did you start out with A-P-A on the road?"

"No, I drove a straight job for three years. I got tired of that. Then I went on city trailer routes for fifteen years, in Jersey and Connecticut, until I had eighteen years with the company. And one day they loaded me up with a whole bunch of stuff, and I said, 'That's it. I'm outta here. I'm not working in the city any more.' I couldn't take it, because we had new dispatchers that were younger, and it just seems hard to work when you have somebody that could be your son or something telling you what to do, how to do it. I was getting older and it was just hard to take. You accept the authority a little more from somebody who's either your equal or older. It's hard. The bosses are getting younger and younger. So I went out on the road."

"The road is different, then?"

"Sure. Out here, I can sit and scream or sing or do whatever I want. Whatever I feel like doing. In a sense this is my ship. I'm the captain of it. As long as I get the freight there in a reasonable period of time, I can do what I want. I don't think I could go back to the city to be ordered to do this, ordered to do that, go over there, do this here, putting up with customers. Most of your customers, you don't have a problem with, but you do have some customers that get up in the morning and look for a problem and you show up." He laughs. "I don't think I could put up with that. The only thing about road driving that I don't like is the hours I have to work."

"Worse than on the dock?"

Unlike city drivers and dockworkers, Ronnie explains, road drivers don't begin work at the same hour every day. " 'When and where needed,' is what the contract says." Ronnie may get home at 5:00 A.M. after a long run that ended at 4:00 A.M. (he has an hour's commute to his home in Middletown, on the Jersey Shore). Then he may be called again as early as noon to notify him of a run at 2:00 P.M. As senior man, twelve years on the road list, Ronnie gets the first call, and so his hours are roughly predictable; but drivers with less seniority "could be awake or asleep or in the middle of a run at any given time of the day or night." Ronnie has accustomed himself to short shrift on sleep. "I normally sleep six. I think a lot of the road drivers only sleep a short while. You start off tired, and then you wake up." He'll take short naps in rest areas and longer naps in terminals while he's waiting for a return trailer. He's already looking forward to the sofa upstairs in the Canton terminal office.

Road drivers for regional less-than-truckload carriers like A-P-A can be assigned runs of two kinds, he explains: a turn, which means a round trip that begins and ends at the driver's home terminal, and a layover, which means a trip that takes a driver up to 500 miles away from home and deposits him there in a motel. (Federal regulations permit a commercial trucker to drive for no more than ten hours before resting another eight hours; and, in the Northeast, ten hours' driving is presumed to carry a driver no more than 500 miles.) Ronnie likes to sleep in his own bed, and so he prefers turns. He also makes more money on them. Road drivers are paid by the mile: $.40925 cents a mile in 1992, with a two-cents-a-mile premium for hauling pups, if the drivers are Teamsters and based in New Jersey.

"Anything over 250 miles is a layover" Ronnie says, "since a round-trip would go over 500 miles. I don't go to Montreal, because not only is the paperwork a pain in the neck to get across the border, but the mileage is very short. It's only 300 and some miles. It doesn't pay. I take runs that will give me a decent day's pay. This run, Canton and back, is 432 miles. If I go through the terminal in Meriden, Connecticut on the way back [which he won't know till he arrives in Canton], it's 442 miles. If I do Baltimore, it's 416, or 432 if I go through Philadelphia. So I try and stay up above 400 miles." (Hauling pups for 400 miles earns him $171.70, plus $16.73 an hour for any time he's on the clock but not driving—for example, the time he takes to hook trailers to his tractor.)

"Richmond is a layover," he continues. "You can't come back from Richmond. It's close to 350 miles. What you might do is go to Richmond, and from Richmond go to the terminal in Lexington, Virginia, before you lay over, or go to Virginia Beach, where we have a daily pickup, and that will give you more than 400 miles." Drivers on layover runs are said to be "in the system," and they need not be routed home the next day. Under the Teamster contract, they may be assigned layovers three nights in a row, and they may be asked, but not forced, to run a fourth night and fifth day. "Other runs I've seen are to go down to Richmond and then come back to Baltimore before laying over. Then you can get up in Baltimore and go to Pittsburgh, or go back down to Richmond. Or you can get stuck up north and they'll run you around Maine and Canada and Vermont."

"Where do they put you up?"

"Red Roof, Comfort Inn, good hotels."

"No shabby motels?"

"No, we had those to start off with, but then they tried to upgrade, because they wanted the drivers to go to sleep easier. They had some sleazy ones where they rent the beds by the hour, where you hear the door slamming in the next room, the moans, and you don't get any sleep."

On the New York side of the George Washington Bridge, we plunge now into a convergence of underpasses beneath high-rise buildings. We emerge and cross in a moment the narrow neck of Manhattan at Washington Heights, and then enter a deep cut, which is enclosed by brick-faced concrete walls rising fifty feet up. This is the Cross Bronx Expressway, site of many a wasted summer afternoon spent cooking in traffic jams in my youth. Thirty years later, it remains probably the most congested stretch of interstate highway in the country, certainly the dirtiest stretch, and apparently the most hated (so revealed recently in a rather whimsical poll of truckdrivers). Ronnie calls it "the worst road in the world" and "torture alley." In the air high above us, city streets cross the expressway at regular intervals, like slats over a crate. Ravaged automobiles line the top of the wall. Beyond them, brick tenements lean back into the dull sky, many staring with burnt-out eyes.

Here, along the roadway, trash in stunning abundance and variety climbs the walls like the flotsam left by a tide. Above the flotsam begin the graffiti, puffy letters crowding one after another in pastel pinks and blues, all meaning to say, obscurely, defiantly, that their writers are alive. Above the reach of the writers' arms, the walls are unadorned, except for an occasional spray of icicles at the emergence of a drain. The road rises, and we flash onto a bridge, then re-enter the cut, which descends for a moment a hundred feet below the level of the streets. Beside us, the large, black-grimed bricks that face the high walls proceed in perfect straight lines. Their design recalls the dressed stone blocks, evenly laid and flawlessly rectangular, with which immigrant masons built the railroad cuts of the urban Northeast, having brought with them from home the Italian genius for working in stone.

The traffic on the Cross Bronx is not really New York's fault. The city lies at a colossal convergence of transportation routes by land, water, and air, connecting everything north and east with everything west and south. The convergence is suffocating, but it is also the reason New York happened. Even when there were only boots, horses, and boats, much of the commerce of North America descended on this spot. As for the filth of the Cross Bronx, Ronnie, who's from Jersey, offers a mild defense of the denizens of the east bank of the Hudson: "They have crews out here picking up the dirt, trying to keep it clean. I guess New Yorkers have an attitude: if they're in dirt, they'll add to it. They get it cleaned up and then it gets dirty again, and when it gets to be filthy, they'll go out and clean it up again."

We're lucky in our timing. Afternoon rush hour has hardly begun, there are no accidents at the moment, and the construction today is only on the other side of the road. Ronnie is advancing through the gears without much interruption. He isn't using the clutch when he shifts; he's meshing the gears according to the speed of the engine, judged by its sound. "If you're an experienced driver, you should be able to shift without the clutch, as long as you're not going uphill or downhill, which puts a strain on the engine." There are only five forward positions in the gear-box, but he actually has nine gears. An aluminum spring-lever attached to the gearshift moves him into an auxiliary high ratio which doubles the top four gears. The reverse gear is also doubled, "but you can't use the high reverse gear unless you're in a wide open space, because you move backward at about twenty-five miles an hour. A little difficult."

Engines built for long hauls across country may be built to 400 horsepower—Ronnie's Mack has 300—and their transmissions may carry a second auxiliary high ratio, giving the cross-country trucker thirteen forward gears, for the attainment of blistering speeds. "You're doing sixty, sixty-five," Ronnie says, "and these drivers pass you like you're standing still. They *move*. They're fully loaded and they pass you like they're empty." Ronnie may catch them on the hills, however; the electronic fuel injection in his 1991 Mack engine sends him up the hills of Rhode Island and Pennsylvania at forty or forty-five miles per hour, instead of the standard thirty or less. But he can't barrel down hills and straight stretches at seventy-five or eighty to make up for time lost crawling uphill, as truckers crave to do, because of an electronic speed governor that A-P-A had Mack install in the engine. The governor constricts the fuel intake when the wheels turn past sixty-two, in the manner of a cruise-control device, but set permanently and only at the high end. A-P-A wants to save on fuel, avoid fines, and prevent accidents.

To keep Ronnie mindful of the proprieties, there's also a tachometer disk recording his speed, for scrutiny by a clerk in A-P-A's Safety Department. Ronnie will tap the brake when downhill momentum rolls his rig past seventy. "That's when they call you in." He adds: "Sixty-three is a safe speed in most states, except Connecticut and Ohio." He means safe from "smokies"— a truckers' sobriquet for highway police. (The name is probably derived from the forest-ranger-style circular-brimmed hats affected by state police in the Northeast.) Occasionally, police in Connecticut will award tickets for speeds as low as fifty-six.

Speed tempts road drivers because they are paid by the mile, not by the hour. Trucklines, too, earn business if they can promise faster delivery. That trucks, as well as cars, use more fuel per mile as their speed increases never used to discourage truckers from speed, because diesel fuel was cheap in the United States, even cheaper than our cheap gasoline. Diesel now costs as much or almost as much as gasoline, in part because of recent increases in state and federal taxes. Cost-conscious trucklines like A-P-A have responded by disciplining drivers' speeds and by demanding fuel economy of truckmakers. Only in the nineties, more than a decade later than the carmakers, have truck manufacturers begun to build electronic engines, as well as truck and trailer bodies of lighter materials. To Ronnie's disgust, the cab of his new Mack is made of fiberglass, the bumpers of mere plastic. (The steel bumpers of his old 1985 Mack R-600 displayed a bank of lights arranged in the shape of an "R," but the new bumper can't support the weight.)

As a result of the new designs, Ronnie's Mack rides at six or seven miles per gallon, depending on the load, compared to four or five miles per gallon in his old tractor—an improvement of about forty or fifty percent. Wind resistance accounts for a further variation in fuel mileage, such that it costs less to drive in summer, when winds are milder, and less, also, to run east, propelled by the prevailing continental winds, than to run west. This is why the roof fairing, which rises like a crest above the tractor cab to deflect headwind over the top of the trailer, is now almost universal on American trucks. Roof fairings are said to reduce fuel consumption by about five percent. Further, aerodynamic cab design has recently become the standard for all the major American truck manufacturers (there are six, of which three—Mack, Freightliner, and Volvo/GM—are owned wholly or in part by European automakers). Thus the hood of Ronnie's tractor slopes and narrows into a snout that drivers have dubbed "the anteater."

Despite their greed for fuel, diesel tractors like Ronnie's are far more efficient than the gasoline engines of automobiles. Fully loaded to 80,000 pounds, the legal limit for equipment and freight combined, Ronnie's rig weighs the equivalent of twenty-seven 3,000-pound cars. While his one engine would burn one gallon of diesel to go six miles, their twenty-seven engines, at thirty miles per gallon each, would together use nearly five-and-a-half gallons of gasoline to go the same six miles.

The advantage of diesel lies in both the engine and the fuel. Like their gasoline cousins, diesel engines are powered by reciprocating pistons, which shoot back and forth within cylinders, and, in their agitation, turn a crankshaft around. The crankshaft is geared to turn the axles. At sixty-two miles per hour on a flat stretch of interstate, the crankshaft in Ronnie's Mack is spinning at 1,800 revolutions per minute—thirty spins per second. (A four-cylinder compact car at sixty-two miles per hour may run at 2,200 revolutions per minute.)

The piston in the cylinder of a gasoline engine is impelled by the explosion of gasoline mixed with air and ignited by a spark. In a diesel engine, the ignition occurs without a spark, simply by the heating of air through compression. Because diesel fuel doesn't explode, it can continue to burn throughout the power-stroke, making the engine more efficient. Diesel also soothes the engine by lubricating the piston, since it is oilier than gasoline: much less refined, closer to the original crude. Also, the air-and-fuel mixture in a gasoline engine is compressed in the cylinder to one-eighth or one-tenth of its original volume, whereas in a diesel engine it is compressed to one-fifteenth of its original size. The result is that the diesel fuel can deliver more power. (If the compression ratio in a gasoline engine were fifteen to one, the explosion would drive the piston backwards—a malfunction which is heard as "pinging.") Still, the trucking industry's appetite for fuel is not dainty. According to *Transportation in America*, the standard almanac of transportation statistics, diesel tractors like Ronnie's have burned about seven percent of all the petroleum used in the United States during the last five years.

Diesel engines are efficient in another way. The 300 horse-power of Ronnie's engine is no greater than a 1976 Chrysler V-8's or a Ford Thunderbird's, but diesel engines are designed to run at top horsepower all the time. An eight-cylinder engine in a luxury car of the 1970s, run at full 300 horsepower, 120 miles per hour down the interstates, would last not much more than a day. A-P-A keeps its diesel tractors for twelve years. While on the road, the company's tractors average 110,000 miles annually. After six years, the engines are rebuilt and the tractors move to the city operation, where engine wear is less intense, and where they're closer to the repair shop. After six more years of pickup and delivery, 30,000 miles a year, a tractor will have run, on the average, 840,000 miles. It heads for A-P-A's leasing subsidiary, or is sold to a local trucker or owner-operator, who might run it another half-a-million.

Improvements in diesel-fuel economy, late in coming, have nevertheless come sooner than controls on diesel as a source of pollution. The black soot in diesel exhaust is carcinogenic, and according to the American Lung Association, heavy-duty trucks and buses produce, on the average, a gallon of soot ("particulates," in technical language) every 575 miles. Congress ordered the development of standards for control of particulates and other diesel-engine pollutants in 1977, but it wasn't until 1988 that the

Environmental Protection Agency—which had been hamstrung and demoralized during the Reagan years, and had been delayed by truckmakers in court—finally imposed pollution standards on diesel engines. The standards are becoming stricter in three phases, the third to be attained in 1994. Ronnie's 1991 Mack engine already meets the 1994 standards, and its exhaust is invisible. But, because most diesel tractors are run for about fifteen years, black diesel soot will be streaming into the wakes of older heavy-duty trucks well into the first decade of the next century. Reduction of the sulphur in diesel fuel will be achieved more quickly. The EPA has required oil refiners to remove eighty percent of the sulphur in diesel by October, 1993, and also to see to it that the fuel they produce is "limited aromatic" (meaning it will stink less). Sulphur oxides are a major element in the production of acid rain.

Ronnie has been driving us east on the New England Thruway, a New York State toll road which the federal government counts as part of Interstate 95. Now, at Greenwich, the highway crosses into Connecticut, where it becomes what used to be called the Connecticut Turnpike. In my Connecticut childhood and youth, I surveyed the sights of this road many hundreds of times, but never from this height. My eyes are eight feet above the pavement. From here, the cars buzzing past our fenders seem paltry and insectile. Ronnie clearly regards them as a form of pest. They are constantly swooping up entrance ramps to crowd him from the right, while others shoot across his bow from the left on their way to the exits. Pointing across me to the tractor's right side, Ronnie says, "People will come out here and get along side of you and then they look at you—you know: 'Ain't you gonna stop and let me in?'—Sure, like I'm gonna go ahead and run you off the road." He adds, "I always say, they got a mental hospital in New York and another in Boston, and they give the patients cars to drive up and down I-95, for therapy."

Automobile drivers merging onto an interstate assume that other cars coming up upon them in the right-hand lane of the highway will either slow down or swing left to let them in. They expect the same of heavy trucks; but trucks often can't manage it. Ronnie can't swing his wheel sharply without tipping over his trailer;

on a crowded highway, there's often no room for a seventy-four-foot-long vehicle to change lanes anyway; and on many highways, he can't enter the left-hand speed lane at all. ("We're not allowed out there. That's a $200 fine.") Slowing down is even harder. With a heavy load, at sixty miles per hour, Ronnie would need nearly 400 feet to stop. A car might need fifty feet. In the Connecticut towns along Long Island Sound, where exit and entrance ramps climb to the elevated turnpike at nearly every mile, Ronnie's eyes are ceaselessly darting back and forth to his mirrors, to check for cars closing in on his left and his right. Sometimes he scolds them when they want him to switch lanes and he can't accommodate them: "Dopey, the road's running out!" He berates them with his horn, a fruity maritime toot which he produces with a yank on a loop of rope by his sunvisor. He says good-humoredly: "I'm going to get into the middle lane here, to get away from some of these bums."

Once he has moved into the middle lane, though, he is exposed to cars in the inside lane who want to pass him on the right, or who simply want to cruise beside him. I sympathize: "This guy in the Nissan has been here on your right for a couple of miles."

Ronnie nods. "I've been watching him to see if he is going to go ahead of me or stay alongside of me. He's looking at me." Ronnie laughs. "Out here, you gotta watch *all* the time. You can't just watch the road. You gotta watch the mirrors, watch ahead of you, look up on top to see if something's falling down. You're constantly looking all over the place."

He adds: "It's not often that the unforeseen occurs. You're usually looking for something to happen, trying to anticipate what somebody's going to do, so most of the time you avoid things. You see something on the side of the road, or you see someone going down the road and slowing down, you start watching for a sudden movement. Maybe they're going to get off the road, maybe they're going to get on the road, or they're going to stop. You start to watch. Most of the time it's defensive driving. If you do things right, there's less chance of them going wrong. There's nothing definite about it, but there's less chance. If you take precautions and try to think things out, there's a good possibility it'll work out better than if you just jump into them without looking at them. That's what I try to do. It doesn't always work, but I try to do it."

Truckers abominate rush hours. "You got all the traffic, it's really sickening to drive up and down the road," Ronnie remarks wearily. It's not only that traffic slows road drivers down and loses them money. During the day, trucks are an ungainly and unwelcome minority—only five percent of the vehicles on interstates during rush hours. The whales and the minnows are a menace to each other, the minnows by their swarming numbers, the whales by the immense momentum of their speed and weight. Ronnie's load is relatively light today, but his tractor and two pups still weigh twenty-five times what my Honda Civic weighs, and they are six times as long. Cross-country trucks tend to be loaded much closer to the federal gross-vehicle-weight limit of 80,000 pounds—equal to thirty-three Honda Civics. As to the length of trailers, state limits vary, from 48 feet in the Northeast to 60 feet in Wyoming.

Even these weight and length limits are fudged, though, in twenty-one states, by tolerance of what truckers call "LCVs" ("longer-combination vehicles"). These leviathans of the interstates may be "triples" (three twenty-eight-foot pups), "turnpike doubles" (two forty-eight-foot trailers pulled in tandem), or "Rocky Mountain doubles" (a forty-eight-foot trailer and a twenty-eight-foot pup). LCVs are usually over 100 feet long—Alaska permits the longest whale, a blue, at 120 feet—and these may weigh well over 100,000 pounds. New York permits the heaviest, at 142,000 pounds. Like Ronnie's doubles, LCVs are generally legal only on the interstates and may be driven only a short distance away from them, usually five miles. But on the interstates, they and passenger cars are strange and dangerous roadfellows.

The high speeds at which longhaul tractor-trailers are driven— thanks to their powerful engines, their hurtling momentum, the superb roads society has built for them, the demands of shippers for fast delivery, and their drivers' desire to get home—make them very resistant to efforts to slow them. Yet the crudest, most unsatisfactory technology in heavy-weight trucks is their air-powered brakes. The air is forced by a compressor mounted on the engine through a system of hoses to the brake chambers, which are positioned beside each wheel. Within each chamber, air pressure thrusts a pin, called a "pushrod," against an S-shaped cam. The cam then rotates, spreading apart a two-flanged brake shoe. The shoe, in turn, is forced against the wheel. This astonishingly cumbersome and old-fashioned mechanism is forever "going out of adjustment," as truckers say. What they mean is that the pushrod in the brake chamber must be positioned just so in order to be thrust by the air against the cam that then spreads the shoe. But, under the pressures of road journeys, the pushrods do not stay just so.

In recent years, trucklines with large fleets like A-P-A's have required truckmakers to install in the brake chambers a mechanical device called an automatic slack adjuster, which repositions the pushrod each time the brake is applied. These "auto-slacks," which the National Highway Traffic Safety Administration recently ruled mandatory for all new trucks, beginning in 1994, have reduced brake failures. However, not every truckline uses them, and the device itself can slip out of adjustment. It also becomes useless if the entire brake system is not frequently maintained by people who know what they are doing. (Federal safety regulations only require annual inspections. A-P-A inspects and services its trucks and tractors every six weeks.) Smaller trucklines and owner-operators—if they are pressed for cash, as they usually are, run older, spottily maintained trucks that lack automatic slack adjusters and are fitted with cheap brake linings and low-cost, light-weight brake shoes. Bad brakes, therefore, contribute to many truck accidents. Along with overweight trailers and drivers' failure to take legally mandated rest periods, brakes are the chief subject of citations when police inspect commercial trucks on the road. A 1992 study by the National Transportation Safety Board found that sixty percent of the 1,520 five-axle tractor-trailers its researchers inspected in five states had brake defects serious enough to warrant parking the rigs off the road.

Even when air brakes are well-maintained and are of the best quality, they are inadequate for cross-country hauling, because the brake shoes quickly overheat during downhill mountain driving. At 600 degrees Fahrenheit, brakes begin to fade, which means they won't slow the wheels no matter how hard the panicked driver stomps on the brake pedal. Therefore, in addition to air brakes, trucks driven on mountains are equipped with loud-blatting engine brakes, which inject air into the cylinders to retard the pistons, or with electromagnets that drag on the revolutions of the driveshaft.

Of the approximately 45,000 deaths on American roads during each of the last few years, about 6,000—thirteen percent—have occurred in accidents involving commercial trucks. Partly because human bodies are often destroyed in these accidents, the blame is hard to assign, but people who study highway accidents judge the main factor in ninety-five percent of such cases to be driver's error. Bad brakes and inclement weather are often secondary causes. In an accident involving only passenger cars or passenger cars and pedestrians, the driving error can most often be traced to alcohol; but when a car meets a truck, the error is usually due, instead, either to the truck driver's fatigue, or, more often, to the car driver's ignorance.

Driver education courses in high schools do not emphasize, and may not even mention, how to stay alive in a truck's company, and auto licensing exams slight the matter or do not test for it at all. It's obvious, though, from the height of Ronnie's cab, that the commuters who keep trying to force him to slow or change lanes don't recognize their own recklessness. The drivers who cruise along Ronnie's right side must not realize that, despite all his mirrors, he may not always know they are there. This is especially true when he is making a turn or rounding a curve, because then his mirrors no longer stand in line with his trailer's side panel, and so they won't reflect a car that is speeding alongside. Even on a straight stretch, the dozen or so feet behind the passenger door in a tractor cab is always a blind spot if the tractor isn't fitted with a round spot mirror on the right fender, as Ronnie's is—but many aren't. Yet some car drivers will ride alongside a big truck in summer just to stay in the shade. If it's turning or if it lacks spot mirrors, even to pass a tractor-trailer on the right is to declare oneself half in love with easeful death.

To follow closely behind a trailer or even a straight truck is as foolish as to ride alongside of one. Truck drivers, and also most bus drivers, cannot see immediately behind their rigs at all. In general, if a car driver is following a truck so closely that he cannot see, up ahead, the truck driver's rectangular "West Coast mirror" jutting out beside the window of the cab, then he can be fairly sure that the truck driver can't see him in the mirror. Car drivers fond of tailgating trucks would do well to contemplate a structure of steel bars, in the shape of an upside-down Greek letter *pi*, that is fitted beneath the back loading doors of most straight trucks and trailers, so that it hangs down between the back wheels. These bars, called "underride guards" or "ICC bars," are a kind of bumper. They reduce the destruction when cars plunge into and under a truck or trailer that has braked unexpectedly in front of them. In the United States, about sixty people a year die in these "underride accidents"—a grisly end.

In the first two decades of this century, as gasoline-powered freight trucks and passenger cars began crowding intercity highways that had been built for horses, the compatibility of motorized freight traffic and passenger traffic was a central concern of traffic planners. It was not taken for granted then, as it is now, that freight trucks and passenger cars should travel the same highways at all. In their trials in modern road building, the early experimenters chose New York as their laboratory, including the New York-to-Boston shore route, which Ronnie is driving this afternoon. (After 1945, the laboratory shifted to Los Angeles.) Since colonial times, the Boston shore route has run along Long Island Sound from the Bronx across Connecticut to the Rhode Island line, whence it follows Block Island Sound and then Narragansett Bay to Providence, from which it crosses overland to Boston. The route was called, and is still called in some places, the Boston Post Road, because it carried the mails, and it is the oldest interstate highway in America. By 1914, the route was traveled by the largest contingent among the 300,000 trucks already populating the country's roads (there are 15 million commercial trucks on American roads now). Although the trucks then were even shorter than Tony's twenty-eight foot straight truck, the earliest strategy to ease traffic on the shore route was to build a new road for trucks. The first plans to build such a route from New York to Bridgeport were laid in 1922.

The plans were abandoned. The route was not built until 1958, in the form of the Connecticut Turnpike. With one exception (the Pennsylvania Turnpike), nothing was done anywhere in the United States to build new routes for freight transport until after the Second World War. In the 1920s, interstate truck routes were merely designated on paper, and on roadsigns, by stringing together existing roads and renaming them as part of a federal highway system open to both trucks and cars. The Boston Post Road became part of U.S. Route 1, which ran, and still runs, along the East Coast from Key West, Florida to Fort Kent, Maine. (For north-south routes, the federal numeration progresses in odd numbers, beginning with Route 1 along the Atlantic and culminating in Route 101 along the Pacific. For east-west routes, the numbers are even, increasing southwards from Route 2, which runs from Houlton, Maine to Puget Sound, to Route 90, which runs from Jacksonville to El Paso.)

Meanwhile, traffic Rasputins in the various states, led by Robert Moses of New York, left the numbering of truck routes to Washington and constructed in real concrete something entirely different: parkways. These were limited-access highways for cars only; the strategy was to reduce congestion on truck routes by separating most of the cars away from them. The Bronx River Parkway, completed in 1923, was the first of many; they were called parkways because they were built as pleasure routes sheltered from commerce. Landscaping with lawns and trees was meant to entice city folk out for Sunday drives. Trucks carrying freight were forbidden. In the late thirties, along a route roughly three miles north of the Boston Post Road, already renamed Route 1, the Hutchinson River Parkway in New York and its continuation in Connecticut, the Merritt Parkway, were built from the Bronx to Milford, halfway between Bridgeport and New Haven. (The Merritt, to this day, is worthy of the parkway name. Swathed in the intense greens of the Connecticut summer, its views still free of billboards and largely even of buildings, its curving lanes still crossed by stonework overpasses that are each differently patterned and variously adorned with finials and floral swags, it remains a startling oxymoron: an express highway of charming beauty.) But the parkways did not, after all, solve the problem of congestion on the truck routes, because cars still crowded onto them along with the trucks, in greater numbers than before. Traffic and accidents on Route 1 remained infamous. The sensible hope that the parkways for cars would lighten the load on the truck routes proved vain. It was not until the seventies that highway-mad Americans acknowledged what now seems perfectly obvious: that more roads attract more traffic, not less.

After World War II, Europe rebuilt its railroads. Even today, European trucks are lighter and fewer than American trucks, a much less dominant presence on Europe's high-speed highways, which were finally built in the 1970s and 1980s. But America made another choice, even though its long, flat distances are far more suited to rail transport than most of the landscapes of Europe. The move away from rail in the United States was conditioned in part by an historical anomaly. Unlike most of the rest of the transportation infrastructure—roads, air lanes and airports, waterways and piers—the American railroad system was entirely owned by private interests. Further, the ownership and management of the railroads, especially in the East, had become incompetent and corrupt. The United States government could not step in to rebuild the railroads without a politically impossible program of expropriation. We built the interstates instead.

The planning for a new federal highway system not only slighted the natural longhaul function of railroads but also rejected the old parkway approach to separating commercial and passenger motor traffic. The interstates were designed instead to accommodate on one roadway both freight and passenger, truck and car. Planning is said to have been grandly initiated by FDR himself, with the drawing of new interstate routes in blue presidential pencil across a forty-eight-state map. The plans had to wait a dozen years for funding, under the Federal Highway Act of 1956, during the administration of Dwight Eisenhower, a highway enthusiast who had been impressed by German troop movements on the early autobahns.

But the northeastern states, ever more strangled by traffic, hadn't been able to wait. Pennsylvania had actually opened the first 160 miles of its turnpike, the country's first limited-access highway for both cars and trucks, in 1940. It was called a turnpike because it was financed by revenue bonds to be paid back through tolls, after the manner of the private log roads and plank roads built before the Civil War. (The pike across the road was turned aside when the traveler paid the toll.) After 1945, New Jersey followed Pennsylvania with its own turnpike while Washington was still dithering. Connecticut authorized its turnpike in 1951 and opened it in 1958, before the feds had built their first mile. California, meanwhile, had begun building its "freeways," so called not because they were actually free, but because they were financed by bonds to be paid off through taxes, instead of through tolls. With their freeways, California, as in other matters of highway design, traffic control, and the deployment of governmental euphemisms, displaced the Northeast and became the model for the country.

The Pennsylvania and New Jersey Turnpikes, and after them the New York Thruway and the Massachusetts and Maine Turnpikes, were meant primarily for long trips, whether by truck or by car. Exit and entry were limited to existing truck routes that crossed the turnpike. Therefore, the road ran unencumbered ten or twenty or more miles between interchanges. Instead of plunging into cities, severing or obliterating neighborhoods in the manner of the Cross Bronx Expressway, and pouring cars and trucks into the downtowns, the early turnpikes skirted cities. This gentler species of highway had few progeny. The Connecticut Turnpike, on which Ronnie is warily driving us now, is of a more dangerous breed, the kind of interstate that highway planners call a "city street." It was bred first in Los Angeles and now dominates every urban landscape in North America. In Connecticut, the turnpike slices through one industrial district after another along Long Island Sound, so that the old brick factories beetle over its pavement. On- and off-ramps connect the turnpike to every important municipal avenue, three or four to a town. In 360 miles from New Jersey to Ohio, the entire Pennsylvania Turnpike has 28 exits; in 110 miles, from Greenwich to New London, the Connecticut Turnpike has 84 exits. This is why commuters are swarming upon Ronnie from both sides, and why the Connecticut Turnpike and the roads like it, in every metropolitan area in the country, are dangerous workplaces for truckers and dangerous routes home for commuters.

On turnpikes with infrequent exits, tollhouses can be placed at the ends of the long exit ramps. On turnpikes that are city streets, there is usually no room for exit-ramp tollhouses, which would anyway have to be impractically numerous. The tollhouses must be built across the main roadway. By stopping all traffic, these "barrier tolls" create congestion and danger. California had the sense to evade the problem on its city-street freeways by not collecting any tolls, but instead relying on taxes, and, again, the federal government followed. (California does collect tolls on bridges, and on them it eventually halved the problem with the ingenious expedient, now also universal, of collecting twice the toll, but on one side only.)

Connecticut's barrier tolls were already infamous for their traffic jams when, on January 19, 1983, a loaded tractor-trailer plowed into the tollhouse at Stratford, east of Bridgeport, crushing three passenger cars, killing seven people, including the trucker, and injuring many others. Five months later, on June 28, 1983, a section of the turnpike bridge over the Mianus River in Greenwich slid into the water in the middle of the night, taking cars, a tractor-trailer, and three lives with it. Abashed and horrified, Connecticut authorized $5 billion to repair its highways, again anticipating Washington by half-a-decade. The barrier tolls were taken down. The Connecticut Turnpike ceased to exist as a separate entity and was absorbed into the federal interstate system. Its very name was abandoned, except by those, like myself, who grew up nearby. It is now merely a stretch of I-95, which, like its forerunner, Route 1, follows the Atlantic Shore from Maine to Florida.

The Connecticut Turnpike was built closer to the shore than the Post Road, and its bridges cross western Connecticut's myriad south-flowing rivers immediately before they meet Long Island Sound. Ronnie hurtles us across one river's mouth after another: the Horseneck, the Mianus, the Rippowam, the Noroton, the Norwalk, the Saugatuck, the Pequonnock, the lovely Housatonic, and finally the West and the Quinnipiac as they meet at New Haven Harbor. From my height I can see that the shores of many of these estuaries are built upon in the same way. Up the right bank, a short pipeline pier ascends to an oil-tank farm. Along the left shore, facing the tank farm, a luxury marina floats on the black water. The two testify together, at its very ports of entry, to Connecticut's status as the most industrialized state in the nation, and, per capita, the richest. Occasionally, high on the point above the mouth of a river, a breezy mansion stands, with its second-floor sleeping-porch boarded up for winter. A sandspit crooks around like an index finger at the farthest reach of each river's long arm. Beyond, the sheet-steel of the Sound lies flat beneath the gray sky of the advancing afternoon.

It has been twenty years since I've seen the New England winter. I well remember the blackened fringes of roadside snow and the bundled bodies, so much thicker than flimsily draped California bodies. I'd forgotten, though, the nakedness of the towns. Their suits and dresses of maple leaves and oak leaves have been stripped away. On my left, across the six lanes of traffic, the health or illness of the shoreline cities is exposed without pity. In some towns, junk is revealed in every back yard; in others, swimming pools. In vigorous retraining for a service economy, Stamford and New Haven are robust. Their office structures, handsome and gleaming, crowd down to the turnpike like young athletes on parade. Norwalk, and Bridgeport especially, have sunk into senescence. Their old red-brick mills line the highwayside in glum desuetude, watching the world go by.

We inch through New Haven in the twilight. Farther east, the traffic clears, and the highway shrinks to four lanes. Ronnie has returned to the right side. As we follow a gradual curve and approach a short bridge, suddenly he brakes and swerves from the right lane into the left. We sweep past two cars poking along in the right lane behind a white twelve-foot delivery van, which must be going over the bridge at no more than thirty-five miles an hour. Its engine is misfiring. Neither of the cars nor the van is lit in the dusk.

In an instant, the van is behind us. For an urban commuter, evading a slowpoke is too brief and routine a happening for comment, but the quality of Ronnie's silence indicates that for him this was more serious.

"He should have had his four-way flashers on," he says, after a minute.

"The van?"

"Yeah."

"What would you have done if a car had been coming up on your left, so there wouldn't have been space to change lanes? Could you have slowed down enough?"

"Maybe not." He adds after a pause: "The foot brake is about the best thing to use, and you look for a place to go. If you're coming up on something, and if there's no place to go, if you can't change lanes, you try to find a space where you can get off the road and not upset the unit." Ronnie has already told me that last week he'd had his first accident in eighteen years. A car skidded on the icy interstate across his path. He drove onto the shoulder, but couldn't avoid hitting the right rear door of the car. No one was hurt.

He says now, "Sometimes you may have to upset the unit. We had one guy, he intentionally went off the road. An accident occurred in front of him and a car was sitting right in his path with people in it. He couldn't stop, so he just drove right off the road. He didn't get hurt. Went out into a field. Here?" Ron laughs without mirth. He would have had to swerve into the bridge railing, and no doubt through it and over it, if he hadn't been able to swerve into the left lane around the misfiring van. "You'd have to say, now whose life am I going to save? The other driver I was mentioning, he saw where he could get off into a field and not kill himself. When it comes to something like this here, though, down in a ravine and a car in front of me, you know, it's like, I'm not going to kill myself. But self-preservation doesn't seem to always hold when you see you're going to kill somebody in front of you, or you might be able to survive if you just went off the road. You don't want to kill anybody, so you try to avoid it, and you might end up killing yourself. That's what's dangerous about this job. You make a mistake and you may not be able to correct it."

"Isn't there always the option of jumping out of the truck? Where I am, in northern California, the logging-truck drivers sometimes jump out if they can't make a hairpin turn."

"It's a questionable thing. Out here on the highway, you'd probably get hurt more than if you stayed with it. If it's moving slow like a logging truck on a hairpin, and you're in a grassy area, you've got a possibility of jumping out and breaking an arm or breaking a leg or something, but if you're moving fast down the highway and you jump, you can't run fast enough if you land on your feet. If there's an area where there are trees or anything like that there, you can't stop, so you're gonna hit, you're gonna tumble, you're gonna slam one of those trees harder than if you stayed in the vehicle."

As I learn from later research, Ronnie's judgments are borne out by statistics. The greatest killers of truck drivers in road accidents are roll-overs, fires, and ejections from the cab; the latter almost always means death.

Ronnie's closest call arose not from a car driver's error or his own, but from bad weather. "I've never gone off the road," he tells me now, "but I've jack-knifed, where the trailer came around towards the tractor. You're no longer in a straight line with the trailer, and you start to lose control." He jokes: "You look out to see what's passing you, because you know there's no one else on the road. Hey, it's the trailer coming around! It was on a bridge on a straight stretch on 380, up towards Scranton. I went to slow down, and the road must have been icy or glazed or something, and I didn't realize it, I just went to touch the brake and the tractor started to cant a bit and the trailer started to come around. But it didn't hit the tractor. I was able to pull out of it and nothing happened. I'm not sure what I did. You just have a lot of things you can do if you jack-knife. You can hit the trolley brake [the handbrake connected to the trailer axle], to get the trailer to go in a different direction, you can change gears, you can turn the wheel the opposite way, there's a bunch of things you can do. I don't remember what happened that time, because you're talking about maybe three or four seconds. It's not something where you have a prolonged time to figure out what to do. You have to do whatever you know and hope that you're doing the right thing."

Ronnie points ahead into the gloom. "In winter, sometimes you don't realize the road's changing. Like you're driving along a road like this here, and the road is wet, okay? You keep looking out of the mirror to watch for a spray off the wheels. If you're getting a spray, the road is still wet. When you don't see the spray, the road is frozen. When the temperature's down and you see water ahead of you, it's not water. It's ice. 'Black ice' is what they call it. You see a shiny spot ahead of you. It's ice. Now. You can't avoid it because you're too close to it. Don't change anything. Maintain your speed. Don't move the vehicle, don't do anything. Go over it, and then you can do something." He continues: "There's a lot of tricks to staying alive. If you can just remember them and follow through with them, it's okay, but sometimes for that instant you don't think, and when for that instant you don't think, that's when something goes wrong."

As we cross the Thames River at New London and leave the shore to climb the low hills of southeastern Connecticut, light snow drifts down and wanders in the headlights. "One time there were three of us riding together in a convoy, on the long hill right up ahead here into Rhode Island. One of the guys was Rudy Trump. It was cold, it had snowed, but the roadway was clear, all the slush and stuff was on the side. We hit the hill up here, and all of a sudden we see Rudy go." Ronnie vocalizes a falsetto call of horror and surprise. "Woo, woo, woo—he hit the guard rail, went down the embankment, and"—Ronnie demonstrates with his hand and forearm bent at the wrist, to show how Rudy's tractor and trailer had doubled up, with their jointure at the rear of the tractor and the front of the trailer leading like the point of a snowplow. "If it had turned around the other way, and he'd gone down backwards like this"—Ronnie demonstrates a descent with the tail of the trailer and the engine of the tractor leading, the plow turned backwards—"the whole unit might have flipped over. It might have dug into the ground and flipped the tractor right over on top of him and anything could have happened. But he went down the other way and landed down at the bottom, and nothing happened. We stopped and went down, it was okay. It was one of those things."

The snow hastens as we approach the Rhode Island line. Ronnie muses, "Once you lose your nerve, you don't drive any more. You're out here, I can't say that you don't have any fear, but you just drive like—if it's snowing, well, the snow's gonna end, and I'll be out of it. You may be driving in it for miles, but that idea is always in your head: well, it's gonna end. You're constantly watching that you don't do anything wrong that would get you into an accident, but you don't worry about it. Once you start to worry, it's all over, because then every time there's a motion in the vehicle, you're thinking you're ready to crash. So you don't even worry about it. You just drive."

Later on in the evening, on the other side of the highway, traffic is inching around a Volkswagen Beetle which has flipped onto its back. Ronnie comments cheerfully: "Someone decided to park upside down." Police cars, an ambulance, and a tow-truck wave their red lights around in the night. Ronnie instructs me in their argot equivalents: 'smokies,' 'a meat wagon,' and 'a draggin' wagon.' He adds: "It's something you see every day. You go along, you see an accident. You don't even slow down to see what the damage was. You see so many, you've seen one, you've seen them all. You just look at it."

Now Ronnie turns off into a travelers' "Welcome Area" just inside the Rhode Island line. This is his regular pit stop, two-thirds of the way to Boston. He halts along the edge of the parking lot, rather than nosing into a parking space, so that he can pull away again without having to back up. Doubles—pups in tandem—are unreliable going backwards, he explains. "You go a few feet and the boggie in the middle starts to turn and the back trailer starts to go the other way." Before turning off the engine, he sets the emergency brakes of the tractor and trailer by pulling out the two "panic buttons" on the dash. A loud hiss and sigh are released as the air under pressure escapes and the brakes engage.

While we're dismounting, a tractor-trailer pulls in behind us. Its driver swings down to the pavement and, without greeting, begins railing against the white van that made Ronnie swerve back near New Haven. His small, middle-aged face is pinched and querulous. "Why can't he have put on his four-ways?"

"He was driving right behind us," Ronnie explains, seeing my surprise and nodding toward the other driver.

The driver turns to me, with a trucker's resentment of the car driver's prejudice: "If there's an accident, it's always the truck driver's fault."

Clearly he's been waiting for Ronnie to make a stop so he could follow Ronnie in and unburden himself. Blame of the white van continues as we walk into the building. Not everyone has attained Ronnie's equanimity about the dangers of the road.

Inside, we stand sipping vending-machine coffee and chatting beside a diorama illustrating Rhode Island's oceanside charms. The round lady who dispenses maps and brochures behind the semi-circular counter comes out to cluck and commiserate; she's used to truckers. To the other driver's litany of sorrows—he still hasn't calmed down—she adds her own: outrage at a recent teachers' strike in Rhode Island. Ronnie interposes swiftly: "Well, you gotta arbitrate. Arbitration is the way to go;" and, shortly, "Well, we better get back on the road." As we step out into the cold, he says, amused, "You told me you're a teacher, so I eased us out of there."

"Marietta, Ohio," says the lettering on the door of the other driver's tractor. Like most truckers at truckstops and rest areas, he's left his tractor running. Some will lock their tractors with a second key. Ronnie turned his engine off. A-P-A frowns on idling, which wastes fuel and ages the engine by building up acid in the oil. According to the American Trucking Associations, an hour of idling is equivalent to 275 miles of driving. Drivers sometimes leave their engines running to power the heater or air-conditioner, or out of fear that the truck won't restart if the engine goes cold. None of these contingencies apply to short stops like ours, but idling is a diehard craft tradition. Ronnie has his own reasons for turning the engine off and taking the key. "I have dreams about coming out and finding my truck gone."

The Ohio driver's pinched face and strained emotions suggest that he has been on the road without much of a break since he left his terminal, even though federal regulations require him to rest for eight hours after he has been driving for ten. Marietta, in southeastern Ohio, is 700 miles from here across Pennsylvania, New Jersey, the New York bottleneck, and Connecticut, probably fifteen hours on the road. Hours-of-service limits are routinely violated in this way by truckload carriers and especially by owner-operators. The limits were imposed by the Interstate Commerce Commision in 1939 as part of the first major spate of federal rule-making for the safe operation of interstate commercial vehicles. The regulations, fifty-three years later, remain in effect. Drivers may actually work longer than ten hours— for fifteen hours altogether, before resting—but only ten of those hours may be spent behind the wheel. Ronnie's time spent hooking to his pups in North Bergen this afternoon would be included in the additional five hours.

There are also cumulative limits. Regional trucklines like A-P-A may run their drivers for no more than sixty hours in seven days; longhaul drivers may run for no more than seventy hours every eight days. The intent is to counteract the mounting weariness of long journeys by forcing a break. Beyond the cumulative limits, federal safety regulations do not restrict the length of long hauls. Ronnie himself, as he has explained to me, cannot be asked to lay over more than four nights away from home; but that is thanks to a clause in the Teamsters' contract. Drivers for truckload companies, very few of which are unionized, are not so fortunate. Without the Teamsters as a watchdog, it is commonplace for longhaul drivers to be dispatched, perfectly legally, on layover journeys of forty-five or even sixty days. Further, longhaul drivers are often forced by their employers to flout the government's hours-of-service regulations, as is the case, so I suspect, with our acquaintance from Ohio.

On the truckload market, a promise of delivery from Los Angeles to Boston is competitive at sixty-eight hours. To drive the 3,250 miles of interstate in those hours, a driver has to average forty-eight miles an hour all across the country without stopping. More plausibly, he will stop three or four times for two or three hours to nap, eat, and refuel. He'll drive for fifty-eight of the sixty-eight hours, averaging fifty-six miles an hour. Except for the speeding to make up for slow climbs, a sixty-eight-hour journey across country can still be legal, and even, perhaps, marginally safe, when drivers work in teams. But, with the exception of husband-and-wife owner-operators, team driving is not the usual practice, because it doubles the labor cost, or, for owner-operators, halves the earnings. It is more profitable to stay awake on amphetamines. Road drivers are required to keep a logbook of hours worked, but it is common practice among long-haul drivers to keep two logbooks, one true one for the employer, and one pretty one, called a "comic book," for the police. If the comic book is transparently false, the fine can reach a thousand dollars

Under the Teamster contract, A-P-A can't keep Ronnie waiting on a layover more than fourteen hours without paying him, but nonunion longhaul employers often keep drivers waiting unpaid between loads for several days in their motels or sleeper berths. Truckload consignees may also delay them, unpaid, all day or all night before allowing them to make their delivery at a factory or warehouse. The eventual permission to back in to be unloaded is often accompanied by an unloading fee levied by the consignee, which the truckload driver must pay, out of his own pocket, to a freelance dockworker known as a "lumper." Forcing drivers to pay for lumping is illegal, but widespread. Lumping fees reduce earnings that are already paltry, considering the stress and danger of these drivers' workplace and the extremes of their hours. Nonunion longhaul truckload drivers generally earn $30,000 to $33,000 a year, about three-fifths what Ronnie makes.

Badly paid, separated by a month or more from home, pressured by deadlines, and wasted by fatigue and amphetamines, these exhausted men are themselves a danger in their workplace. Ronnie fears them. He says when I ask him about it: "Sometimes when you listen to the radio, you'll hear a driver say that he left California on this date and he's up here and now he's going back there and it's less than a week, so you know he didn't sleep much. They'll tell you, 'I was here and I was there, and now I gotta be over here and over at this point at this time,' and it's too many miles. You couldn't cover that many miles and still be off eight hours at a time. It's evident that these guys are pulling over on the side and getting a couple hours sleep." He apostrophizes them with some heat: "Hey, y'know, it's okay if you run coast to coast, just so long as you get sleep and you're wide awake when you're operating your vehicle. If you're going to get an hour's sleep and then drive for another eight or ten hours, and then get another hour's sleep, your body's got to get fatigued, your judgment is going to get poor and you're going to do something that you shouldn't do." Fatigue is the destroyer of patience. Ronnie says: "You're out here with some people with very fragile nerves, and they're a menace to the road. Everything bothers them. You listen to the radio, you hear a guy cursing this car that's going slow in front of him, or somebody else that cut him off and wants to run him off the road. You're out here with someone that could kill people."

Another menace—the swarm of aging, poorly maintained tractors and trailers that descended upon the interstates after trucking deregulation in 1980—has, to some extent, receded. Ronnie explains, with the broad understanding of industry issues that I've heard from other A-P-A line workers: "When they brought in deregulation, they put a lot of junk on the road. A lot of people felt that with deregulation they could get a truck and they could make a living. Well, they found out they weren't making a living, because there were just too many people in the industry and there wasn't enough freight. So they had to sacrifice something. They had to put fuel in the vehicle, and they had to make payments on the vehicle, and they had to have food, so they had to sacrifice repairs, and you had junk running on the road. Bad tires, bad brakes, bad equipment in general. Now the inspectors are out there. So you're going to have to take better care of your equipment."

Doctrinaire deregulators in Washington were reluctant to admit that their scripture could contain an imperfection, but protests against the flood of junk equipment—"killer trucks," the media called them—led eventually to much more vigorous enforcement of safety regulations for commercial vehicles. Launched in 1984 with 120 Department of Transportation inspectors, the federal Motor Carrier Safety Assistance Program now funds, in addition, 1,500 state inspectors, both state police and officials of state motor vehicle departments. This is why Ronnie brings his logbook up to date before we leave the parking lot at the Rhode Island welcome area. "There's usually a D.O.T. van around the rest area up ahead." We'll also be passing a weigh station, a "scalehouse" or "coop," where, if it's open, Ronnie might have to stop for his rig to be weighed and to be inspected for safety violations.

As we roar back out onto the highway, Ronnie says, pointing: "Sometimes you'll see the D.O.T. van in the median up here ahead. He'll look at a vehicle going by, and if there's one that looks like it's driving heavy, 'I'll try it with this one.' If it's riding high, there's no sense in even bothering with it." Inspectors on the watch for overloaded trailers will look for what they call "over-deflection of tires," as well as a sagging suspension and a slug-gish climb of a hill. "He'll come up along side of you and put the red lights on. You go up to the next service area or rest area, and he'll put the portable scales down. Then maybe he'll get his creeper out, the thing that mechanics use to go under a vehicle, four wheels on it and a little head cushion, and he'll go under the tractor, he'll go under the trailer, to check if the brakes are properly adjusted, if you have any oil leaks, if you have an ex-treme play in the wheels. He checks the rims, the air pressure, the air hose, the suspension. He's what they call a creeper cop."

Tonight the creeper cop is not in sight, and farther on, neither of the weigh stations on the two sides of the highway is open. (They are manned in rotation; in Connecticut, for example, the scales are open for one shift a day, three days out of every five.) When they are open, most of the truckers approaching the scales will be forewarned on their CB radios by other drivers. If their logbooks are out of date or obviously doctored (if, for example, the logs are belied by toll receipts or truck-stop receipts, which a creeper cop can demand to see), or if the drivers were too obviously exhausted or stoned, they will stop in a rest area to sleep before reaching the weigh station. In response, inspectors haunt rest areas. Ronnie has seen inspectors roust sleeping long-haul drivers from their cabs and make them urinate in a bottle if they seem incoherent.

The urine test measures the presence of marijuana, cocaine, opiates, phencyclidine (PCP), and amphetamines. Positive results require confirmation by a follow-up blood test, which is more reliable. Commercial truck drivers now must take the test in five separate situations: during their required biennial physical exams, upon hiring by a new employer, when an employer or a law-enforcement officer suspects they're under the influence, when they've been involved in an accident and cited for it, and when their name comes up for random testing, which an employer must impose on half of its commercial drivers every year. Truck drivers, like car drivers, may also be required to take a roadside breathalyzer test for alcohol. The legal limit for alcohol for commercial drivers, however, is .04 percent of the blood, as opposed to .10 percent for car drivers in most states. It is against federal regulations for a commercial driver to drink any alcohol while on duty or during the four hours previous to reporting for work.

Truck drivers must also show inspectors their national commercial driver's license, a requirement new in April, 1992. While many states have had strict requirements as to age, training, and a record of safe driving before permitting commercial driving, nineteen states have had no specific requirements at all. A sixteen-year-old who had never mounted a tractor could climb in and, if he could get it started, legally drive 80,000 pounds down the highways. It was common, also, for truck drivers to carry licenses from several states, in order to spread out their violations through several computer banks. (The man who plowed into the Stratford barrier toll on the Connecticut Turnpike had eighteen violations on his various records.) The intent of the national license is to make that impossible.

Ronnie has been "placed out of service"—made to park his rig in a weigh station—only once, here in Rhode Island, for out-of-adjustment brakes. He waited for a mechanic to drive down from the Canton terminal to fix them. "The inspections are a nuisance," he says now, "but they're a good thing. They're catching the guys who don't sleep, and they're getting the junk off the road. You don't see as many vehicles in an area where there's an inspection. Years ago, you would see quite a few of them there, because there were just so many people out with junk. So I think the inspections are a good thing."

"Here we are in downtown Providence," Ronnie announces. As in many American cities, the interstate in Providence is an elevated roadway that wraps and chokes the center of town. The darkened office buildings peer out rather bug-eyed over their concrete collar. As we sweep by, moving our perspective along the rows of high-rises, the white stone capitol building appears to wander among them, its illuminated turrets and domes entirely out of place, like an unrecognized avatar. Suddenly, we overtake the white van again. "This guy is still limping along, with no flashers. They ought to put him on the side." It's well past 7:00 P.M., the rush hour is over, the six-lane road is nearly empty, and Ronnie sweeps around the van easily. In another five minutes, we enter Massachusetts. We've crossed Rhode Island in half-an-hour. "Yeah," says Ronnie, affirming the state's CB sobriquet: "It's the ministate." (Connecticut is nicknamed "the Gestapo state" and "the Communist state" because of the vigor of its highway police.) After twenty-five more miles northward, Ronnie descends from I-95 onto a state highway lined with malls. A-P-A's Canton terminal lies beyond them in an industrial park.

There's no guard shack at Canton, and Ronnie turns in through the gate in the chainlink fence. The terminal is a single 45,000-square-foot rectangular building, with a two-bay maintenance hangar protruding forward toward the gate. City tractors are parked along the fence; along the terminal walls, trailers and straight trucks are lined up at right angles to the doors, like a row of nursing piglets at their sow. Ronnie parks in the yard. He slips on his jacket, gathers up his manifests, and dismounts. It's 7:50. We've been on the road five hours and twenty minutes, including the stop at the Rhode Island welcome area, and have covered 216 miles.

We walk up a ramp to the front door. Inside, a small drivers' room with vending machines and picnic-style tables extends along a windowed transom. Behind the transom, an office pool with a dozen desks is inhabited now only by two or three night billers. We cross the room to another door which leads out to the dock.

Unlike the North Bergen dock, this one can be seen in its entirety at a glance: a single room roughly 200 feet long and wide,
with eighty-six doors. Clearly, this is North Bergen's progeny.
The center of the floor is piled high with drums, crates, and
cartons standing in rows that are divided by lanes. A single wider
lane sweeps around the periphery. Hilos are backing out of doors,
dockmen are wheeling carts, competing boomboxes are blaring.
There is no dragline, however, which explains the lack of crashes
amid a din much milder than North Bergen's. Steve Shea, night
supervisor, blond and burly, presides from his free-standing
wooden carrel at the far end of the dock. Ronnie introduces me,
then takes his leave. He's going to nap on a sofa in a room on
the second floor above the office pool.

Canton is A-P-A's second largest terminal. It is one of six major A-P-A terminals along the eastern seaboard, which, together,
transship about the same amount of freight as North Bergen does
alone. Canton itself handles 500 to 600 shipments outbound every
twenty-four hours, and about the same inbound, a total of 800,000
to one million pounds, as Jack Poor, the terminal manager, told
me when I first visited Canton last summer.

Tonight, Steve Shea and the other night supervisor, Billy Egan,
young, dark, and muscular, have twelve dockmen loading straight
trucks and city trailers for morning pedal runs. The terminal's
drivers pick up and deliver in Boston, Worcester, New Bedford,
Providence, and points in between. The night men are also loading outbound road trailers to be hauled to other terminals, perhaps ten to North Bergen and another twenty to other A-P-A
terminals in the Northeast. Philadelphia, Baltimore, and Buffalo,
each between 250 and 500 miles from here, are layovers for the
road drivers, too far for a round trip. Closer runs, to North Bergen and to terminals in Maine, Vermont, Connecticut, and eastern New York State, are turns.

Steve repairs often to the phone in his carrel for a call to the
central linehaul office in North Bergen, to plot the movement of
road trailers between terminals. The need to dispatch trailers
"cubed out" (full) to and from thirty-two terminals, while keeping promises of overnight delivery, and at the same time shuffling drivers so that none is on the road beyond his legal hours,

requires not only a computer logistics program but the specialized cortex of the linehaul dispatcher. In the North Bergen linehaul office, it is common to see dispatchers processing two phone
calls at once, one receiver held to each ear, the voices of two
dock supervisors in different states entering from either side.

The two pup trailers Ronnie just hauled to Canton are an instance of linehaul complexity. The lead pup was loaded in Baltimore, the back pup in Cleveland, both with freight consigned
to Massachusetts, Vermont, and Maine. The pups were brought
separately from Baltimore and Cleveland to North Bergen and
were joined there for Ronnie to haul to Canton; for them, North
Bergen acted merely as a switching yard. Here in Canton, Steve
will have the Massachusetts freight stripped from Ronnie's pups
and reloaded into city trucks for delivery tomorrow, and the
Vermont freight will be reloaded for linehaul to one of A-P-A's
two terminals there. The Maine freight, perhaps, will remain on
the pups for further hauling tonight, after more Maine freight
has been brought on to complete the loads.

There is no Sam Chominsky or Brian Nallen at the Canton
terminal to rule the dock by night and day, no Vinny Carnavale
to oversee the dispatchers, no linehaul office, no billing supervisor. Steve Shea and Billy Egan at night, Jack Poor and his two
dispatchers by day, are the entirety of terminal management.
They organize the loads, route the trucks, shape the men, supervise the billing. The dockmen, too, are generalists: they all
have access to hilos, and when they've cubed out a trailer they
jump down into the lot, make the hook to a tractor, pull the
trailer out into the yard, lock the door, close the seal around it,
sometimes fuel the tank, and snoop around the chassis for the
pre-trip inspection, so that all Ronnie will have to do when a
night biller wakes him up is to pocket his manifest and drive.
Some road drivers who make short turns to and from smaller
terminals, such as Bangor to Portland, or Portland to North
Reading, north of Boston, will finish out the night on the dock,
or they'll load their own trailer before they haul it. North Bergen's nice divisions of responsibilities, its cavernous dock, and
its torrential flow of freight are the awe of workers at other terminals. They, in turn, are envied in North Bergen for the blurred

borders of their job descriptions. "Here and North Bergen is like night and day," I have heard at several terminals.

Andy Park, though, who built up the Canton terminal as its manager in the 1970s, and who now, as vice-president for operations, oversees all the terminals, cautions: "It's looser, less regimented in the other terminals, but it's not any less intense." In fact, I remember meeting Jack Poor's two dispatchers, Bob Jose and Tom Whittles, on an earlier visit to Canton; the pitch of their madness in the cage of their carrels was as high as Pete Leota's in North Bergen, if not higher. To prove their terminal's zeal is every match for North Bergen's, they regaled me, each finishing the other's sentence, with the story of the Canton pedal driver whose forward gears froze just before the end of his run. The driver, David Setterland, backed up three miles, with a trailer, uphill, in winter, to make his last delivery.

Ronnie's next assignment will be to haul a van trailer to the Meriden, Connecticut terminal, halfway between New Haven and Hartford. I've been watching Billy Egan and one of the dockmen build the load: thirty-two shipments weighing 35,678 pounds in 241 pieces, all consigned for delivery tomorrow to Connecticut towns. Billy and the dockman, Andy Meyers, have already stacked cartons to the roof in the van's nose, and they are now passing each other in hilos, rumbling in and out of the van with drums and skids on their blades. They're done in a few minutes. Billy jams empty pallets upright in the tail to keep the skid freight from shifting on the run. While he works, another dockman backs in Ronnie's tractor to hook up to the trailer, making the trailer jump. Andy Meyers, who seems not yet twenty, pulls down the dock door, jumps down onto the yard, sighs, climbs into Ronnie's tractor, drives the rig out a dozen feet, jumps down, closes the swing doors to the van, locks and seals them, climbs back in the tractor, and pulls farther into the yard. A night mechanic has already done the fueling. Billy Egan meanwhile bands the load's strip tickets together and sends them overhead through a pneumatic tube, which crosses the dock, breaches the wall, and emerges in the office pool. A night biller will generate Ronnie's manifest from the strip tickets. It's nearly time to go.

Inside the drivers' room, Ronnie is already leaning on the transom and joking with one of the billers. As we lounge at one of the picnic tables to wait for the manifest, I tell Ronnie about certain linguistic investigations that I've made on the dock, while I was asking about the terminal. Not only are the supervisors here named Egan and Shea, I tell Ronnie, instead of Trentacosti and Falgiano and the rest of the Neapolitan telephone book, as in North Bergen, but a terminal here is not a terminal at all; it's a barn—actually, a "bahn." Steve supplied me with other regional variants of craft argot: a drum is a barrel (and so a drum truck is a barrel truck); a hilo is a chisel; a driver is a jockey. Ronnie, who seems far wider awake than I ever feel after a forty-minute nap, is absolutely tickled by this. He says he's always twitting—has in fact just been twitting—the billers in Canton about their Yankee r's and a's. "I ask 'em: 'Can I have a cup of cahfee?' " He opens his mouth to exaggerate: "Caaaahhfee?" (He himself says something like "cawfee," but with a very quick closed "oo," made with rounded lips, before the "aw." It's the diagnostic New-York-area dipthong that one hears even more clearly in the region's unique "because": be-coo-awss, almost rhyming with "loss.")

Outside, the snow has stopped. The wet pavement has not yet frozen. We trade observations about regional accents. Ronnie informs me of shades of distinction between New York and New Jersey dialect, which I myself have never distinguished. I take the opportunity to ask him about his childhood.

"I grew up on the Heights in Jersey City," he tells me, "between Journal Square and Union City, in a white area—mixed Italian and Polish. My mother I know was born in downtown Jersey City; that was an Italian area. I spent most of my life in a mixed area. That's the reason I don't have a southern accent, like you might expect with a black person, and my kids don't have a southern accent, and I don't know anything about southern food. I remember when I was stationed in Alabama, in the Army Chemical Corps. I couldn't understand the accent down there at first, how they talked with their mouths closed." He sucks in his cheeks to mimic a muffled Deep South drawl. "Like when a girl in a store asked me 'Y'all want a sack?' for what I'd bought, I thought she meant a burlap bag.

"Environment breeds character," Ronnie continues. "If I'd grown up in a black neighborhood, I might have a different outlook. I didn't have the black exposure that you would have living in a black neighborhood, so I would say that my attitude would be more a white view of things than a black view of things. All the things that I did were things that most people would do in a white neighborhood. The prejudice that you would get going from one neighborhood to another I didn't get much of, because I was in my own neighborhood, I was there. It wasn't that I was going into another neighborhood. Back then, it would be easier for me to feel comfortable in a white neighborhood than in a black neighborhood because I was there. Now, it doesn't make any difference to me. But it's what your previous environment has been. What your basis is."

I ask him what he means by a different outlook, and he offers an instance. "A person coming out of a black neighborhood, a neighborhood that hasn't been mixed, and walking into a restaurant, let's say a long restaurant, might walk all the way down to the other end of the restaurant and sit next to a another person of the same race. A white person coming out of a neighborhood that hasn't been mixed might have the same attitude. 'Let me look for somebody that I can associate with.' Whereas I'd go in and take the first seat that was available, because it doesn't make any difference to me. In that respect I have a different outlook.

"My girl friends when I was young," he says, "they were whatever was available. Didn't matter. Spanish, Chinese, Italian, didn't matter. Most of the guys I was friends with were white. I personally feel that growing up in a mixed neighborhood gives you a better outlook on life than if you grow up in one neighborhood—Italian, Jewish, white, black, green, blue. Then subconsciously you're prejudiced against other people. Growing up in a mixed neighborhood is, I think, a good idea. And then traveling enhances it, because you get views from other people. Just staying in one spot really is a loss. My attitude works for me. For example, when I used to do selling. I think once I start to talk to someone, it breaks the ice over their first seeing me. You see a person, and until they say something, they have an opinion, and then their opinion changes based on whatever you do or say. For me, it's helped a lot."

Put otherwise, white strangers' first impression of Ronnie is that he's black, but then when they hear him speak, their "opinion changes," as he says—in other words, they forget to apply to him as an individual whatever they feel about black people in general. Ronnie ascribes this remarkable feat of interpersonal engineering to his lack of a southern accent and to his growing up in a multiracial neighborhood. It has never occurred to me that much of white Northerners' racial animosity toward blacks may actually be regional animosity toward southerners, as evidenced in their speech. But this is what Ronnie is saying. His own regional accent exposes him instead to expectations, not necessarily positive, concerning people from New York and New Jersey. "It's an advantage," he says, "except when I go out of state. If I talk to someone who expects the southern accent, I usually have to repeat what I say, because they've tuned into the southern accent. 'What did you say? Again, slowly . . . Oh! You don't have a southern accent.' "

We're silent for a while, and then he says, "My father died when I was, I don't know, seven years old. I don't know where his folks came from, but to me it sounds like he came from the Carolinas, something sticks in my mind. If we were older, maybe we would've went to visit, but at that time, there wasn't much money around. We were all on relief and just about making ends meet. Fortunately, we had the family house. My grandmother and grandfather had a house, so everybody lived there. Otherwise who knows where I'd be."

"They were your mother's parents?"

"Yeah. My grandmother was a schoolteacher, my grandfather was a railroad worker. They came from the islands. It's not Antigua, but somewhere around there. Whatever island it was I don't know. When I was like sixteen or seventeen we'd gotten some papers: some relative had left us something down there. If my dumb brother had gone and checked on it, we could've had property there. (Ronnie's brother, Thomas, who died in 1981 of asbestosis contracted in Navy engine rooms, was five years his senior). All we had to do was find out what the property down there was and decide whether we wanted it. It might not have been anything, and then again it might have been a spot that somebody wanted to build a hotel on. But my brother wasn't one to do anything for anybody. As long as he could go chase a skirt around—you know: 'I'll take care of it. I got things to do.' " Ronnie laughs.

He continues, "Part of Antigua is called Parham,"—Ronnie's last name. He drops the 'h' and pronounces it "Parem," rhyming with the verb "carom." A village on the east coast of the island carries the name, and Ronnie had to see the place, to look for roots, and, maybe, for investment. "I went to Antigua with my wife, Thelma. The island's only about fifteen miles square. It was British at the time. The only thing they grew on that island was sugar cane, and they'd built a hotel with a casino, so they had tourism. A guy had a concession there for juke boxes and pool tables, and I was going to buy the concession. Fifteen thousand dollars for the whole thing. I wanted to buy it. But my wife said she wasn't staying on any island out in the middle of the ocean. They only had a handful of stores and no place to go. So"—he laughs—"I didn't buy the business. Well, maybe it worked out just as well.

"It seemed nice there, but it was *really* laid back. The attitude on the island was, 'Don't do today what you can do tomorrow.' *Nobody* hurried. My wife was so aggravated. Like, we were at the hotel, and she wanted a cup of coffee. A woman came over with the saucer, went back, she got the spoon, went back, and got the cup. And all my wife was saying: 'You see that? you see that? She's going again. You see that?' "

The light snow has stopped, and Ronnie is watching for black ice on the road. To my surprise, after leaving Canton, he turned north onto I-95, rather than south, and drove fifteen miles towards Boston. He then turned west onto the Massachusetts Turnpike. We're on the Boston-to-Hartford route, and we'll descend on the Meriden terminal from the north. Ronnie could have cut a slightly shorter route more directly southwest across Rhode Island via U.S. Route 44, but he doesn't leave the interstates if he can help it. Most road drivers don't, unless they're evading weigh stations, police ambush, or tolls. Narrower highways are far slower and far more dangerous, especially in winter. Ronnie regales me with the perils of Vermont: "They got roads up there that were made for bicycles. I was following a fellow to the Burlington terminal along a highway that you could legally go on, it's wide enough to take trucks, but when you're used to driving on something like this here, and then you get on something like that there, it seems like you're driving through a straw. Every time somebody would pass me, I'd lean over to the right because I thought they were going to hit my mirror. Anyway, we're coming around this bend, and the other guy says on the radio, 'I'm gonna swing wide here. Put your high beams on so people know you're coming.' I put on my brights, I swing wide, and I look at the back of his trailer, and it looks like we're going into somebody's garage. It's a railroad underpass. I went to that terminal twice. I said I ain't going up *there* any more."

It's after 8:00 P.M. now, and even near Boston the harassments of heavy automobile traffic have subsided. The balance of traffic has begun to shift gradually, and Ronnie says that by 10:00, as more and more trailers are cubed out in less-than-truckload terminals and dispatched, trucks will begin to replace automobiles as the dominant species on the road. Truckload operators, too, prefer the night. "The run only pays so much. If it takes you longer, in fact you'll lose money. In the daytime, with all the traffic, the accidents, delay here, delay there, you have no idea when you're going to get back. At night, it's nice." The disadvantage, of course, is that there's nothing to look at. "You just see lights. You go by lights, you pick up this building, that sign over there. You make that same run in the daytime, you don't know where you're at." The time is passed not with looking but with talking: tuning into late-night talk shows, recording thoughts on a microcassette, chatting on the CB. This night, Ronnie passes the time by filling me in on his past.

"I went to grade school, then high school, but I wasn't making it in high school. I was making money, and I didn't feel like I needed any more education. I was always hustling, wheeling and dealing, I'd buy stuff and add a few bucks onto it and sell it. I was the kind of person to make money, I was never without money. For me, I think, it was: 'Well, why do I have to go to college? I can make money now. I can make more money than my teachers, I can make more money than my brother. Why should I go to school?' Later on in life you find out why you should. But at the time it doesn't make any sense.

"I quit high school in the ninth grade and worked in a factory that built floats for parades. I was a receiving clerk, and for a little while I was assistant purchasing agent, and that paid about $80 a week thirty-some years ago, and on weekends I used to get $100 a day to move the floats and take them through parades, and so I just had money.

"In 1958, I went into the Army Chemical Corps. I was an instructor in communications and did radio repair on aircraft. Most of the times you went up with the pilot. I'd already learned to fly. So the pilot says: 'Oh well, you fly. Then I don't have to.' So I'd end up flying. I haven't flown since."

"How did you get into radios?"

"A fellow who lived next door to me did amateur radio. He used to be on the air in the evenings. At that time there was a lot of interference because radios weren't as perfected as they are now. A commercial receiver that you used for your house to listen to broadcasts would pick up just about anything. The neighbor next door would get on the air and blot out whatever was coming through to our radio, so it used to be a fight between him and my grandmother and the Lone Ranger, because my grandmother would be listening to the Lone Ranger and he'd be on the air trying to call someone, and he'd blot the Lone Ranger out. My grandmother would be banging on the radio— the fellow's name was Herbie—'*Herbie, get off the air get off the air! I can't get the Lone Ranger!*'

"That's what got me interested in it. I started going over to see what Herbie's equipment was. I more or less got fascinated with it. And later on they had a local school for communications and I went to that to learn what you had to learn in order to get a license. You had to learn Morse Code, you had to learn general theory of radio and how it works, how to build radios. I went through it and got a license."

Ronnie earned his high school diploma in the service, and after his discharge, he went back to the float factory. "I lived in New York and I didn't find it bad. I had two apartments, one in Greenwich Village and one on upper Broadway, plus my mother's house in Jersey."

"You sublet one of the apartments?"

"No. Convenience. I had somebody living in both of them. Two apartments, three girlfriends. It's one of those things. When you have money, you flaunt it. I had it and I didn't need it."

"Then you got married?"

"Well, yeah. You have to grow up sometime."

Not long after they were married, Ronnie and Thelma, who had grown up in Queens, moved to a suburb, "a nice neighborhood, a mixed neigborhood" in Middletown, on the Jersey Shore. The commute takes Ronnie a little over an hour, but he wanted to re-create for his children the comparatively untroubled surroundings of his own youth. "What it is, is environment breeds character. Where I live, you park in front of the house, park in the driveway, lock the car, leave it open, it doesn't make any difference. People who live in the city, they think every place is a jungle like where they live. They don't know what it's like to be anywhere else. They don't know what the environment is." Ronnie's children, Kenneth and Debra, both in their early twenties, still live at home. Kenneth has another semester at community college and will go on to a four-year college in the fall for a degree in electronics. He won an A-P-A scholarship, but even so the expenses mean Ronnie won't retire next year, his thirtieth as a Teamster. "Dad might have to come up with some money."

"Have you thought of what you'll do when you retire?"

"Well, I've thought of an Amway business. Network marketing. I'm having some difficulty with it, because with this job I don't really have time to promote it. But I've always done selling. Years ago I used to hustle things out of my car. I used to go to jobbers in New York on Sunday to the Jewish area, and then there were other places I could go to on Saturday, and then on Thursday and Friday nights I would peddle what I'd bought. I'd mark it up, but usually it was still cheaper than people could buy it in a store. It was convenient for them because I would show up at a bar that I used to frequent, I was never a real big drinker, but I could go in, have a couple drinks, buy a few drinks, make a few sales, I'd make my three or four hundred in two days."

Another second passion, then: or, perhaps, a first passion that has not been fulfilled. I say: "Now I remember Armand telling me you used to sell shirts after work in the drivers' room, when you were on a city run."

"Well, I never have time to do much in it now. Right now I'm trying to do MCI. I sign people up for long-distance service with MCI through Amway. They give you a sign-up card." He delivers a summary of his sales pitch for me, and then says: "I can almost guarantee you, if you tell Arthur you rode with me, the first thing he'll say, he's going to ask you, 'What did he sell you?' "

And, in fact, when we stop for dinner at a cafeteria in a service area beside the Massachusetts Turnpike, Ronnie pulls an Amway brochure from his overnight bag and explains the advantages, for me and for himself, of joining his sales network.

"Did you every think of becoming a salesman for A-P-A?"

"Yeah, Arnold Imperatore, when he was alive, he was always after me to go into sales."

"Why didn't you?"

He gives the answer I have heard from several others who have refused promotion at A-P-A: "Well, I didn't feel I had the education."

Our talk drifts to the Teamsters, and, again, Ronnie echoes the sentiments I have heard from John and Tony and others. He is grateful for the protections the union has secured for him, scornful of the corruption that has debased it, and hopeful that the recent election of reformers to the leadership of the International will bring change. He adds: "Unions are good and bad. They're good in that they get you a lot of benefits that the industry in general wouldn't give employees otherwise. But they're bad in that they limit individuals in what work they can do." Despite his complaint this afternoon that A-P-A requires, in terms of effort, a day-and-a-half's worth of work for a day's pay,

Ronnie is contemptuous of work rules that limit a worker's enterprise. "Like the painter who has to stop painting the wall and
wait for a carpenter to come by to pull the nail out." He sees
how work limitations can lead to featherbedding. "Like on the
trains, when they changed to diesel, they didn't need the firemen because there was no coal. But the work rules said you
needed a fireman. There are a lot of things like that there. The
auto industry had a guaranteed wage so whether you worked or
not, you got paid. I think that's bogus. I don't see how anybody
could stay in business if you're going to pay someone and they're
not going to produce anything."

When he was driving for the city operation, Ronnie felt the
weight of A-P-A's demands on its workers. But once he had become a road driver and had thus secured his distance from the
harassments of dispatchers over the radio, he was able, from
that distance, to place his loyalty with the purposes of the company. "Employee-wise," he says now of the company's zeal for
productivity, "it seems like a lousy attitude. But management-
wise, it's the right way to run a business." Despite his modest
role in the community Arthur founded and his subdued expectations for himself, he respects A-P-A as a businessman would
respect it. He doesn't see his point of view as in the least excep-
tional.

"Most of the labor you talk to at A-P-A are capable of running
their own businesses. Not all of them do, but most of them have
the mentality to do it. One fella, a switcher in the yard, has his
own band, another fella had a bar, a few of the drivers have had
their own trucks or have something that they do other than
trucking."

My first thought upon meeting Ronnie returns, and I tell him,
not certain what he'll think: "Frankly, I looked at you, I saw
your face, and I thought, 'Oh. Another A-P-A aristocrat.' "

Ronnie laughs loudly. He's pleased. He's ready with a narrative that shows he has understood my thought far more quickly
than I did. He takes the word "aristocrat" in its secondary sense
of the superior rank in any group—in his case, the elite of his
craft. "We went to Brown's one year, a big resort in the Cats-

kills, for one of our five-year affairs. It was a very funny thing, because we all showed up in tuxes, in business suits, and the only indication that we were truck drivers was that we were consuming a lot of alcohol at the bar. And the people that were around us kept walking around saying, 'Are you sure these are the truck drivers? They look like business people. They don't act like truck drivers. These people are opening doors and talking like normal people. They're not all cursing and fighting. They *can't* be truck drivers.' "

I ask him what he thinks of Arthur, and he says without hesitation, "Arthur and I get along real well as personal friends. Whenever I got a savings bond for safe driving or a card or something, he used to personally write on it. We hit it off real well together, and we've been friends for years. If I had a problem, I'd go in and talk it over with him. If I thought about something, we'd sit down. When he sees me with my wife, he goes up to her without talking to me and jokes, 'How'd you ever get stuck with this guy?' or something of that nature. For some reason we just hit it off well." He's not speaking of a friendship sustained by meetings at each other's homes, but of a professional friendship warmed by personal respect. When Ronnie was driving a city run, Arthur used to call Ronnie up to his office in the mornings for coffee and keep him in conversation until Sam De Piano, then the terminal manager, came looking for his missing driver. Arthur would sigh: "You see who really runs this place." Ronnie adds, "Arthur's a person I really look up to. Not just because he's my boss, but just as someone you look up to because of the person they are. He just has a nice personality."

On the road again, we're riding southwest on I-84. ("Here we are in Connecticut, the State of Confusion, which makes rules by the day.") This is the old Wilbur Cross Highway, rebuilt to ten lanes in the late 1980s. Cars in the passing lanes are few, by now outnumbered, as Ronnie predicted, by the trucks in the two right-hand lanes. At twenty minutes to midnight, we shoot through Hartford, which is darkened and silent, and join I-91, which climbs the long hill southward out of the Connecticut River valley. On these heights, Ronnie is seeing ice for the first time, and as he leaves one curve he loses traction for a moment. "You accelerate and the engine's going faster, but the vehicle isn't going faster." He keeps his speed steady and moves out of it.

Soon he turns off to approach the Meriden terminal through a night landscape of streetlights, illuminated signs, and dark shapes against a darker sky. The terminal is only slightly smaller than Canton's, with a dock in the center of a fenced yard and a drivers' room inside with picnic tables and vending machines. Ronnie's next trailer, which he'll haul to North Bergen, is ready to be hooked, so the stop will be brief: manifest handed in at the transom, time-clock punched in, nature relieved, coffee sipped, logbook updated, a brief chat with another waiting driver about the mysteries of finding one's way to the A-P-A's Long Island terminal, which is secreted behind a dump; then the new manifest collected (28,209 pounds, 24 shipments in 618 pieces) together with a manila envelope, fat with customs documents for an international shipment. In a few minutes, we're back in the tractor, with the new van behind, ready for the last leg of the journey.

Now we glide downhill into New Haven and slip onto I-95, going west. Here the two conduits of New-York-bound commerce from New England—I-91 from the north, and I-95 from the east—have merged. On both sides, the highway is charged with ceaseless streams of tractor-trailers. Westbound, on our side, we travel with a slowly shifting cluster of square-backed black shapes, each outlined with yellow body-lights and underscored with red tail-lights. Across the median, on the eastbound lanes, a double current flows by us in a pleasing sparkle of lights. First the white headlights, which do not dazzle eyes at the height of ours; then the yellow marker-lights that frame the tractor's brow and circle over the roof fairings like diadems; sometimes the company letters, illuminated on the fairings, each in its corporate color and design; last the stream of body-lights along the floor-line and roof-line of each trailer as it passes. The flow of lights has the beauty and spookiness of a night world. What society declined to build for heavy trucks—their own system of highways—they have claimed for themselves nevertheless, by default, between midnight and dawn. Not one car is to be seen darting across the stream; not a single pickup truck or delivery van; not even a straight truck. The road drivers have come into full possession of their workplace. I say to Ronnie, "This is a different I-95 than the one we rode this afternoon." He nods.

Most of the trailers gliding past are rectangular "dry vans," like Ronnie's, but other kinds of trailers swim among them. First, the other vans: refrigerated trailers, called "reefers," with their louvered coolers mounted on their front panels; open-tops, also known as rag-tops, for the blue tarpulins that cover their freight; and drop-frames, mostly household-goods moving vans and United Parcel Service linehaul pups, their low bellies drooping toward the roadway. Then the platform trailers: the flatbeds, humped with mysterious shapes beneath their tarpaulins, and the low-boys, dropped between the axles to make a lowered resting place for construction equipment, which might otherwise be decapitated by an overpass. Next the tank trucks, for liquids, for gases, and for powders; the hoppers, for earth, for gravel, and for stone; and the louvered livestock vans, called possum-bellies, for their double-tiered floors. Lastly the car-carriers, longest of these fish, sixty-five feet by dispensation from Detroit's Washington friends. Their double-stacked autos shake and jerk in their chains.

The panels of the vans are moving billboards that announce their species. They aim to seduce with block capitals. I can read them when the roadway becomes a harshly lit city street through the shoreline towns. Most numerous are the food-peddlers, who think their names alone will do: SHOP RITE, WHITE ROSE, A & P; then the loquacious meatpackers: PURDUE, FRESH YOUNG CHICKENS; JAC PAC, PORTIONED MEAT PROD-UCTS; ALLEN'S, THE QUALITY CHICKEN PEOPLE; ROBIN-SON BEEF CO., DISTRIBUTORS OF WESTERN BOXED BEEF. The nationwide truckload carriers, hauling trailerfuls anywhere for anyone, are painted nose to tail in company colors: WERNER ENTERPRISES, midnight blue; SCHNEIDER NATIONAL VAN CARRIERS, tangerine; J.B. HUNT TRANSPORTATION, white, with yellow name-sign; MIDLAND, the Canadian intruder, green. The less-than-truckload nationals swim by, the big three and the little three, their names marching across their trailers' flanks:

YELLOW, ROADWAY, CF (Consolidated Freigthways); OVER-
NITE, CAROLINA, ABF (Arkansas Best Freight). The big north-
eastern regionals form their own school; PRESTON, ST.
JOHNSBURY, TNT RED STAR, NEW PENN, and A-P-A. From
every species, acronyms flash their genetic codes: P & P, H & H,
OUI, ACL, CRST, P. A. T. S, and G. O. D.

Ronnie's CB crackles with the night talk of the road. Plucking
his mike from its perch on the dash, he says, "How are things
going westbound?"

In a few seconds a voice responds, so reformulated into a spit-
ting static that I can't understand the words. Ronnie translates:
"Nothing going on down to Stamford," adding, "You get used
to the radio after a while."

"Nothing going on?"

"Means, no radar, no traffic problems."

"So he'll have just come from Stamford."

"Yeah. The conversation you have on the radio usually per-
tains to what's happening on the road—if there's any smokies,
if there's any accidents, any traffic backed up. It's usually that.
Or you might pick up somebody that's local, who can tell you
exactly how to get to where you have to go. It's practical, to
keep in contact, keep abreast of what's going on. I was down in
Maryland a few weeks ago and they had a major accident down
there, and I had to get off the highway and get back on again.
You know, 'Should I get off on this road? Are there any low
bridges on it?' That's the whole thing."

The radio rattles with brief messages. Ronnie calls to a UPS
driver, whose drop-frame pups he's been following, to let him
know he'll be inching up along his left: "Buster Brown, can I get
by?" Another driver warns of a speed trap. Ronnie comments:
"The language that's used on the radio in real life is not what
you might think of as 'CB language.' If you hear people talking
in 'CB language' "—he chants sardonically with jazz beat and
Ozark twang: " 'I hear where you're comin' from, I understan'
what you're sayin'—things that don't sound like normal English,
then it's somebody who's trying to act like a truck driver, or he
just got a CB and he wants everybody to think he knows what
he's doing. He puts on a southern accent, so you ask him, 'What

state are you from?' " Ronnie answers for him sarcastically: " 'New Jersey. I live in Rutherford.' "

He adds, "You don't hear the women on the CB trying to drum up business so much any more. There used to be a lot of action at the truckstops." Ronnie mimics a truckstop siren (a "lot lizard," in truckers' parlance): " 'Why don't you pull in? I'll see you when you pull in. Flash your lights so I know where you are!' But now with the AIDS and the herpes, with the cops coming in and out of there, they go in and pick the lot lizards up and take them away. A lot of them have decided not to go to the truckstops, because if they go to the truckstops then maybe they go to jail."

In the daytime, the talk on the radio will often review the merits of women's legs visible in cars going by below. "That livens things up, because you got nothing else going on out here." Ronnie demonstrates "the trucker's third eye" with a sudden craning of his neck toward his side window. In this context, women are called merely "seat covers." "And then there are the exhibitionists. If they see that you're looking, they make adjustments so that you'll look a little longer." He recommends: "You could write a book about all the things you see from up here. But I won't go into it."

CB traffic bulletins sometimes develop into convoy conversations among three or four drivers traveling together, "with everybody putting in their two cents." Sometimes Ronnie and a chance CB acquaintance will move onto another channel "and shoot the bull, just to use up time, because the more you talk, the shorter the distance." Names are not generally exchanged, although the drivers may discuss by name the trucklines they drive for, and they may mention their radio call-names, their "handles." Ronnie's handle is Nomad One.

"The other day on the New Jersey Turnpike going to Maryland," he recalls, "I got to talking with a guy who knew somebody I knew. Usually you run out of things to talk about, but we knew some things about the same people, and we started talking about old jobs. It ended up almost a four-hour conversation. We were talking, we were talking, we covered about 180 miles. I didn't see him. I think he was behind me."

It is a strange craft fraternity. The members share a workplace and its dangers; they watch each other's rigs pass, they converse in electrified voices, but they almost never meet in the flesh. The relief offered by truckstops is very partial. There and also in turnpike service areas that do not cater directly to truckers, drivers will spot each other. "If you're in a restaurant and you're sitting by yourself," Ronnie says, "and somebody comes in, they'll sit down and carry on a conversation." Especially for longhaul drivers, though, these nameless meal-length acquaintances have little likelihood of being renewed.

Ronnie has the poise and fluency of a man gifted in gregariousness—he can laugh, pun, mimic, narrate, and sell after five or ten hours on the road; but for others, truckstop conversations consist of desultory complaints and exhausted monologues. A picture of a truckstop near Portsmouth, New Hampshire, remains in my mind. At a horseshoe-shaped lunch counter, a middle-aged driver with a broken-down hat and a broken-down back was speaking a soliloquy. His topic was the grievance he suffered from his estranged wife, who had gone to court in a distant state to wring child-support from him. His listeners, besides myself, were a fuzz-cheeked boy in a baseball cap—probably not eighteen, certainly not yet twenty-one, as truck drivers legally must be—who perked up only at the mention of the aggrieved driver's vintage car, which had been repossessed; also a silent man in his thirties, with a natty black fedora and black goatee; next to him, a young and enormous fatty who, as he ate, stared with impassioned gluttony at four high-mounded dinner plates, neatly arranged before him on the counter; and finally the vigorous waitress. Only she, on each of her returns to the counter, responded with brief acknowledgments at the end of the complaining driver's paragraphs. That was part of her job. The others said nothing. They were too tired. Finally the waitress had heard enough and cut the soliloquist off with: "I have five children, and I never got a dime from a man for any of them."

A better, rarer contact occurs in emergencies. "You see someone broken down on the side of the road," Ronnie says, "you call and say, 'Well, give me your vehicle number, your name, and I'll tell your company where you're at.' You stop at the next service area. You go in, usually you call collect, and you tell them what the situation is, where their driver is, and they'll get somebody out. But if it's wintertime and it's real cold, you'll maybe stop with the driver and sit with him, let's say in your cab, and have somebody else make the phone call. In the wintertime, you don't want to leave someone sitting in the cab if that engine isn't running."

In general, though, what road drivers share is loneliness. It's not only that their workstations are enclosed and solitary. It's that they're rarely home. Even Ronnie, who drives turns, so that he can be home every night, has mentioned often during our long ride together that he "has no time." He won't be home from this trip till well after 5:00 A.M. Including his commute, his workday will have lasted seventeen hours. If he punches out at 4:00 A.M., he may be called for the next day's haul as early as 12:00 noon, and probably no later than 2:30.

When his children were small, he was still driving a city run. "As tired as I was, I'd come home, sit on the bed, read 'em a story. If I had small children now, it would really be lousy, because you just don't have the time." Despite allowances in the union contract for paid personal days, Ronnie found it hard when he was a city driver to secure a day off for family time. "Something would come up, my son was in a soccer game, my daughter was in a play at school, a championship, a graduation, a one-time thing. 'Well, I'm going to see my kid, because I don't have any time with them as it is.' You call in, and the dispatcher gives you a hard time." Ronnie quotes a typical dispute. " 'Well, I won't be in today.'—'No. *You gotta come in.*'—'I ain't coming in. I got a personal'—'*Well you can't take it now. We're busy now. You can't take any days off. You have to work.*' " Ronnie learned to call in sick at such times. "So, hey. You lose a day's pay, but hey, what's more important, a day's pay or seeing your children grow up?"

Once he left the city and went on the road, time at home was even scarcer. "I try to do things, like volunteering for the Boy

Scouts for their jamborees on the air, where the scouts learn to operate amateur radios, but when you go home, go to sleep, get up and go back to work, it limits what you can do."

Nevertheless, because he works under union rules and for a company managed by people with a sense of decency, Ronnie's schedule is far more humane than that of most other road drivers. "The job is bad enough where you're only home for an hour or two a day. These jobs where you're away for months make a very difficult life for a young person with young children. A lot of guys get into it, figure you can make the money, so lemme get into it. One of the problems is, a woman gets married, she wants to have somebody home, and the guy's gone all the time. You find a few wives that can tolerate it, understand it, stick it out, but a lot of them just can't handle it. 'I didn't get married to be alone.' The marriage lasts for a little while, then *pff*, it's all over."

The sacrifice of family life for the lure of the freedom of the road is, for most men, unsustainable. I've mentioned that a hundred-percent turnover among drivers is commonplace among longhaul truckload operators, which means that, on the average, they replace their entire road list every year. Two-hundred-percent turnover—the new workforce replaced, on the average, every six months—is not unknown. In the last few years, turnover among drivers has become the greatest single problem in the longhaul truckload industry, and it has begun to retard economic growth. Truckload operators now buy each other in order to gain drivers, and the large nationwide carriers, led by J. B. Hunt, are loading more and more of their freight into containers and shipping them by rail on flatcars, partly to save on fuel and equipment costs, partly because they can't hire enough drivers.

Other trucklines have turned to professional recruiters, who lure young men onto the road with dreams of the road cowboy's freedom. Then the men quit, if they can, when they find that the freedom is a trap and the myth is a fraud. Their breezy and beckoning open road proves to be cluttered and perilous, and their heroic steed is after all no faithful companion, as the country singers imagine, but an unreliable machine that speeds along the edge of being murderous. Nor do the drivers find they have escaped the restraints and houndings of employers. The non-union trucklines, besides paying poorly, require, by their deadlines, high speeds, long journeys, and inhuman hours. Nevertheless, the drivers are the ones who are fined if they are caught. The trucklines must pay the fines if trailers are overloaded or poorly maintained, but the drivers are the ones whose lives are put at risk. Owner-operators pay all the fines. A Connecticut state trooper who specializes in commercial vehicle enforcement told me that individual drivers, or, when it is present, the Teamsters, will sometimes tip off the police when a driver is forced to take out a rig that is overweight or otherwise unsafe.

In effect, trucking deregulation removed restraints upon the trucklines and the shippers, while roadside inspections increased restraints upon the drivers, whose conditions of employment require them to break the law and defy common sense. Regulation of the economic behavior of employers has been replaced by regulation of the personal behavior of employees. As we were warned by Alexis de Tocqueville, that early prognosticator of America's strengths and vulnerabilities, a weakening of local associations in order to make way for individualism opens the way to tyranny from the top. The longhaul road drivers' situation recalls Tocqueville's warning. Their companies, which are fragmented by chaotic turnover and, often, by a preference for hiring owner-operators on short-term contracts, lack any sense of community, and the drivers have no union to embody a craft solidarity. The drivers are loners at the mercy of economic conditions and the police. When they climb behind the wheel, far from escaping the counters, benches, and desks to which they had been tied, nailed, and clinched—far from claiming the freedom of the open road, as country singers pretend—longhaul truck drivers enter a life of alienation and bondage.

On the one hand, Ronnie is contemptuous of road cowboys, and fearful of them, because their speed and recklessness threaten his life. When a driver squawks over his CB a warning about a "smokey with a hair drier" (a state trooper with a radar gun), Ronnie remonstrates wearily, but not with his microphone on, "Just keep to a reasonable rate of speed and there's no problem." On the other hand, he pities the cowboys for the price they are paying. He suggests how he would advise them if he were asked: "The road is not a job for a young person to stay in. To get in, get something, get out, it's okay. Let me rephrase that: not just the road: the trucking business. Get in, get what you can, get out; to get a job where you can work like a normal person would be much better. You make less money, but a least you have a normal life." He adds, "I just hope my son goes somewhere with the computers. I would like him to get some kind of a job where he can get out of it early, he can have some free time, and not have a job like I have."

Ronnie himself, though, despite his relentless schedule and his solitude, does not feel duped by the myth of the road. He may be pressured, but he does not feel exploited. "A-P-A is a good company," he says, "and the money is good. I've been able to pay for the things I've wanted to pay for and I've gone places I've wanted to go, plus the places the company has taken us to." Nor does feel alienated: he may work in solitude, but he does not see himself as being alone. His freedom from the commands of city dispatchers would be too dearly bought with isolation if he did not feel, nevertheless, that he belongs to A-P-A, that he commands respect and affection in the company, and that he is protected by it and by the union contract as much as possible from the dangers of his workplace. His schedule, while intense, is sustainable. As a senior driver, he can choose his runs. His equipment, imperfect though it is, is of the newest and the best. His membership in an elite, and at the same time his physical separation from it, create a balance between freedom and belonging, between individual and community—that blending of the two American dreams which is, I think, the unspoken striving of all of us.

Suddenly we enter a long underpass. As we shoot through, I see up above us the aircraft-warning lights, blue and white, atop the dark towers of the George Washington Bridge. The CB crackles: "Hey, Ronnie."

An A-P-A tractor-trailer sweeps past us off the bridge, on its way out. It's the shop steward, Billy McKeever, code-named Lightfoot, headed for Canton.

Ronnie: "I'm going home."

Billy: "At least you're going in the right direction for once."

"I didn't expect us to get back this quickly," I say.

"It's always shorter going back," Ronnie agrees, and analyzes: "Illusion. You feel like you're going faster. It's psychological. You cover the same mileage both ways, so it can't be any shorter than getting out there."

As we rumble down the hill toward Tonnelle Avenue, Ronnie says, "I think the thing that keeps you going is not necessarily what money you can make in it, but what you personally get out of it, and I'm happy out here on the road. I used to have the same thing when I was flying. I don't know, you feel, you have that air of superiority because you're doing something that somebody else is not doing, and I think you get that in driving. You're traveling around, and a lot of people don't go more than ten miles away from where they live to go to work. Here you're traveling to this state, that state, so you just feel different about it."

Up ahead, the A-P-A diamond glows on the sign at the corner of Tonnelle and 88th Street. We jounce to a stop at the long red light. We're alone on the street. It's 4:02 A.M. Ronnie says: "I enjoy the driving, I enjoy the scenery. I wouldn't say there's any sort of a challenge in doing what I do. But I am content in doing it. It's an enjoyable thing to do. I'm out here, I'm my own boss, I go fast, I go slow, I stop, as long as I get the freight there in a reasonable time, I do whatever I feel like doing. So it is more of a relaxed job. But what you gain on one end, you lose on the other. A relaxed job, but you have no home life." The compromise belongs to any life: "You get a piece of it, but you can't have it all." He turns into the steep stub of 88th Street and roars downhill in low gear toward the gate.

5. Acres of Diamonds

Arthur Imperatore, duly introduced with superlatives, takes the microphone comfortably. ("We get a lot of this kind of encomia," he tells me later.) A few feet behind him, the Hudson River slaps against pilings in its rush towards New York Bay. The breeze that rarely fails here lifts Arthur's white hair. July sunlight, already bright at 9:00 A.M., glances off his forehead and off the gray decking on which some fifty folding chairs have been set up for dignitaries, their aides, and the press. They are here at the waterfront to honor a new expansion of a public bus service that will bring more commuters to meet Arthur's Port Imperial Ferry. The ferry boats connect Arthur's property here in Weehawken, New Jersey, to midtown and downtown Manhattan. The expansion of a bus service is not an event that would normally haul the Governor of New Jersey out of Trenton, along with two dozen legislators, mayors, city councilmembers, and public agency directors from two states, and, besides, *The New York Times*. The event, really, is Arthur. At sixty-six, he still insists on accomplishing things others consider too unlikely to attempt—in this case, re-establishing the long-defunct New York–New Jersey ferry service across the Hudson, and running it without public subsidy, in fact making a substantial profit on it by its fifth year.

The dignitaries have come, too, perhaps, to refresh themselves with the sight of what must be the most dazzling of all visions of Manhattan. The entire sweep of the famous island from South Ferry to the George Washington Bridge lies across the dark water, seeming much closer than half a mile, with the World Trade Center, the Empire State Building, the Chrysler Building, and New York Life striving upward with a thousand other up-start high-rises, jostling together toward the blue like cornstalks in a field. The sun flashes from a thousand glass facades. Stand-ing here beside Arthur's ferry terminal, I remember the intima-tions of glory that drew me to those buildings as a young man, as it has drawn so many others. From here, what one sees is not the gritty substance of the real metropolis, but its bodiless mi-rage floating on the waves, the Platonic Idea of urban majesty, silent and shining on a breezy morning.

"The waterfront," as everybody at A-P-A calls Arthur's 365 acres of riverbank, is a two-and-a-half-mile-long strip of flat landfill lying just above water level on the Jersey side of the river, at the base of the Palisades. It is one of the few large tracts of unde-veloped real estate remaining within twenty-five miles of Times Square. Arthur heard about it in September, 1981, and four days later bought it for seven-and-three-quarters of a million, cash. (Ten years later, its estimated worth exceeds $100 million.) It had been a major terminal and switching yard, long since aban-doned, of the late New York Central Railroad and the New York, Ontario, and Western Railroad; the railroads' successor, the Penn Central, was bankrupt, and the trustees were shedding the as-sets. When Arthur bought it, the railyard was a wilderness of rusted rails, junked rolling stock, sunken barges, squatters' shacks, and eleven hundred trashed automobiles, all patrolled by packs of feral dogs. Rotted pilings protruded from the water like stumps of brown teeth. But where others saw a civic nuisance, Arthur saw something else: a new, privately managed city. He would call it Port Imperial. It would have condominiums, offices, banks, stores, parks, schools, churches, everything. He had left the truckline in Armand Pohan's hands. Port Imperial would be his new opus.

In the ensuing few years, while he dreamed in consultation with expensive planners and architects, he had the old railyard swept clean. It is mostly lawn now, the rails and the junk sold for scrap, the barges towed, the teeth pulled, the interlopers gone.

A two-lane road runs the length of the property, and arbors of flowers arch over the sidewalks. There is a marina, a golf driving range, Arthur's Landing (the high-toned restaurant and object of truckline jokes), and the ferry, which now carries 8,000 riders on an average day. The idea for the ferry arrived when Arthur was crossing the river in the company yacht—Arthur can usually recollect when and where his lasting ideas arose, and by what associations of thought. It took less than four minutes that day for the yacht to cross from New Jersey to New York, fewer minutes, Arthur realized, than drivers are often stalled at a single midtown stoplight. His Weehawken waterfront was closer to Manhattan than most of Manhattan was. The residents of the future Port Imperial, and of the old ridge-top towns above it, he realized, could commute to New York by ferry.

The Palisades that stand behind us as Arthur speaks to the dignitaries this morning are an almost vertical riverside cliff, at this point 150 feet high. North of the George Washington Bridge, where the cliffs reach 300 feet and the flat land at their base is narrow, the Palisades are an interstate park, which was established in 1900. South of the bridge, the flats vary from a few hundred feet to nearly a mile wide in Jersey City. In the nineteenth century, towns and now-defunct factories and wharves were built upon the deep muck of the flats and also, in many places, partway up the face of the cliff. Here, in Arthur's old railyard, where the muck is mostly coal cinders, 170 feet deep in some places, little was built, and the cliff has few scars. Its face is draped with a temperate jungle of tulip trees, yellow poplars, oaks, and sweetgum, all looped and bound by thick gray ropes of wild grapevine. The towns of Weehawken, fashionable until fifty years ago, and of West New York, long a first haven for immigrants, stand back from the top of the cliff. If I turn around and look up from the ferry terminal, I can see the turreted wooden mansions from the 1890s and the brick apartment houses from the 1920s lining Boulevard East in their faded smartness and gazing over the stone parapet at the view. When Arthur was a boy among the West New York tenements in the 1930s, he used to cross the toney cliffside neighborhoods and climb halfway down the Palisades. He'd find a jutting boulder, build a fire among the grapevines, roast sweet potatoes and smoke cigarettes with his buddies, and look across the river at New York.

To revive the Hudson River ferry was considered daft: Arthur's folly. But Arthur is used to his ideas being an occasion for scorn first, and flattery afterward. "The first month," he admits now to his audience in the folding chairs, "we couldn't give the ferry service away. On the first day, December 3, 1986, we had either twenty-three or twenty-six people who were riding free. In fact we gave the first month of service free just to introduce people to the system. And it was predicted it wouldn't work. But I remember the time when the fare was four cents to midtown on the old New York Central–West Shore Ferry that operated out of here for somewhere around a hundred years, and people have attributed to me some genius, y'know, but the fact is it was just memory of the ferry when I was a kid, when I used to sneak on, walking down the 'ferry hill' so-called here, and I learned to take the ferry to go over to New York, to take the subway up to Yankee Stadium to see a ballgame, all for sixty-five cents, between getting into the bleachers and the transportation." (The entertainment expense, even then, was a matter of careful note.) "And so it was easy for me to see the beginning of something that would serve people. Along the way I've had a lot of help with my idea. Some people predicted disaster and failure, but others were believers. We had a great experience working together. It took twenty-seven months and cost one million in the process, just for lawyers and consultants, but we got the job done and started the service."

With friendly words tailored to each, Arthur introduces the people who helped, and some who may have hindered. He proceeds to extol the political and economic virtues of "private-public cooperation," exemplified today by the expansion, funded in part by himself, of New Jersey Transit public bus routes that will bring riders to his privately owned ferry. As he moves toward a closing, he interrupts himself. He cocks his eye at a stocky man, conspicuous by a lack of coat and tie, whom Arthur has just noticed standing beside a New Jersey Transit bus that has been parked immediately behind the crowd. Arthur says, deadpan and without pause, "I'm running for shop steward of the Fairview garage against Elan here, and I'm doing pretty well I'm told, and he's a little nervous I see this morning, because he knows I've been picking up votes along the way." The crowd laughs, and Elan Erenkranc, the bus driver and union steward, is delighted; his broad face grins. He wasn't on the list of dignitaries prepared by Arthur's publicity aide. But despite years of rubbing shoulders with the great (who, like everyone else, are moths drawn to the candle of money), Arthur still feels more comfortable, probably, with Elan the busdriver—a workingman as Arthur himself once was—than with anyone else in the audience. (To me he remarks later in the day: "I get along wonderfully with the busdrivers here. Wonderfully. Why? They're damn good people. I'm right at home with those bastards.") At last he introduces the New Jersey Governor, James Florio, who, with his prizefighter's face and stubborn schoolboy manner, addresses the microphone, praises Arthur ("a model of what private-sector entrepreneurial skills are all about"), offers his own optimistic homily on public-private cooperation, and defends his record.

Now half the reporters surge upon the Governor, and the other half upon Arthur. Arthur rests one grandfatherly hand on the thin shoulder of a youth starting out at the *Hudson County Dispatch*, and another on the tweedy shoulder of a young matron from a Bergen County weekly; their questions are eager, their manner respectful. Not included in this loose and friendly huddle is the scrawny figure in a baseball cap from the *Bergen County Record*. His shirt is rumpled and his tie he left at home, which Arthur clearly considers unprofessional. Perhaps the reporter's own standards are equally disgusted by the friendly huddle. His questions are nasal with irony, which Arthur ignores. *The New York Times* reporter is not in evidence; she must be interviewing Florio. The journalists around Arthur want to know about his frustrations in building his dream city. A decade has passed since the brilliant purchase, and nothing has been built on the property except the ferry, the marina, the restaurant, and the golf driving range. The great plans remain plans. The towns of

Weehawken and West New York have not been willing to approve Arthur's proposals for any buildings above fifteen stories: any, that is, that would rise above the top of the Palisades.

The fifty or so high-rises that were built along the top of the cliffs between Jersey City and Fort Lee during the sixties and seventies have been political embarrassments. They block the views and the sunlight in the old neighborhoods, and they have defaced the noble lines of the Palisades. While a few would have elegance if they were elsewhere, most would be ugly anywhere. But Arthur needed height in order to justify his investment; he wanted forty stories, not fifteen.

Local opponents to Arthur's proposals had only to point a few blocks north to the Galaxy Apartments, a condominum in three tubular high-rises, fifty stories tall. The condominiums tower over the entire cliff-frontage of Guttenberg, a narrow strip of a town just north of West New York. That Guttenberg had allowed well-heeled newcomers to extinguish the town's three enviable, and three only, charms—the pleasantly modest scale of its housing, the breezy walk along the Palisades, and the unparalleled view of New York—was a precedent fatal to Arthur's own plans. His proposal for a six-billion-dollar, thirty-year development envisioned nine million square feet of commercial space and seven million square feet of residential space for 40,000 inhabitants. Canals would lead to a square that would recall the Piazza San Marco in Venice; an 800-foot tower would be modeled after a drawing by Leonardo da Vinci. Despite Arthur's door-to-door lobbying in West New York and Weehawken, his neighbors found his proposals overwhelming and too foreign to their sense of their towns. Arthur's lack of experience in real estate was a further caution. Ruth Elsasser, president of the Weehawken Environment Committee, expressing the kind of sentiment that prevailed, called Arthur's planned high-rises "a monstrous mistake."

Reluctant neighbors were not the only obstacle. More recently, a partnership Arthur formed with another developer, Hartz Mountain Properties, to build a smaller project at the south end of the waterfront, has gone sour. Lawsuits have ended in a settlement to dissolve the partnership. Finally, financing for real estate, above all commercial real estate, has dried up. No one will lend when there is more than a twenty percent vacancy rate in the New York area office towers that are already built. After ten years, then, Arthur's waterfront is still greensward, with the cliff of jungle behind, the cool sweep of water in front, and the mirage of New York beyond. The dream of Port Imperial is, as Armand puts it, "an idea whose time is gone."

Arthur doesn't want to talk about all that to the reporters today. He soothes them: "My old Italian mother used to say: 'Everything happens for the best.' " He wants to talk about the ferry: in particular, he wants them to understand how it competes for riders with subsidized public transportation. He's got all the figures he wants the journalists to write down: comparative fares, subsidy formulas, transit times. But his publicity aide is dancing on the periphery. He's shaking down his sleeve at Arthur and holding up his watch. There's a meeting with Tom Downs, the New Jersey State Transportation Commissioner, on the second-floor lounge of the restaurant, about the conversion of a railroad tunnel that runs through the base of the Palisades from the Meadowlands to Arthur's waterfront. Turning the tunnel into a trolley route or a bus way would help meet the second major objection, after height, to development of the waterfront: the paucity of transportation access from the rest of New Jersey. Riders can reach the ferry now only via River Road, a narrow street that winds along the bottom of the cliff.

The meeting in the restaurant starts briskly (Downs: "What do you want from us, Arthur?"—Arthur: "Straight talk and quick decisions") and ends hopefully. An agreement in principle to convert the tunnel to a trolley route can be expected, although early funding is doubtful. But I can see at the meeting that Arthur is distracted. Something's bugging him. Afterward, on our way to his Lincoln in the parking lot, Arthur asks the New Jersey Transit dispatcher at the bus stop: "How's the ridership been?" He's already told his audience at the ribbon cutting that his breakeven point for daily ferry traffic has risen by two thousand riders, not only because of the expense of the added New Jersey

Transit connections, but even more because of the increase in private connecting buses on the Manhattan side, where Arthur is paying the full cost.

He tells the dispatcher: "I have been losing sleep, to tell you the truth, but I also lost sleep over the original ferry. I'll tell you what's bothering me. Our relationship with you fellas, so far, and what we've done is excellent. We've been doing mailings, we're doing television. The Jersey side will come. What I'm really upset about is the other side of the river, with the charter bus company, because it was our error. We put out too many of their buses in Manhattan. We should've used our own little vans, but we didn't have enough drivers." To a rider who's stopped to listen, he adds reassurance that is actually meant for himself: "You know why it's going to work? Because it's right. It's absolutely right, to fulfill a need for a service. We'll be having a couple thousand more people a day, you'll see."

We run into Dick Melosh, who retired in 1985 as executive vice-president of A-P-A, where he began as a diesel mechanic. He has a gray crewcut, a bullet face, a round belly, and a cigar. He's been coming up from Florida in the summers to advise at the waterfront. Melosh asks: "How was the ceremony?"

"The usual bullshit," Arthur answers. "Fifteen advance men, standing around doing nothing."

Idleness grates on Arthur's principles, but Melosh isn't interested in philosophy. Needling Arthur a little, Melosh says around his cigar, "The ceremony was okay. It all depends on how much money it cost you."

"I'm a little shook up this morning," Arthur tells me, as we ease into his Lincoln. "With all the promotion we've done, we're getting very few new riders." He reassures himself: "It's okay. The logic is there. The logic is sound. I don't just make idle predictions. I know I'm right." He swings to a stop on the shoulder of the exit road, opens the door, picks up a half of a plastic cup from the gravel, and puts it on the floormat by his feet. He noticed it on the way in. "This is what really bothers me. I've got a new man just hired to take charge of this stuff, a head groundskeeper, he's quite talented, too, and this bothers me a lot, because he's ridden past that stuff more than once today, I'm sure. I watch the store. I always have."

Arthur crosses River Road and guides the Lincoln up a cobble-stone alley that winds up the face of the Palisades. On our way up, we enter an unexpected tunnel: it is formed by the Galaxy Apartments' footings, which stand over the alley and the cliff-face like the legs of a brontosaurus. The alley emerges at the top of the cliff onto Boulevard East. We turn west on 72nd Street across the crown of the ridge. This is a working-class neighbor-hood of two-story houses with stoops, heavily inhabited, clean but worn, declining with a slowness perceptible not by the year but by the decade. I'm assuming that we'll drive across the ridge and dip down the other side of it to A-P-A at the edge of the swamp. Instead, Arthur turns left onto Palisade Avenue, head-ing us south, along the spine of the ridge. We leave Guttenberg and enter the town of West New York. Here poorer brick tene-ments raise the skyline to six stories, and the jagged teeth of their storefront signs speak Spanish. Once Italian, West New York is now Cuban. Other North Jersey ridge and swamp towns still cleave to unchanging old-world identities: Carteret, Polish; Fairview and Cliffside Park, Italian. To the few outsiders who visit these neighborhoods, all seem alike, equally crowded and undistinguished, an unbroken conurbation without any varia-tion except for a gradation from rich to poor. To their residents, though, North Jersey is not the continuous city it seems—not, except for Newark, a city at all—but a series of adjacent small towns.

Half-a-million Jersey residents commute to New York, and they have turned some of the towns near the George Washington Bridge, like Fort Lee and Englewood, partly into suburbs of Manhattan. But many among the working-class populace of West New York, Weehawken, North Bergen, and their sister towns may visit Manhattan no more than two or three times a year. To forget New York's existence, of course, would not be possible. As we drive along the ridge-top, the grid of streets at nearly every corner reveals a glimpse, as through a narrow window, of the castellated island across the water. To these ridge towns, though, Manhattan's presence is a defining background, rather than the foreground where life is lived. It is a human-made equivalent of Denver's backdrop of Rocky Mountains, say, or of Tucson's Sonora Desert, or of Salt Lake City's Wasatch Range and inland sea. Contained by their river, their swamp, and the castle across the Hudson, these towns look inward. Their provincialism and their memories of an old-world past have, in general, retarded alienation and fragmentation into the American mass. (There may be a shopping mall somewhere on this ridge, but I have not seen one. There's really no room for one.) The towns' reluctance to change may have frustrated Arthur's dreams as a developer, but it has strengthened his success as a trucker. It is no accident that, in recruiting a loyal populace for the small town of his A-P-A, Arthur has found his citizens among ethnic enclaves like North Jersey and South Boston.

Arthur parks near the corner of 51st Street. The line of five-story brick walkups gives way, at the corner, to a low, yellow-brick, four-door garage and, beside it, a small, square, two-story flat-roofed brick house. Joined to the back of the little house is a two-story wooden addition, faced with white clapboard, with a pitched roof. Without explanation, Arthur opens the door with a key on his ring. As he does, I'm startled to notice that below one of the three doorbells, the name "Imperatore" is typed under yellowed tape. I know Arthur moves about between his duplex in Manhattan, his apartment near the waterfront, his horse-farm in Pennsylvania, and his yacht; and I know that, as much as he likes fine things, he also likes working people; but this? Down the shabby hall, past doors to the two apartments in the front house, up steps to a door to the house in back: Arthur knocks. "I grew up here," he says.

A man in a tee-shirt answers. He's in his seventies, bald, smiling, delighted at Arthur's surprise visit. This is Andrew Imperatore, sixth oldest of the ten Imperatore siblings. I remember now that one of the brothers prefers to remain in West New York. Andrew worked for Eddie Imperatore in Eddie's furniture store in Union City; they were the only two of the seven Imperatore brothers whose work was not A-P-A. Arthur tells me later that he bought the house from his mother's estate after her death in 1975 and gave it over to Andrew's use as long as he wanted it.

Downstairs, the house is a single room, less that twenty feet long, an L-shape with the kitchen the shorter and the living room the longer arm. Here, Arthur tells me, an ironing board extended the dinner table so that the younger kids could fit. There were three sisters and seven brothers, of whom Arthur was the second-youngest sibling. The children slept packed into the second bedroom upstairs or on sofas in the living room. Arthur points to the windowpanes that were thick with ice on winter mornings when there wasn't enough coal for the furnace in the basement.

Andrew's wife presses coffee on us, but Arthur won't stay. In his three-piece beige summer suit, he's out of place in this room now. In his youth, when he still wore workingman's clothes, before his energy began to cool with maturity, one wonders how the walls of this crowded little house could have contained his restiveness. The force that restrained him, it seems to me as Arthur tells me now of his childhood, was his mother. "She was my idol and my teacher," he says. "She insisted on absolute integrity, and that standard has been and is still with us to this day. She was a very strong woman. I never saw her flinch at any problem, and her life was studded with problems, because my father was drunk every day. She would never give into it."

In the front, yellow-brick half of the joined houses, Arthur's parents ran a vegetable store. "I never saw my father when he wasn't drunk," Arthur says, as we drive away from the place. "Every night he threatened to kill us. I hated my father and feared him. My mother was strong, very staunch," he repeats. "She would never give in to it."

Arthur was determined to redeem his father's degradation and to prove himself worthy of his mother's courage. The medium of redemption would be work. Arthur began work at seven, on his father's produce truck. Next he mopped floors at the neighborhood candy store, and by the age of ten he was being paid fifty cents a day "and a baloney sandwich and a soda." While in high school, he held a full-time job as a Western Union messenger. "I was driven by the Depression, by the fear of poverty. We literally worried about starvation. My mother favored me because I had the drive to succeed. All during my lifetime I was her favorite." There was "always a certain amount of anger and resentment," Arthur says, among his siblings.

His sister Anna Kortrey told me on another day: "Arthur made fifty dollars a week, working for Western Union, and that was during the Depression. He pedaled his bike and made more money than a friend of his who had a car. He was always a go-getter. When he was twelve, he started saying he would be a millionaire."

She added: "For the Imperatore children, life was terrible. We had no childhood. None of us can relax, even today. We weren't shown any love at all. There was a lot of fighting." The older brothers, particularly, fought with their drunken father, and in his brothers' absence, Arthur as a child felt insecure, Anna said. "That was the reason he had drive."

All of the children worked. Eddie, the eldest son, worked in the vegetable store. "The daughters had to clean and care for the kids," Anna said. (Her charge was Arthur.) At seventy-seven, Anna is still angry that, because of her childcare duties, she was not allowed to go to high school.

The solidarity of the children, in the face of parental relentlessness and sternness, set another of Arthur's patterns. "The children were very close," Anna told me. It was natural that the brothers, looking for a livelihood after their return from World War II, should decide to go into business together. That the business was trucking was almost a matter of chance.

"My kid brother Harold, who had an impish nature," Arthur tells me now, "used to do a little skit when we were discussing what we should do. 'We can drive, can't we?' he'd say. 'So let's buy a truck.' In early 1947, two of the brothers, Gene and Arnold, proceeded to buy a used Army ordnance truck for $700 and to paint "Imperatore Brothers Moving and Trucking" on the panels. Harold and George joined the firm, and a second used Army truck joined the fleet.

At first, Arthur kept his distance. His counselors in high school had told him he should go to college, because, as Arthur says,

"I was a smart guy." In the war he had enrolled in officers' training school and served as a navigator on B-29s with the rank of second lieutenant, and upon discharge he enrolled in night school while he sold Fuller Brushes during the day. But it was hard to wait. "I was too anxious to get started with life"—by which he meant starting to build a fortune. "I couldn't contain myself." His brothers' trucks and their business meetings around the dinner table in the house on Palisade Avenue tempted him, except that he couldn't abide their lack of zeal in the pursuit of customers. He finally exploded one day upon walking in from his Fuller Brush beat to find four supposed truck drivers lounging at the table during working hours. "Get out there and work," he shouted, "or get my name off that truck." The upshot was a reformulated partnership of five brothers, with Arthur as boss— as *primus inter pares*, as he says now. "I told my brothers that if anyone could do a better job, at any time, then he could be boss," and they agreed—an agreement of which Arthur reminded them in later years whenever the brothers became restive. Arthur doesn't mention it to me, but I suspect his mother's special trust in him must have been a factor in his ascendancy.

For the first month, the Imperatore Brothers' terminal was one of the brick car-garages next to the house. Inside the house, on the peninsular counter that still separates the kitchen from the living room, Arthur manned the phone on dispatch in the morning while his brothers drove. Then, in the afternoon, his mother ran dispatch, while Arthur went out to sell. Later that year, for $800, they bought out A & P Trucking Corp., eight blocks north at 210 59th Street, with two battered trucks and a garage with a six-foot loading dock. Because the seller, one Albert Amorino, had already bought advertising with the A & P Trucking name, the Imperatores adopted the name for their own company, judging it cheaper to repaint the panels on their own original trucks than to buy new advertising. (The second "A" in A-P-A was added in the late fifties to settle a lawsuit by the Great Atlantic and Pacific Tea Company, the supermarket chain known as "the A & P." A-P-A, therefore, stands for nothing, unless it be, according to company jokes, for "Always Please Arthur" or "Arthur's Private Army.")

A snowstorm eventually downed the old 59th Street garage, but Arthur can point out other landmarks of his youth as we inch north again, since almost nothing has been torn down in these neighborhoods for decades. Here are the schools on 54th Street, 56th, and 57th; there on the corner is the Hudson County Bank, a stone pilastered temple. "I had my first bank account there in 1935, when I was ten. I still have my stock certificates there. Everything I own is in that safe deposit box." Referring to the waterfront, Arthur says, sounding still a little mystified, "I own a third of this town now."

Along this avenue and up and down the ridge, A & P Trucking moved "anything to make a buck," Arthur says: food, chemicals, building materials, household goods, junk freight. Arthur gives the example of a half-ton commercial refrigerator the brothers hauled from West New York twelve miles northwest to Paterson for four dollars. The first year the company grossed $23,000, and in the second year, "we were starting to generate a sizeable amount of less-than-truckload shipments, and the six-foot dock at 59th Street had become quickly obsolete as we added trucks and some people. The freight that we pulled through there was such that the dock couldn't accommodate it, so we had to make do, we had to make up for the lack of efficiency by just doing a lot more work. We were double-handling freight" —stacking freight onto a truck to clear space on the dock, and then stripping it off again—"and we sometimes triple-handled freight. We learned early in the game to do sequential loading."

In November, 1948, A & P Trucking made its first move to the swamp's edge, to a 3,500-square-foot garage on 40th Street and Tonnelle Avenue. The new garage had two wide doors that fit eight of the company's fifteen trucks. Sam De Piano, the North Bergen terminal manager until his retirement in 1983, said of the 40th Street garage: "We had four brothers, two nieces, a third girl, and myself in one fifteen-by-fifteen room. Arthur had a private office, but it was so small that he had to climb over his desk to get to his chair. Sometimes we'd lose the trucks down the rear end in the mud in the yard. We parked the extra trucks on a street a mile away."

Marty Marino, who replaced Harold Imperatore in 1954 as Director of Traffic after Harold died of kidney failure, said of the early years: "A-P-A was hell then. There wasn't any money. We all worked eighteen hours a day. I don't think the brothers took a salary all the time. I remember running to the bank to cash checks and running back in time to meet the payroll. Arthur never slept."

By 1950, the brothers were moving from driving into management. George joined Arthur in sales; he retired as vice-president for sales in 1986. Arnold was vice-president for operations until his death in a helicopter crash in 1975. Gene, who retired in 1975, was dock supervisor. Marie Tierney, the eldest sibling, was office manager. Arthur himself drove trucks only as a substitute, and from the beginning he was salesman, deal-maker, planner, philosopher, teacher, and boss. "The brothers were Mr. Arthur, Mr. Arnold, Mr. George, and Mr. Gene," Bruce Zeman, now director of purchasing, recalled. "You couldn't say Mr. Imperatore, because if you did, all four of them would turn around."

"It wasn't a business, it was a family," Arthur says. But for his brothers and the employees, it was a second family. They went home in the evening, or in the morning; they forgot A-P-A on the weekends. For Arthur it was different. He had no second passion.

Armand told me on another day, "Everything in my father's life was his business. There was no separation whatsoever between business and everything else. If he met somebody on the outside that he liked, he'd want to involve them in the business. If he was working with someone in the business, he'd want to bring them home to the house, and at any hour of the day or night, so there was no separation of the one from the other. The average owner of a bagel store or a deli lives this kind of life, where the business is downstairs and you live in the back room or upstairs; in fact, that's how Arthur grew up, where the vegetable store was downstairs and the family lived in back of the store and on the second floor. So the continuum between business and family was part of his life. His mother was the first dispatcher and bookkeeper. *My* mother was the next bookkeeper."

Arthur acknowledges: "I was so driven and so determined. In the early years I had no outlets whatsoever. I hardly had any other interest. I couldn't read a book. I wouldn't go to a ballgame or a movie. My whole cerebral life was based on commitment to learning and growing a company. It was kind of screwy in a way. In twenty years, I took one week of vacation. Ask Armand—*he* remembers. I have an insecurity that's driven me, that's maybe given my children, starting with Armand, a lot about which to have deep consternation, if not serious worry, but that's my nature. I was very insecure and it may not look it, but I guess it's the truth." Eventually, in the 1970s, Arthur sought out psychotherapy to help him learn to moderate his obsession with work.

The drive for wealth is not a single phenomenon, because money is desired as a means: for some, a means to power; for others, to luxury and ease; for others, to status. For Arthur, it was a means to redeem himself and his siblings from the humiliations of their childhood, a redemption that was not only material, but moral. He says, as he drives us back to the waterfront, "I'm gifted with certain talents. I guess it goes back to when I was a little kid. I felt in the presence of the Almighty that I understood something about myself in terms of these gifts and therefore I should optimize the talent I was given to make the world a little better in ways in which I might have the chance to do." It would never have occurred to him to flee his surroundings and escape across the river to seek his fortune alone among the high-rises. His mission was to lift up his own piece of the world, together with the people around him, with the materials that fell to hand. Trucks themselves were "nothing special," he says. That they became the materials was chance, occasioned by his kid brother's whim.

Manufacturing jobs reached their historical high in Manhattan in 1946. After the war, factories began moving into the outer New York City boroughs and into Westchester and the neighboring counties of Long Island, Connecticut, and New Jersey. Well into the 1960s, the New York metropolitan area was the country's leading manufacturing region, and one-third of the jobs in the region were in factories. (In 1992, by contrast, twelve percent of the jobs in the New York–New Jersey region were in manufacturing, compared to seventeen percent nationwide. As a source of work, the making of things has yielded to the provision of services, not only in New York and New Jersey, but in the entire country.) In the late 1940s and the 1950s, however, when the Imperatore brothers were establishing themselves, their business drew, as Arthur says now, "on a very, very dynamic market in the greater New York–New Jersey area. There was plenty of room to do business, because there were really more customers than there were good operators doing the kind of work that eventually we came to do." Arthur not only pursued the junk freight and the small shipments that the then-established carriers considered burdensome, but he followed the flow of jobs out of Manhattan into Jersey and the outer boroughs. "The big trucklines, say in 1948 to '52, would go from Newark to Manhattan. They wouldn't go into Brooklyn or Queens or the Bronx, so I saw this early in the game as an opening. In effect, we took the leavings."

Industrialism then showed more of the rawness of previous generations than it does now. The freight was different from Tony DeRosa's and John Occhiogrosso's civilized crates and cartons, and it called forth a different sort of man. Tony and John are actually two generations removed from the men that Arthur and his brothers first hired in the late 1940s. I learned about the early drivers from Harold "Smokey" Petsch, Jr., himself a member of the middle generation of A-P-A drivers, now in his mid-fifties, with short-cropped hair the color of his nickname, and a round, blazing-red face. Harold was seventeen in 1954 when he began at A-P-A as a driver's helper, following the lead of his father, the late Harold "Pappy" Petsch, Sr. "He was one of the older generation, one of the very, very tough characters," Harold Jr. said of his father when I interviewed him on another day. "Burly, cigar-smoking, swearing and cursing, he'd punch you in the head to settle a dispute. He left school in the eighth or ninth grade, but he was a shrewd character and knew how to handle freight. You'd use a Johnson bar, like a flat-tipped crowbar, to lift crates, then you'd use a wedge, or a pipe, to roll it, you'd use ropes and handtrucks to handle big bales of cotton, or piece-goods, or rubber. All the other people you'd meet of that generation were tough like he was. Today you don't need the physical freight-handling skills.

"I started going down to the ocean piers when I was sixteen," Harold continued. "Dirty and smoky, cashews and pistachios in the cargo-nets, for some reason it was very exciting to me. Everything was handled by hand, piece by piece. There were hardly any banded skids, there was no shrinkwrapping. Now everything is finished goods in a container, and you don't see it or smell it. You move it once. But in those days, you moved it six or seven times." Trucks back then, Harold explained, were connecting links in the manufacturing process, moving goods from workstation to workstation as the goods evolved. "You'd bring the raw materials from the ship to the plant or the ware-house." Then the truckers would move the goods once or twice or more in semi-manufactured states, again as finished compo-nents, and finally as complete, assembled products, which had to be shipped first from factory to warehouse, and then from warehouse to store.

The trucks, too, were in an earlier stage of evolution. "You had to have iron men to drive them," Harold recalled. The windshields opened outward at the bottom, and the clutch and brake pedals and gearshift emerged through open holes in the floor, through which cold, heat, fumes, and noise streamed. In the winter, "You wrapped a rag around the base of the gearshift to stop the draft," Larry Estes, who has driven trucks in Western Maine for forty years, told me when I visited A-P-A's Scarbor-ough, Maine terminal. "The union rules said you had to have a heater and a defroster in the cab, but it didn't say they had to work. In the cold weather you had to keep the windshield open to keep it from fogging. You dressed for it. The engines were weaker, too, and you had to shift down a lot. It was much harder work. And the brakes weren't as good. That's one thing the union did. They pushed and pushed for better equipment."

"You'd hit a pothole and chip a tooth because of the poor suspension," Harold Petsch said. He recalled his first trip across the mountains into Pennsylvania before the building of the in-terstates. "You'd snake up the hills on those two-lane roads in very low gear. I was grinding up one hill, and a truck bumped me from behind. He pushed me over the hill. I found out that's how it was done."

In their first years as truckers, the Imperatore brothers knew very little about the trucking industry. "They were dealing with a business they hadn't grown up in," Harold said. "They got into it because it sounded simple." To some extent, it was simple when they were still driving their own trucks, without any employees besides a bookkeeper. They had no occasion to clash with hardbitten truckmen like Pappy Petsch, Harold's father. But becoming Pappy's boss and telling him what route to drive and what freight to load turned out not to be simple at all. Sam De Piano, A-P-A's first terminal manager, explained it to me this way: "The first words out of those oldtimers' mouths was 'Go fuck yourself.' They'd fight at the drop of a pin." Even if they took the load without protest, "those guys knew how to get lost," Harold Jr. said. "So Arthur's challenge was how to keep track of them once they'd left the terminal."

"Trucking in the 1950s," Arthur found, "was the toughest, most brutal business you could imagine. Our industry was victimized by the sweeping power of the Teamsters and the influence they had over the workingman. The abuses of the law were rife, they were daily; they would happen all day long. The working people would punch in and they would try to screw the boss, and I was very paranoiac about this. I was very fearful, because I knew that if we lost control of the people, if we allowed precedents . . ."—it's not a sentence Arthur wants to contemplate finishing, even forty years later.

The International Brotherhood of Teamsters, Chauffeurs, Warehousemen, and Helpers of America had existed since 1903, but it had grown as a loose confederation of independent locals, which now number more than 600 in the United States and Canada. To bind these locals into a single power was the partly successful life-work of two presidents of the International, Jimmy Hoffa and his predecessor, Dave Beck. Beck was a Westerner, president of a Seattle local; Hoffa was a Midwesterner, president of a local in Detroit. During the 1930s, 1940s, and 1950s Beck and then Hoffa moved beyond their cities to organize their regions. They negotiated multi-employer contracts that specified wages, benefits, work rules, and grievance procedures for many of the unionized trucklines in their areas. But until the 1960s, the locals in the East remained almost completely autonomous. Walter Shea, who until 1991 was an international vice-president of the Teamsters, and who began as Hoffa's aide in the 1950s, told me that officials of the Teamsters International "just didn't go up to New York, New Jersey, or New England" before the 1960s. "Nobody messed with them."

Virtually every American labor union continues to draw its goals in some part from the tradition of utopian socialism that has inspired the labor movement since its beginnings in Europe over 150 years ago. In the case of the Teamsters, union socialism, with its straight-arrow idealism and militant commitment to working-class solidarity, was particularly strong in the upper Midwest before World War II, under the leadership of Farrell Dobbs. (Leftist idealism resurfaced in the Teamsters in the recent insurgency of the Teamsters for a Democratic Union, an advocacy group that supported and largely ensured the election of a reform president of the International, Ron Carey, in 1991.)

Despite this tradition, a right-wing countertrend began overwhelming the leftists in most American unions in the 1930s. Because the rightist unions strayed from the guidance of idealism, they sometimes succumbed to corruption. Business abetted the corruption, because dishonest union officials could be bought; government abetted it, because it feared union leftism. (Until well into the 1960s, the Federal Bureau of Investigation under J. Edgar Hoover hounded union leftists and ignored Mafia infiltration of rightist unions, having taken the preposterous public position that the Mafia didn't exist.) In the Teamsters, corruption infected the International and many locals, most notoriously the autonomous locals of the New York area. Of most concern to the young A-P-A was Local 560, the largest local in New Jersey, based in Union City, a ridge-top town just south of Weehawken. Local 560 was the operations base of Anthony "Tony Pro" Provenzano, a capo in the Genovese Mafia family, a convicted extortioner and murderer who died in prison in 1988.

When A & P Trucking consisted of five Imperatore brothers and two nieces, it was beneath the union's notice. But union pressure grew as the brothers began to hire. Arthur delayed, although he knew it was inevitable that his truckline would be organized. He issued a promise that when he reached his goal of building his own terminal, he would sign a union contract. Meanwhile, his brothers deflected the pressure from Tony Provenzano's Local 560 by joining Local 617, a much smaller rival of 560. The brothers joined as truck drivers, though they were not properly employees. A friend of Arthur's who was an official in a local manufacturing union suggested the feint and made the introduction. The sidestep into Local 617 was "a critical choice," Arthur recalls. "I would not have fared well with 560, because they were such thugs. They all wound up killed or in prison." Local 617 was then run by one Nick Armatrudi—"a bad guy, a liar, and a politician"—but he was not a Provenzano.

In 1950, Arthur bought an abandoned one-acre coal yard off 85th Street in North Bergen. In the next year, two more adjacent acres were bought, and the first dock, 7,500 square feet, now the southeast corner of the North Bergen dock, and the first offices, now the office mezzanine, were built at a cost of $135,000. In March, 1952, A-P-A signed its first union agreement, with Local 617.

In working with the Teamsters, Arthur and his brothers could choose among four alternatives, which, generally speaking, American corporations have followed in their relationships with employee unions. One alternative is for the employer to capitulate. That choice commonly entails union control of hiring and work-rules, a control which can lead to the abuses of absenteeism, contractual overmanning (featherbedding), lax discipline, and theft. Another alternative is for the employer to weaken the union, perhaps destroy it or drive it out, with the resulting bosses' abuses common to nonunion shops: poor pay, skimpy benefits, unsafe working conditions, and arbitrary discipline. Both of these alternatives are adversarial, involving defeat or victory, or, more commonly, a prolonged struggle in which every contract negotiation and every grievance procedure becomes a battlefield in the class war.

A third and a fourth alternative involve cooperation and the establishment of a stable *modus vivendi*. Cooperation can be honorable, involving full performance of mutually beneficial agreements. Cooperation can also be dishonorable, often criminal, enacted most often through pension fraud and sweetheart deals, by which the employer pays out less to the workers than the contract specifies. The employer bribes the union officials to keep silent, and the union officials silence the employees by intimidation and violence. All four of these alternatives have been employed in the post-war history of the trucking industry in its relation to the Teamsters.

From the first, the Imperatores chose the alternative of honorable cooperation. When the early drivers told Arthur they were going to organize, he recalls now, "I told them I would never sign an agreement until I could live up to it. I said when I would sign an agreement, it would only be at a time when I knew I could live up to it and not bankrupt the company." While his intent to operate according to the terms of his contract with the union would seem unexceptionable in most industries in most places, in the environment of the New York–New Jersey trucking industry, his approach was eccentric, if not actually unique. It was threatening to his competition, whom he despised as "gyp companies" because they operated under sweetheart deals; it was threatening to the corrupt union locals that thrived upon bribery and intimidation. "Arthur took a lot of abuse, even from the other trucklines," Harold Petsch, Jr., told me. "He was just a local carrier, and he bumped heads with the so-called giants of the industry, most of whom are out of business now. They looked at him as a crazy kid causing more trouble than it was worth." (Harold was shop steward at A-P-A for seventeen years; he retired from road driving in 1991 and joined Local 617 as business agent. His retirement made Ronnie Parham senior man on the road list.)

The telling corollary of Arthur's intent to live up to the letter of the union agreement was that he intended the same for the union and for the employees represented by the union. They, too, were going to live up to the agreement. If A-P-A was going to pay the full union wage and yet compete with established companies which, through sweetheart deals, were paying less than full wages, then A-P-A was going to have to push the men to work harder. The company was going to have to make the likes of Pappy Petsch perform according to Arthur's idea of productivity.

Arthur knew what he wanted, but he didn't know how to achieve it. The logistics of moving less-than-truckload freight in New York and New Jersey turned out to be far from simple, and the stubbornness of an independent craft tradition baffled and infuriated him. When the men were slow to increase their productivity through harder work, Arthur's response was to become an abusive and feared martinet. His greatest weapon was his insomnia. No one knew when to expect him on the dock. "Arthur was known to come down to the dock at 3:00 A.M.," Harold Jr. said. "He would see things going bad and he would plain go crazy, scream and holler and throw things and all kinds of theatrics. In the early years it was serious, but later on, I surmise, he realized it worked. Whoever heard of the company president coming down at three in the morning? Usually in most companies your president is just a picture on the wall."

Armand calls them "Arthur's wardances." Wearing sneakers, he would appear suddenly, and if men were moving too slowly or lounging on company time, he would, as Arthur says now, "abuse them, abuse them, abuse them. I was in a constant state of rage." He would throw the change in his pocket at their feet, shouting that if they wanted to steal from him, here was more. He was once so beside himself, several people have told me, that he dropped his pants, bent over to present his behind, and bawled to the men, "If you guys want to fuck me, go ahead and fuck me!"

The night billers worked on the mezzanine then, overlooking the dock. "You knew when Arthur was on the dock," they told me. "It was: 'Arthur's here.' "

"And what would he say?" I asked them.

They shook their heads and laughed.

"I couldn't talk about it."

"It was not printable."

"When he came up to see you on the mezzanine, what was he like?" I asked.

"Oh, here he was a gentleman," Mary O'Gorman said, "a perfect gentleman. But I meant the times when he was on the dock, and he saw everything in disarray, and the men weren't functioning like they should. He was talking to men."

"He can be very hard, even cruel, but on the other hand he's very soft and generous, and he's never been hard to me," Harold told me. "Not to say I've never argued with him, but he's never screamed at me. If you met his standards, he was good to you. If you didn't, he could abuse the hell out of you, especially verbally. He's very fast with the language, swearing and carrying on. The fifties and sixties were the stormy years, when he had a love-hate relationship with the employees."

Arthur rarely hit an employee, although Bill McKernan, president of Local 617 since 1957, recalls one or two fights, which, he says, Arthur lost. The fisticuffs Arthur usually left to Sam De Piano, the North Bergen terminal manager then. A bantam of a man bristling with nervous energy, with a full head of gray-black hair and great popping eyes, Sam at seventy-two is still a fearsome presence. He told me: "I used my fists. I wouldn't be afraid to fight the men, and I fought with a lot of drivers. I'd catch guys goofing off. I'd say, 'Get off the yard now. I'm not going to listen to you.' " (In other words, he was suspending them without pay for the rest of the day). "I'd hand my wristwatch to the supervisor, go up against the driver, and let him hit first so the company wouldn't get sued. Then I'd hit him. I knew how to use my hands. I'm little, but I'm fast. Next day we'd be friends. I never held a grudge. If you do your job, I'm your friend. If you don't do your job, I'm going to beat the shit out of you."

Arthur was a terror to his managers as well. "You'd look at him and shiver," recalled Marty Marino, who retired in 1984 as director of traffic. When I asked Sam De Piano his view of Arthur, he said, "Truthfully? Arthur was a bastard. He was a nut. He wanted to be number one, he was power hungry. We were going to be the biggest and the best, and he instilled that in everyone. And we did become the best, the best on the East

Coast. We had the best equipment in the area. We made the drivers feel like salesmen." In his answer, without noticing it, Sam moved from resentment to pride, acknowledging that Arthur's rages, while unpleasant, worked.

"Arthur controlled his brothers with nine fists," Sam said, but the metaphor is natural to Sam; the fists were verbal. Arthur acknowledges: "In 1960, I forced my brothers to choose: either give me fifty-one percent to take control, or else let me put the business in shape and then turn it over to them in two years." They gave him control, and eventually he bought them out entirely.

It was the presence of Arnold Imperatore, the next-oldest brother, that allowed Arthur to act the wild man. Arnold played soft to Arthur's hard. Armand recalls: "Arnold had a soft heart and was loved by many people. Arthur would come through and shake things up and get people upset. They'd tell Arnold: 'He's upset. He wants us to do X. But how are we going to do it?' and Arnold would smooth it down. 'Don't worry. Here's how we'll do it.' Arnold could be hard if he found out you were lying to him. But softness was his basic style. He liked to go down and have spaghetti and beer with the guys and shoot the shit."

To Arthur's wardances the men replied in kind. In the mid-1950s, the company suffered four wildcat strikes. Most were led by a driver named Roy Miller, whom Arthur remembers as "a very skillfull, lying bastard who could take my weaknesses, my temper, my swearing—I mean trucking isn't Sunday school, y'know—and he would pow-wow with the drivers, and he manufactured what he deemed to be a major contractual issue of drivers handling freight on the dock. He was trying to effect a limitation on the work, create work classifications, and we would never go back to that. When it came to getting a dollar's worth of work for a dollar's worth of pay, I would never yield. Never. I wouldn't give a god damn what the particular issue was, if I thought I was right."

Marty Marino, the retired director of traffic, shook his head as he recalled the strikes. "In those days, to take on the union—none of the other carriers did that." The brothers, including Arthur, drove trucks through the picket lines. George Imperatore and one of the strikers went to jail together after the worker brandished a gun at George and George threatened to run his truck over the worker. Another of the men pushed a boulder off a bridge onto the cab of Arnold Imperatore's truck. The strikes each ended in a draw, with the Imperatores gaining respect for not backing down, but the impasse remaining: the brothers continued to insist on harder work than other trucklines required, but they didn't know how to inspire it or enforce it, except by yelling.

For Arthur, the greatest infuriation was the restriction on his power to fire. In the trucking boom of the fifties, when the company was growing rapidly and there was a shortage of drivers, Arthur would sometimes scour the Hudson County bars to find men to haul the freight. Then the fifteen days of probation would pass, and suddenly the barfly was a permanent employee. Under the Teamster agreements, dismissal of employees for poor productivity is almost impossible. (Usually, unproductive workers can be eased out for other faults common to poor productivity: absenteeism, tardiness, theft of time.) In his wild early days, Arthur kept stubbing his toes on the barriers to dismissal. "He didn't understand the rules in those days," Harold Petsch told me. "He wouldn't build a file. He'd hire drunks and thieves, then fire them and get burned and have to take them back, and pay back pay." Arthur complained in a later speech, "Marriage is not nearly as close, especially these days, as the working relationship of an employee with an employer under today's labor agreements in the motor freight industry."

By the late 1950s, Arthur tells me now, "I hated the business. I never expected I would make money. I planned to leave it. I was going to build the company for my brothers and then just let them have it and leave." Then a snowstorm changed his course. In 1960, the city of Reading, Pennsylvania, where A-P-A had recently opened its first branch terminal, was shut down by a blizzard. Arthur, who happened to be on the site, went out onto the lot with a driver to shovel off the snow. Soon Arthur was busy shoveling, while the driver was busy complaining because snow removal wasn't mentioned in his job description. And this was an employee who as far as Arthur could see should

have been grateful: he had just completed his probationary period and had been placed on the permanent list. The boss's rage
was about to boil over into the snow when a sudden epiphany
froze it. It was A-P-A that had hired this fake of a worker; the
mistake was therefore A-P-A's.

"I got a reading on this man's character," Arthur recalls, "and
after the snowstorm ended, I went back to North Bergen and
told my brother Arnold, 'This is the worst man you ever hired.'
I said, 'I predict he will create a strike, and I can't tell you why.'
He was not at all discourteous, you see. Arnold was all upset.
But we'd learned from all the strikes we'd had in the fifties, and
we were going to grow now. We were a two-terminal operation.
It was ever more critical that we retain control of the quality of
the people we hired. The denouement with respect to that particular guy in Reading? He almost created a strike. Jesus Christ,
he was awful. How do you like that?"

Admitting responsiblity is always a source of power. If the
man in the snowstorm was there through A-P-A's fault, then
A-P-A could correct the fault. The result was the company's defensive hiring process. "The system I evolved in 1960," Arthur
says, "was the salvation, one of the most important foundations,
one of the rocks on which the company was built. That was when
we went into industrial engineering, into polygraphs, into security checks. We analyzed people's handwriting—all kinds of
things. We used to do retail credit checks on people, check with
their neighbors, check with people who had union affiliation,
check everybody out like we were paranoiac." Arthur said later
in one of his speeches, "The number one requirement for quali-
fication in our company, far more importantly that any other
aspect or attribute, is character: honesty and loyalty."

Arthur elaborates for me now: "You have to start with the
right people. You have to have people with good character. They
have to have a sense of purpose, a sense of self. A certain amount
of ego is necessary, because otherwise—if a man, doing our kind
of work particularly, doesn't have a strong personality, a strong
ego, a strong sense of right and wrong, a strong sense of professional purpose, he's like a reed in the wind. Each one influences
the others around him, which is one of the things you see in the

emotional dynamo of a company like A-P-A. No one lives in isolation. No one's just *here*. He's interacting with everyone else and becomes part of the mass psychology."

Arthur would recruit and train a new kind of truckman. "He broke the mold," says Bill McKernan, the president of Local 617. But as for the Pappy Petsches of the older generation, Arthur resigned himself to struggling with them until old age would retire them. Then, during the same year, he also discovered a substitute for the wardances, or, at least, a supplement to them. He had Harold Weisberg, Augie Pagnozzi's early predecessor and A-P-A's first time-study man, draw the fifteen-foot flowchart that set the first productivity standards for each of the company's operations. Weisberg's flowchart identified 225 stages in the movement of freight and of the paperwork that accompanied it; an optimum performance time was assigned to each. (Now re-vered as a turning point in the company's history, the flowchart became the basis of Augie Pagnozzi's computerized productivity measurements.) At last, Arthur had an objective description of what he wanted. The old hands could be given new rules that could be enforced without recourse to personal recriminations. Arthur's yelling ceased to be an unpleasant sole strategy and became instead a bad habit hard to break.

Gradually, during the 1960s and 1970s, the climate of the com-pany changed to something more formal, more predictable and fair, though if anything more intense. As A-P-A doubled and redoubled in revenues and in geographic reach, the new em-ployees were trained, from the first, to work in accord with mea-surable standards. There were no more wildcat strikes. The union locals resisted the writing of specific productivity standards into the contracts, Harold Petsch told me, but "they accepted Ar-thur's language of a fair day's work for a fair day's pay, because they figured it couldn't be measured. Then A-P-A figured out a way to measure it."

The insoluble had become soluble. Arthur was reinvigorated. In 1960, "I got the inspiration of the systems," he says now, "and I decided that I loved the business. I took the challenge and I figured to hell with money"—which he had been restlessly dreaming about seeking elsewhere—"I'd build this machine. To say I wasn't interested in money would not be accurate. But as a result of these insights, I felt the urge to really concentrate on quality and to disregard my childhood dream of a big success in business. I eschewed money for the sake of money."

⸺⸺⸺⸺⸺⸺

Arthur has driven us back to the waterfront now, and we're sitting with coffee and cheese sandwiches at a café table with a view of the ferry slip and the river. The café occupies the center of the *Jamestown*, a 206-foot retired car-ferry that once plied Narragansett Bay in Rhode Island between Newport and Jamestown Island. Arthur had it towed to Weehawken and then moored to serve as dock and floating terminal for his passenger ferries across the Hudson.

Arthur has chosen our table as a vantage point from which to judge how much new ridership has been drawn by recent advertising and the new bus connections. Lunch-hour passengers are hurrying past us on either side of the café tables, and Arthur's blue-and-white, square-jawed, ninety-foot ferryboats roar into the slip every ten minutes, each disgorging fifty to a hundred riders, but it's soon clear to Arthur that the new passengers are too few. He's overextended; the new break-even point is not being reached, and the ferry's profits will evaporate for a while.

Arthur's frustrated, but at the same time undiscouraged. He's always progressed by trial and error. He says now between bites of his sandwich, "We went through many stages at the truckline, just like at the ferry. We were kind of scatterbrained, y'know. We really had to undergo a transformation in our thinking, to make the totality happen. That's when we started hiring defensively and measuring productivity. What we really learned was, I suppose, how important it was to learn. It was hard to develop a credo, a philosophy of life, at twenty-one years of age, when you're drawing five dollars a week and working like an animal. But I know now that at the beginning of any enterprise you do experimentation, you do observation, you do, let's call it a kind of pragmatic research, and then you draw from that your conclusions as to the best way to operate, whether it's the ferry or the freight dock at the truckline, whether it's maintenance, city delivery, dispatch, whatever. And you create a language. I created a language early in the years of the company. I was basically a teacher. I would discover what I thought was a piece of truth, and then would teach it, teach it, repeat it."

Arthur didn't conceal his struggles; he played them out on the floor of the terminal. "He poked his way through learning experiences," Harold Petsch told me. "He tried many things and they weren't always right. He wasn't always the brilliant truckman. He got smart as he went along. One disaster was a conveyor-belt system that was electrically powered and would empty the truck and then you'd sort the freight on it. There were all sorts of bridges and rollers and overpasses for the hilos. The theory was it would save time, but it just didn't work, because the freight would go by too fast to deal with, to read the labels, and the heavy freight would smash the light stuff. It cost a lot of money. Arthur always had a good imagination and he wasn't afraid to try things. You have to give him credit. But that was one of the worst. We had to tear the whole damn thing out."

The compensation for the errors of an undisciplined imagination, as Harold suggested, is the ability to see possibilities that others do not see. Arthur's seeing a glittering waterfront city in the wreckage of an abandoned railyard, and a ferry on a river where everyone else believed ferries were dead, are only recent evidence of his sculptor's gift for seeing the finished image in the block of uncarved stone. He saw the chance for both fortune and community in the shorthaul, small-shipment sector of a raw and corrupt industry. He saw honor and elegance in the daily routines of truck drivers and dockmen. A person with more sophisticated schooling and more disciplined emotions might not have danced the wardances, but would not have understood, in an epiphany during a snowstorm, the essential principles of the legendary productivity of the mature A-P-A. Although A-P-A can now serve as a checklist for the institutional virtues extolled by the consulting gurus of corporate culture, Arthur hasn't read a single one of their books. He very rarely takes time to read books. I do not think this is an accident. I wonder if the entrepreneur's ability to see what others cannot see can be taught at all—indeed whether two years at business school are more likely to suppress it.

"If you really want to dream and accomplish something," Arthur says now, "and have a lot of fun seeing something grow almost literally out of the ground into a viable entity of one sort or another, you have to be half-crazy. You have to be really driven enough." Craziness is a word Arthur is willing to use about himself and also about the effect his blizzard of intuited possibilities inevitably exerts upon the people around him, because they have to dig their way out of the snowdrifts.

On another day, Armand described it to me this way: "Arthur is more like an artist than he is like an executive. Because really, as an executive, you have to filter and screen what you say very, very carefully, since people are hanging on every word you say when you're a leader. And if you don't want them to fly in four different directions, you have to be careful about expressing contradictory feelings and ideas to them. You sort of have to wage that battle in your own head and bring it closer to a conclusion before you throw it out for general consumption. But that's never been Arthur's way of doing things. He thinks aloud, and when you do that a lot, you end up expressing contradictory ideas and getting people running in all different directions. They assume that they are to act on whatever it is that you're saying.

"Now around here," Armand continued, "people who are more of the inner circle have learned not to jump at the first expression of an idea out of Arthur's mouth. I mean, Arthur might say, 'Why don't we start running buses between here and Florida, and a ferry service as well?' The uninitiated person will run out the door saying, 'That's what the man wants. Let me start doing it.' People who have been around Arthur a while don't usually jump at that first thing. They wait till he says it a second or a third time, because he's engaged in a process of thinking out loud. But it's sometimes misleading for new people, or people on the outside. Arthur will say something and someone will run off and start doing something and he'll come back to Arthur and say, 'Well, here it is,' and Arthur will say, 'I didn't want that.' And they'll say, 'Well, but you *said*.'—'Hell, ah, y'know, aren't

I allowed to think out loud? Can't I speculate? But I certainly didn't etch that in stone.' "

"Everybody has to go through this?" I asked Armand.

"Yes. There are exploiters on the outside who will take off on what Arthur has said and see it as an opportunity for self-enrichment in some way or another, and then they get caught short. There are lots of such people. Arthur will meet somebody who'll say, 'Arthur, what you really need is a, whatever, a sky-hook'—anything. And Arthur will say," (here Armand beat his desk, imitating) " 'That's a damn good idea. We ought to look into that. Call Bruce Zeman, he's our man in charge of purchasing. Maybe we ought to get three or four of those.' " Armand laughed. "Now this person says, 'Ah! I'm in fat city.' So he calls Bruce Zeman and says" (Armand's voice turned cool, masterful), " 'I was just talking to Mr. Imperatore, and he said I should arrange with you for the purchase of three or four skyhooks.'

"So Bruce, who deals with this as much as or more than anybody, says," (voice unimpressed), " 'Hey, wait a minute. Send me in a proposal and we'll discuss it further.' "—(Eager) " 'Well, Mr. Imperatore said that he didn't, that he wanted this right away. He didn't want to lose any time at all.' And Arthur may have said that. Bruce'll say," (severe), " 'Just a minute. I know Mr. Imperatore a lot better than you do, and that's not what he meant.'

"So, Arthur can get very steamed up for a very brief time about an idea—he can be very stimulated by it, talk about it, take it to a far extreme, but he doesn't necessarily mean to go do it. He's fantasizing out loud. And if he were an artist or a writer, you'd understand it a lot better than when you see it in the context of an executive. Even if he were in advertising, or a marketing executive, someone in the so-called creative end of business, when they are brainstorming, then you'd accept it too, but from someone who is also an operating executive, it's very, very discombobulating to a lot of people. Operating executives usually don't do that sort of thing. But that is the role he has taken, and the role that he has traditionally wanted people to play around him: that he is Odysseus and we tie him to the mast and stop up our ears, but he has to hear the siren song. That's been his prerogative, and we are to best serve him by letting him be a wild, creative person and then placing parameters on him."

Arthur knows he has to watch himself. He tells me now: "We've put up a golf driving range here on the waterfront, and we may open a golf school. There was a television program done on golf for Channel Five about three weeks ago. Some guy came in from California, I forget his name, to do the program, and he came out here to the waterfront to film our golf driving range. So I asked him, what would he do with this property? He said, well, he'd run a golf school. I thought, my God, wonderful, we'll run a golf school here! I've got to go fight that one out with Armand, y'know, because he's really going to be upset when I tell him about this one. I think I have told him—no, I think I may have dictated it on his voice mail." Arthur laughs his gentle chuckle. "I drive Armand crazy. I have to be careful talking around him."

Arthur is not going to be able to sit at a café table any longer without dealing with the overcommitment of buses on the New York side, today's minor piece of craziness. He begins to rise, but a ferry rider accosts him.

"Excuse me."

Arthur, still seated: "Hi."

She is chic, dark-haired, roly-poly, costume jewelry à la mode. "How are you? I got a question."

Arthur shakes his head. "I got a bellyache. Don't annoy me."

She laughs, tries to continue. He says, "Siddown. Be quiet."

Laughing, still standing, she tells him: "I bought my ferry pass last week. Then you come out with the announcement—"

Arthur, anticipating, interrupting: "Right—"

"That you can add to the bus—"

"Right, and I don't know the—"

"How do I convert the ticket for the rest of this month?"

"I don't know. Ask the cashier."

"I did. She doesn't know the fare."

"She still doesn't know it?"

"She doesn't know it. She had to call on the phone, and I said I'd better get the ferry—"

Arthur: "Jesus Christ. Go ahead. What you'll do is—you'll come back tonight. They'll know it."

She: "All right."

"You'll pay more money!"

"Yeah!" She hurries off for the boat.

"Do you know her personally?" I ask Arthur, not entirely accustomed yet to his ease with strangers.

"I just know her from the ferry. I may know a million people."

Arthur stacks our lunch plates and coffee cups and punches them past the "Thank You" flap in a rubbish barrel, then leads the way across the *Jamestown's* semi-circular steel deck, painted blue, at which a ferryboat has now docked between rows of tall piles. Boarding with the crowd, we skirt the doors to the closed deck below and climb by steep steps to the open deck above. With a blat of the horn and a roar of engines in reverse, the ferry churns its way out of the slip, then backs around so that it faces New York. We head across the water.

The breeze is cool, but not so stiff as to require us to shout. The water below is swift and rumpled, black without white-caps. Ahead, the sun glitters and winks on the high-rises in the noon haze.

Arthur is a familiar sight to ferry riders at noontime. As they greet him, he answers them variously:

"I can tell you must be Italian."

She: "Right!"

This one he misses: "We have this service for nice Jewish ladies."

Rider: "I'm Italian."

A couple holding hands on the bench across from us offer that she is Korean and he Italian, and that they are engaged.

Arthur: "Koreans are good at business."

The young man: "We're about to open a pharmacy."

Arthur: "You see? I knew."

With its speed—four minutes across—the exhilarating air, and the vision of Manhattan that reminds commuters what drew them to the island in the first place, it is easy to see why the ferry has wooed these riders away from rival routes. Not only have they escaped noxious confinement in bus, subway, or automobile tunnel beneath the river, but Arthur has saved them about half-

an-hour a day, which, for middle-class professionals, New York-
ers especially, is a gift beyond the joys of money. Since the Port
Imperial ferry was established in 1986, about a dozen other
ferries have followed on various routes across the Hudson, New
York Harbor, and the East River, and New York City and New
York State are now planning to subsidize yet more. The
new ferries, together with the undaunted survivor, the Staten
Island Ferry, still carry less than five percent of commuters to
Manhattan. But their riders speak with the zeal of the converted.
"Before the overwhelming assault on my senses, I just like a few
Buddha-like moments," a woman told *The New York Times* for a
later feature on Arthur's ferry.

Today Arthur is cheered by a lady with these encomia: "You
know, Mr. Imperatore, I've been meaning to write you a letter.
I think this ferry service is wonderful. You've done a wonderful
job. One of these days I'll get to write you a letter. You forget to
write the good stuff."

"No," he tells her, "we get great satisfaction. People are constantly telling us. We get nice Jewish ladies who have all kinds
of suggestions and complaints." (The rider smiles; this time Arthur's hit it.) "But they always compliment us. It's wonderful."

She: "It's wonderful."

"But," Arthur begins—

The "but" is that there's still the question of how to bring
riders to the pier on the Jersey side when the street access for
private automobiles is inadequate. Arthur is ready to explain today's expansion of bus connections and his new break-even point,
but she waves that away, interrupting:

"No 'buts.' It's wonderful."

Now the ferry eases into the New York slip; the boss is aboard,
and a captain who docks with a bump will be rebuked, within
the hearing of any riders who care to listen. Here on the riverbank at 38th Street, west of Twelfth Avenue, Arthur owns a
parcel large enough for a one-room terminal, a terrace, and a
walkway down to a small pier. Wooden planter boxes, un-
painted in the California style, fill every corner and interstice
with shrubs and flowers. Arthur's parcel adjoins a city-owned
yard where the ferry's connecting buses line up according to their

various destinations in Manhattan. Beside the yard stands an old roofed ocean pier that serves as a garage for the buses. "We just signed a lease with the city," Arthur tells me. "We control all this land."

He's on an inspection tour now, watching the store. He hails the supervisor of the New York pier. "How are you?" The supervisor, dark-complexioned, pockmarked, heavily moustached, doesn't see what Arthur sees. Between two of the doors to the bus garage, just next to the path marked by white pavement striping for pedestrians to follow to the terminal, Arthur notices a storm-drain grate with half of its grid missing, leaving a gap wide enough to catch and break an ankle. "That's an error. You see, that's an error." He and I fetch orange traffic-warning cones to place over the hole. Then, from behind the shrub in a planter box at the corner of the garage, where the pedestrian strip reaches the steps to the pier, Arthur fishes out a Marlboro cigarette box that was wedged into the dirt. "Not only do they trash the place, but they're very ingenious about where they throw their trash, so that it's ever more difficult to find it. They don't just trash it, y'know. They want to make life more difficult." He's disgusted with the supervisor of the pier. The man has two strikes for today, and his batting average is already abysmal. "The guy is a phony. He could be a case history, illustrative of something," Arthur suggests to me, mindful of a writer's needs. "A phony bastard. I want to fire him."

"Why don't you?"

"Sooner or later, he'll fire himself. I want to let the organization function. It's the way I teach, and it's a way for us to evaluate our own managers." He has in mind the newly hired supervising groundskeeper on the other side of the river—the man who missed the plastic cup that Arthur stopped the Lincoln to pick up by the roadside this morning. "If I teach *him,* and *he* can inculcate, then I'm ahead. I'm in my role as teacher once again. Always, always teaching. I guess I must enjoy it."

Now a short young man in a dark three-piece suit, with slicked-back dark hair and a briefcase at one end of his right arm, accosts Arthur with his woes. He waited on Wall Street for an hour for the charter company's connecting bus. Arthur immediately shifts from fact-finding to damage control. He learns the young man's name, the name of his downtown law firm and of his home town (Fort Lee, on the Jersey side of the George Washington Bridge). The gears of Arthur's memory for names and faces revolve: he went to high school with the lawyer's aunt. He knew the man's father, too, and asks after them both. The lawyer is both flattered and mollified. But Arthur is distressed. "The charter outfit has good hardware," he tells both of us, "but their people are bad. Not bad, but mediocre."

A boat is leaving—two are at work at midday, passing each other in midstream—and we move down the walkway with the crowd. The new break-even point presses on his thoughts, and he tells a rider as we board, "We're climbing another mountain. It's a loser, a big loser now. But that's all right. It'll come."

We ride back to Jersey on the lower deck. As we dock against the *Jamestown*, Arthur stands aside from the stream of disembarking riders, then hails two dockhands and their captain as they amble off the boat on their way to lunch. "How are you, how are you?" Arthur says. "You need my genius out there?" Suntanned, dressed in white polo shirts, shorts, and sneakers, the dockhands laugh and sail past. Their captain, tall, wearing long pants and dress shoes, more attentive to the boss, halts. "How's it going?" Arthur says. "You need a haircut?" He reaches out, and between the second and third fingers of his right hand, he scissors the captain's shoulder-length hair.

Heartily, but perhaps a little irritated, too, the captain says, "New shoes today, haircut tomorrow."

"We'll take up a collection for you. All right," Arthur sighs, dismissing him.

"Think he'll get one?" I ask.

"He'll get one."

I laugh; Arthur doesn't. "He's a good guy. I was a little surprised. See, I don't like . . . to me, hair . . . ." Arthur fixes me with his soft, slightly weary brown eyes. "You used to have long hair. Huh? I remember, in the 1960s. We used to debate that in the family."

In my own memory, my appearance during my college years, when I was an occasional dinner guest at Armand's home, was nothing worse than fashionably unkempt, but my hair was long enough to trouble Arthur's working-class conservatism. He was apprehensive lest his brilliant stepson be misled by "those Harvard influences," by which he meant people like me. Even now, any appearance other than clean-cut, especially in a manager, suggests laxness and sloppiness to him. He says now, "To me, the haircut relates to the whole man. That guy's a captain, so he has to be a kind of model. He's a little chunk of the organization. He interacts. You don't live alone. Everything you do, everything you say, your whole being is involved in the body politic of the whole organization, and discipline is the key to safety and skillful operation. Because people emulate what they see around them in the way of leadership. They don't learn from reading. They don't learn from hearing. They get pounded through the senses. I've found in my experience that people learn from what they see."

Seeing a long-haired supervisor can exert the same dispiriting effect on workers as seeing plastic litter on the asphalt of the terminal or ancient grime on the panel of a trailer. Arthur agrees with Ronnie Parham's dictum that environment breeds character. "Each terminal," Arthur said in a 1974 speech to trucking managment trainees, "has a climate all its own which becomes part of the conditioning process of each working man. Thus our terminals are kept immaculately clean and in a high state of repair. When each of our men steps into our terminal each day, he becomes influenced in the way we choose him to be."

Now we stop by the terminal manager's office, a cubbyhole in the *Jamestown* with a port-hole window. Arthur gives instructions about the broken grate on the New York side. "It's a miserable little problem, but it's serious." On the way out, still troubleshooting, not forgetting the lady with the costume jewelry who couldn't convert her ticket, Arthur leans across the counter of the ticket window, face to the wicket, and chides the cashier for not knowing the new fares. "It all comes under the administrative agreements with New Jersey Transit. You have to understand it perfectly." His tone is gentle; it's not really her fault. The waterfront management should already have instructed her. "Ask them," Arthur says, adding, because he knows a scolding from him can upset an unseasoned employee for days: "It's not a big deal. The customers know we'll make it right."

As we walk up the blue-carpeted ramp that connects the *Jamestown* to land, Arthur halts in mid-sentence to me, and with raised hand hails a young couple brushing by. "How are you?" The two stop, held by Arthur's gaze. He hasn't seen them before, and with his new break-even point, new riders must be won over.

"All right," the young woman answers him sharply. "Okay," the young man grunts suspiciously. This may not be New York, but it almost is. Both of them carry briefcases and are dressed for the office buildings that shine across the water.

"Is this your first ferry ride?" Arthur says. His voice and his loose-lipped smile, which is slightly raised on the left side, express avuncular warmth and comradely New York irony.

"No," the woman says, looking at her companion.

Arthur holds out his hand. "I'm Arthur Imperatore. I own the ferry."

Now come the broad smiles: of course they have heard of the trucking magnate who started the ferry for his neighbors. The two riders say at once: "Oh, are you?" and "Nice to meet you. It really looks very nice." All shake hands, then Arthur lets them go with, "I need the business."

Arthur's frankness and gregariousness are at once delightful and challenging. In North Jersey, certainly in New York, in fact in most cities anywhere in the late twentieth century, one doesn't stop strangers for conversation the way Arthur stops strangers. Most people brush past someone wishing to accost them, but it would be next to impossible to brush past Arthur. There is nothing unsettling or nervous about the intensity of his energy; he doesn't twist or fidget, his hands are still, his voice calm and ironic, his laugh gentle. He has, rather, a mastered intensity, which, because it is disciplined, is all the more riveting.

A-P-A's vice-president for operations, Andy Park, recalled: "This is the thing that Arthur's a genius at—besides his business genius—this is the thing I've never seen anything like: his ability to get people's attention and get people to respond. Like when we were opening the Toronto terminal, we had the yacht on

Lake Ontario to entertain a boatful of customers. It was a gorgeous day, a magnificent view. Everyone was clustered around Arthur, listening to him. They didn't look at a building or a tree."

"What was he saying to them?" I asked Andy.

"He was telling stories."

For Arthur, dominating others is honorable if it is a means of leadership toward, in his phrase, 'high purpose,' and, further, if it is free of deceit. He told me on another day, "My whole life is based on trust and being trusted, trusting as best I can, and living with other people, people whom I can respect. There are times I have to exploit people. I'm not saying I'm Goody Two-Shoes. But I don't do it deliberately; I mean, I buy services from a person. I don't have to fall in love with him. But if I can, I like to. I guess that's how my heart works and how my brain works, how my stomach works. I would like to like people. I would like, if I could, to love people. I know that's not possible, universally; otherwise they'd cart me off to the looney bin. But the fact is I have this sense that ordinary but good people are the salt of the earth. They are not celebrated, not appreciated. And so I, without making words, in my actions try to show that appreciation. I will praise sometimes a lot, sometimes not enough. But I guess if there's one characteristic I have, it is to acknowledge a person, even if I don't like him, or even if I do like him a lot but don't like what he's doing on the job, let's say. I acknowledge. I try to be as truthful as I can, and sometimes that's painful. But by God people don't accuse me of doubletalk, and I don't engage in that kind of folderol. I don't just make words, that I know of. I probably talk too much at times, but that's my weakness. I suppose I like people to know where I stand."

"He is totally open and frank," Armand told me. "He tells strangers how he's been in psychotherapy for twenty years." (I myself heard him mention that during a radio interview. The psychotherapy has helped him not only to slow down and even take occasional vacations, but also to cool his temper.) "He's like a great leader of men or like a great stage comedian," Armand continued; "what others repress, he expresses. He dares to do and say what the rest of us don't dare to, because we're inhibited. He controls it, but in a specialized way."

His lack of inhibition, together with his commitment to honor, combine to create an impetuous courage that has the appearance of stubbornness and sometimes foolishness, but which, nevertheless, commands people's admiration. Bill McKernan, the Teamsters Local 617 president, was the first person to tell me of a winter morning rainstorm that flooded the North Bergen yard. (Flooding a foot deep, even two feet deep, is not uncommon at the terminal, where the water table lies just beneath the asphalt. A-P-A people call it Lake Imperatore. Crossing it, the tractors plow wakes like baleen whales.) Electrical outlets are mounted in the fences around the yard, because diesel engines need to be heated in cold weather before they will start. Heaters installed under the hood are plugged in overnight to the outlets in the fence. That morning, the wires leading to a few of the tractors were immersed in the lake, and fearing electrocution, the trucks' drivers were refusing to pull the plugs and drive. The shop steward called Bill McKernan to come over from the union office; someone else called Arthur. When Arthur arrived, he pushed past everyone else who was standing around, waded up to the fence, grabbed the plugs, yanked them out, and stalked off the lot. "Arthur's sometimes a little flaky," Bill offered as a moral, "but I'll give him credit for balls." Yet it is this same uninhibited, stubborn impetuosity, this "flakiness," that has allowed Arthur to impose his systems, create his community, and stand up to the mob.

⸻

In the Lincoln again, we drive the mile south along the riverfront to the headquarters of Arthur's real estate company, Arcorp Properties. The waterfront offices occupy one remodeled wing of a large, open, two-story structure that looks like a rusted parking garage. This is the "banana pier," built by United Fruit Company in the 1940s. Ships used to dock here bearing Central American fruit, which was then reloaded onto boxcars. Arthur parks at the south end of the pier, and we charge upstairs and down the corridor.

Compared to the Florentine library at the truckline, Arthur's office here is simple, with a sofa and armchairs along one wall, sliding doors leading out to the roof, and windows framing rectangles of Manhattan. Only the boss's desk hints at his taste for the ornate: dragons in mother-of-pearl inlay disport themselves on its teak panels. Arthur sits and punches on the intercom the number of the waterfront manager, Tom Scullen. He tells Tom to scale back the charter bus routes on the New York side. The Sixth Avenue runs should be cut out, the Wall Street runs reduced. "Address this with urgency." Then he calls Burt Trebour and instructs him to accelerate the hiring of new drivers for Arcorp Properties' own mini-buses, so that the charter buses can be replaced with the ferry's own buses and the charter contract terminated. He wants his own people on the street to ensure that no more young lawyers from Fort Lee waste an hour on a downtown streetcorner. His tone to Burt, friendly and forthright, signals that this is not the Arthur who speculates and thinks aloud, but the Arthur who's made up his mind.

Hunched forward over his desk, Arthur leafs through his pink stack of phone messages, then plows in. He calls Tony DeFino, mayor of West New York, to invite him to join the crowd on the *Imperator*, the company yacht, for the annual July Fourth cruise on New York Harbor to watch the evening's two fireworks shows (Macy's on the East River and A-P-A's own on the Hudson.) Next he phones the president of New York University, where—ever hopeful that his own inspiration can be breathed into others—Arthur is endowing a chair in entrepreneurship at the business school. He explains to the president that the money will be forthcoming upon the sale of a Manet. As he's talking, Kathleen Husoskey, his secretary, hurries in:

"Mr. Imperatore, do you want to talk to Jared Smith?"

"No. He's nothing but a pain in the ass. You can tell him so. In those words. Quote."

In her office adjacent, I can hear her say, "May I take a message?"

Arthur tells me, "He's a fundraiser."

Soon, on a new call, Arthur is stalled, too. "No," he says into the phone, "I'd prefer to wait. There's some modest urgency about this, all right? So can you give him a note and tell him I'm on? I'm a big wheel—What? Well, I don't know if I'm a bigger wheel or a smaller wheel, but I know that it's a pain in the tail to get calls through."

"Why don't you have Kathleen place your calls?" I ask him.

Arthur shakes his head, still scowling at the phone. "It takes too much time." He adds, "If any one of these people said, 'Yes sir,' I'd fall over. I'd fall over. It'd be dangerous."

Now Augie Pagnozzi, chief industrial engineer for all of Arthur's enterprises, eases in to remind Arthur that he'll be at his sister's house on the Jersey Shore for a two-week vacation. It's already Monday afternoon, but Augie still hasn't gotten away; he's wearing a pink polo shirt and blue pastel pants, but he's carrying his briefcase. He feels responsible for the overblown routing of the charter buses, because he's the one who designed the routes.

Arthur greets him with mournful exaggeration: "We got a problem with those buses. It's costing me too much money. I'm having trouble sleeping. We're getting no business. I'm going broke soon. There's a guy named Trump who's having troubles. I'm not there yet and I don't want to get there. Melosh says I'm going to end up like him. Why did I do this, Augie?"

"We didn't have enough of our own drivers," Augie reminds him.

Arthur nods. He tells Augie that he's already asked Burt to accelerate the hiring. "We'll have to move step by step."

While he's been talking with Augie, he's also been shuffling his mail, asking Kathleen about checks she's given him to sign, and talking on the phone:

"It was a great vacation," he tells whoever is on the line now. "One week in Antibes. I hated to come back. Why did I? Because I'm a schmuck. I'm sixty-six and my best friend says I ought to quit. No danger of that. I'm not quitting."

Augie is used to threading his way through a disjointed conversation with Arthur, but I have been finding it disconcerting. When I ask Armand about it later, he nods and says, "It's a way he has of controlling the agenda."

Augie's not ready for the Shore yet. He heads for a meeting with Tom Scullen, to scale back the routes. "I'll call you every day," he tells Arthur.

"Yeah, call me, Augie."

In a company with many loyal, sometimes fiercely devoted employees, Augie stands out as one who comes closest to being a personal disciple of Arthur's. He's chief industrial engineer not only of A-P-A but of the waterfront, of Arthur's other real estate ventures, and of the A-P-A subsidiaries: the truck-leasing operation, the newspaper-delivery outfits, the small truckload line. That means he goes wherever Arthur feels like sending him, including other companies that Arthur wants to help. (With Arthur's consent, Augie once advised a company which leases A-P-A trucks that they were leasing far too many.)

Like many others at A-P-A, Augie works twelve- to fourteen-hour days, but, unlike others, he works them six and even seven days a week. He's a bachelor in his forties; with his long-legged, slouched gait, his rumpled sweater-vests, his wavy gray hair, blinking gaze, and solemn mastery of intricate systems, he strikes an odd, and much-liked, figure at brisk, clean-cut, humorous A-P-A.

I interviewed Augie in his cubbyhole office on the mezzanine above the dock, while the computers under his aegis chugged out their charts and reports in the office pool outside his door. He spoke of Arthur with emotion.

"Arthur's a genius. He can read people. He knows who to kick in the ass, who to stroke, who to pat on the head. He knows I need a kick in the ass. He always give you respect. No matter who he is with—sometimes he's with famous people—he always introduces you, says what you do, how long you've been with the company. When he comes to the office, he greets everybody and remembers something about them. If he doesn't know them, he introduces himself.

"I always say I have the best job at A-P-A and I also have the worst hours. I don't want to tell you how many hours I work. If I have to come in Saturday to get the job done, I come in Saturday. If I have to come in Sunday, I come in Sunday. That's not a problem with me. I once worked twenty days straight."

I asked him, as I have others, what kept him going all those hours.

"Loyalty to Arthur. He's like a father to me. A-P-A is my family. I grew up at A-P-A." Family loyalty is a shield against executive headhunters. "A number of people have gotten offers from other companies, and for more money. But you don't go. Why? It's loyalty. There are a lot of people who are loyal to him, at all levels of the company. Not just managers. There are drivers, dockmen, secretaries, mechanics, janitors. What can I say? *You* know Arthur. Arthur's Arthur."

At A-P-A, "Arthur's Arthur" is the explanation of last resort for the boss's unexplainable contradictions: his self-taught eloquence, his brilliant mistakes, his fine tastes in things and simple tastes in people, his drive for fortune and his readiness to share it, his stubbornness and restiveness, his domineering gentleness, his crafty furies.

On another occasion, Augie told me, "A-P-A is my career, yes, but it's really my life. People think I'm crazy. Arthur calls me in the middle of the night. But he also calls me on Christmas morning."

He told me that after that twenty-day stint of work—Arthur had loaned him to *The New York Times,* to advise the newspaper's managers how to rationalize their delivery systems—Arthur then asked him to fly to Chicago to scout out a failing truckline as a possible acquisition. Exhausted, Augie unburdened himself to Armand, who told him not to go. Armand said he'd call Arthur on Augie's behalf, but then didn't get to it. A few days later, Arthur called Augie.

"How was Chicago?"

"I didn't go."

Then Augie was summoned to the waterfront, "and Arthur dressed me up one side and then down the other in case he missed any spots. 'When I say do something, you do it.' "

"Didn't you tell him?" I asked.

No; Augie said nothing to Arthur about Armand's intervention. He returned to A-P-A, where he passed Armand on the stairs, and Armand said, "Oh, I got to call Arthur on that Chicago trip." "Yeah," was all Augie said. Armand made the call. That night, Arthur called Augie at home to apologize. "Why didn't you tell me?"

Augie's presence has calmed Arthur now, as I suspect it often does. Arthur's relieved, too, that the overreaching contract with the charter line will now be curtailed. He's ready to return reporters' calls.

First a local weekly, to field questions about traffic on River Road. "You little squirt, what do you want?—Naah, I got a lot of affection for you. I think you write very well; that's why I called you back."

Next a *Times* editor, who has an apology that the story on this morning's dockside ribbon-cutting will not make the paper. To him, Arthur's response is respectful and formal. "I appreciate your going to this length. There was a *Times* reporter here. I shouldn't have called anyway, but dammit, I think it's a story." Even though Arthur's trucks and drivers deliver the *Times*, and even though he's often a guest on the fourteenth floor to advise the newspaper's executives about their troubled relations with their labor, the educated men on 43rd Street still intimidate the trucker from North Bergen. He cannot feel that he belongs on their social level—which is why he has none of the trouble with his workers that they have with theirs.

We're done here for today. Arthur sighs, "There's nothing on my desk that requires me to work or to do some good for the world. It's all bullshit." As we make our way downstairs to the Lincoln, he adds, a little sadly, "I don't have much to do these days."

As Arthur drives us toward the north gate of the property, a young man in an old car is tailgating us. To discourage speeding, reduce liability, and encourage mutual respect, Arthur has had speed-bumps set in the waterfront streets, but the tailgater has less patience than the thirty-mile-per-hour speed limit calls for. Arthur is fuming. He's hunched over the wheel, gripping it with both hands. "This is what drives me crazy." His anger may compromise his caution, but it doesn't dull his craftiness. He keeps driving till he's just past an unmanned guardshack in the middle of the street, then halts. The tailgater stops short beside the shack; to get around Arthur now, he'll have to back up and drive around the shack. Before he can, Arthur whirls out of the Lincoln, leans through the tailgater's open window, and berates him for reckless driving on private property. The man nods meekly. As quickly as he left it, Arthur is back in the Lincoln. It isn't the first time he has confronted traffic violators, here and on the New York side. "I believe in the rules," he tells me. "I'm lucky I haven't gotten killed."

In fact, Arthur is lucky, in the way that many people who succeed in carving circumstances according to their will have the luck, or the wit, to be present when circumstances are ready. In 1960, when Arthur determined after the Reading snowstorm to eschew money for the sake of money and to concentrate on quality, as he says, the American economy was prepared to reward brains and drive in the trucking industry. Manufacturing was in ascendance, while the railroads were in decline. Washington had just undertaken the largest road-building project in human history. The new diesel tractors were far more powerful and efficient than their predecessors. At the same time, a new generation of truckmen like Harold Petsch, Jr., about ten years younger than Arthur, and Bill McKernan, about ten years older, was growing up around him, not only on the dock and behind the wheel, but in the union. After Arthur's wardances on the North Bergen dock and the wildcat strikes of the 1950s, A-P-A's relations with the Teamsters evolved from war to truce, and from truce to a friendly, although still wary, alliance. The company's growth owes as much to its successful relations with the union as to its skillful exploitation of the interstates and the diesel engine.

In 1957, Bill McKernan ran for president of Local 617 and unseated the old guard. In 1991, now seventy-four, thin and bespectacled, with a gravelly voice, a puckish smile, and a full head of white hair that flops over his forehead in schoolboyish bangs, Bill is still president. He began in the Teamsters in the 1930s as a cold-storage warehouseman. "I got shot up in the war and came back as a clerk, and I organized the office," he told me, with a still-proud smile, in an interview at Local 617's headquarters on Central Avenue in Jersey City. Like many other younger union men in the 1950s, Bill had not been entranced with the chair throwing and nose breaking that, he says, was the rule at union meetings. "The members would look up to the arrogant

and boisterous guys in the black shoes and black hat and tie,"
he told me. " 'Here comes a gangster who'll stand up to the
boss.' " At the same time, the gangster union officers were collecting dues in the bars and then denying the dues had been
paid. Bill was elected on a campaign promise to install, in the
union office, a cash register that would print receipts. Loan
sharking, too—usurous loans forced on members by threats of
violence—was rife in Local 617, as it commonly is in crooked
union locals, and not only in the Teamsters. The old shop stewards "would take the dues and give out loans and take care of
the boys," Bill said (by "the boys" he meant the mob). In order
to force out the crooked henchmen of the old guard, Bill also
initiated direct election of the shop stewards, who represent the
workers at each job site.

During the same years, at the Teamsters International, a partial reform was gathering force under the presidency of Jimmy
Hoffa. Hoffa's ambition was to organize the entire American
trucking industry under a single contract. He envisioned a single
code of wages, benefits, work rules, and grievance processes,
and uniform procedures for hiring, dismissal, and seniority for
all trucklines and their employees throughout the country. In
the 1950s, his goal was achieved in his own Midwestern base.
In the 1960s, he turned his focus to the autonomous, fragmented
locals of the Northeast.

"There were 150 different agreements in the East in the 1950s,"
Walter Shea, Hoffa's aide, and later a vice-president of the International, recalled when I interviewed him. "I went with Hoffa
up and down the East Coast from Maine to Baltimore to persuade the locals to agree to a national contract. Hoffa was a master. He charmed the local union powers. They were awed by his
knowledge of it all. He went from 6:00 A.M. to 1:00 A.M., a
hundred meetings a day. It was his pet rock, his obsession." In
1964 his barnstorming was rewarded with the signing of the first
National Master Freight Agreement. The National Agreement has
continued to be renewed every three years; the latest contract
runs from April, 1991, through March, 1994. In the mid-1970s—
at the height of the Teasmsters' power and at the apogee of the
union's membership, at over two million—the National Master

Freight Agreement covered 302,000 drivers, dockworkers, and mechanics working for 1,700 trucklines, both truckload and less-than-truckload. (Workers for the United Parcel Service—with 140,000 members the largest single Teamster employer—are covered by a separate contract.)

Hoffa's National Master Freight Agreement imposed a coherent and uniform code of work rules and uniform scale of labor costs on Arthur and on all his competitors. It was, and in much of the less-than-truckload sector still is, a form of regulation that complemented the now-defunct government regulation of freight prices and routes. The National Agreement "provided stability and made the game easy to follow. It made everyone equal," Harold Petsch said when I interviewed him. "I don't think the trucking industry would have grown after the war by leaps and bounds the way it did without the Teamsters."

But Hoffa's reforms were only partial, because in his drive for unification he allied himself not with union socialists but with the Mafia. Arthur was involved in the negotiations for the National Agreements in the sixties and seventies, just as Armand has been more recently; Arthur recalls, "Hoffa was a very smart guy and a strange man. He was brilliant. He was honest in some parts, and corrupt in others, a real paradox." In order to accumulate power and to persuade the locals to join in a National Agreement, Hoffa for his part agreed to accommodate the mob, which, as Arthur says, "controlled anything they wanted to." What the mob wanted to control above all was the union pension funds. In particular, the mob coveted the consolidated Central States Pension Fund, then and now the largest employment benefit fund controlled by the union. With over a billion dollars in assets available for lending during the 1970s, the Central States Pension Fund was in effect a large bank operating with virtually no regulatory control. The fund became a source of venture capital for organized crime. It built Las Vegas.

In New Jersey, the union pension fund that covered A-P-A employees was controlled by Tony Provenzano's crime organization based in Local 560. In 1974, however, Bill McKernan succeeded in creating for Local 617 members a separate pension fund outside of Tony Pro's control. Nowadays, the independent Local

617 funds are invested in stock and bond accounts managed by financial advisors from the Philadelphia Main Line, and Armand and Burt Trebour sit on the funds' board as employer representatives. Unlike many Teamster funds, Local 617's health fund is solvent and its pension fund is fully funded. (Armand has some background as a pension-fund watchdog. In 1974, as an assistant prosecutor for Hudson County, he put five county pension commissioners, including the county supervisor, behind bars for pension fraud.)

This alliance of an honest company with an honest union local had to be recreated each time A-P-A expanded into a new area. During the 1960s, A-P-A established terminals in Scranton, Allentown, Philadelphia, and Lancaster, in Pennsylvania; in Albany and in Newburgh, which is halfway between New York and Albany on the Hudson; in Boston; and in Old Bethpage, Long Island. Where the local was corrupt, Arthur had to demonstrate to the union officials that A-P-A would not strike deals. In every case, whatever the local's morals, the employees themselves had to be persuaded to work according to A-P-A's standards, to be measured, badgered, and driven. The obvious way to escape the need to convert the local people—to build an entirely new A-P-A terminal in the new area and to man it with transplanted North Bergen believers—was not usually possible under federal trucking regulations as they existed before 1980. Expansion was generally feasible only through purchase of an existing company, and the existing workforce came with the deal.

As we cross the ridge now on 79th Street in North Bergen on our way back to A-P-A, I ask Arthur about his company's expansion into new union territories.

He's ready with a narrative about his move into New England. "That's an interesting story—one night in Boston with Billy McCarthy," he tells me. "I went up when I bought that company there, Henry Jenkins Transportation, didn't I ever tell you that story? I went up to see McCarthy. I sat with him and Jenkins and a guy from the First National Bank of Boston, just the four of us. By then Jenkins was almost bankrupt, and the bank had called me to see if we were willing to go to Boston. The New England area was always the area in which good companies founder. So I was unwilling. But I finally decided to review this Jenkins thing. So I went up to see McCarthy."

The Billy McCarthy in Arthur's story is William J. McCarthy, who was president of Teamsters Local 25 in Boston from 1956 to 1991, when he was unseated by a local reformer, George Cashman. McCarthy eventually rose to the presidency of the Teamsters International, serving from 1988 to early 1992, when he retired under a consent decree with the United States Department of Justice and was replaced with the election of another reformer, Ron Carey. McCarthy's name retains the old-country pronunciation: "M'Cartie."

Arthur leans forward over the steering wheel, the better to pound the rim when required. In his story, it was June, 1967. Arthur was 41, McCarthy 47. "I said to Billy, 'Do you know who I am?' So, y'know, these guys never quite answer you. They use the language of grunts, grimaces, nonverbal, unless they really want you to know something, in which event the flow of language can be very rich and colorful. Well, he had to know who I was. People would talk about how we treat our workers. That is the Achilles' heel of any corrupt union person. If you have a good relationship with the working employees, especially our kind of employee, they stay with you long-term, they get to know you. You have to trust them, they have to trust the employer. You have to build that if you can, you build respect, you build a good working relationship, and that gets around. That's telegraphed all over the industry. And McCarthy would have gotten to know that; anybody would. So he was already aware that he couldn't muscle us. And they don't really care for that shit, anyway. It's better for them, you see, if an employer's tough enough to stand up to guys.

"So I said, 'Listen. I'm going to tell you who I am and what I do and the way I want to operate in New England.' I said, 'I don't want any bullshit.' I said, 'I know you hate the Guineas from New York, you hate the Jews from New York. I'm a Guinea from New York, and I'm telling you how I operate. I know this fucking business as well as anybody in shoes, and I know how to manage men. And one thing I'll do up here is live with the agreement. I'll make it work. I cut no corners. But I don't want any bullshit.' I said, 'I just don't want any militation, any militancy on your part. If I do what I'm supposed to do, I will live with my people, they will become my allies, and they will become my biggest supporters. Just stay the hell out of my hair.' He agreed to that. So we were ready to do the deal.

"Now, before we took over the operation, we had a meeting. You ever hear the story of that? A great meeting. I bused all these people in the Jenkins company to Boston, to 1200 Beacon Street, for a Saturday meeting. I brought up fourteen of our people to meet them. I brought up truck drivers, dockmen, and mechanics. I brought up some really wonderful old guys, some young guys. We had about 400 men in that room. Jenkins had five terminals, so I say 400, maybe it was 350, I mean it was a big group. I gave a long speech. I told them about all our systems of control, I told them we have these ways of checking on productivity and that's what we sell.

"I said, 'I ain't coming unless you guys tell me to come. Now I'm telling you just what you're going to get into when you associate with me.' I told them how we run the company, with honesty, the whole philosophy, and I told them specifically about the systems. And then some fellow way in the back raised his hand. I think his name was Jimmy Punch. He became one of our staunchest allies. He said, 'Listen. Imperatore, I don't like this idea. I'm an honest man.'—I'd told him, y'see, how honest we were, how if people do their work they don't ever have to worry—"

I interrupt Arthur, "The guy was saying, 'Why all these systems?' How come you weren't just going to trust him, without having to measure him?"

Arthur nods. "He was asking, 'How come you don't trust me?' So I said to him, 'What did I just tell you?' I said, 'What's your name?' He said, 'Jimmy Punch.' I said, 'What did I just tell you? that if you're making a record, it's on the *record*, and if we're competent people, and we don't want trouble—we know how to make it for you when you need trouble—but if we have good people, and you're one of them, and you're doing your work, then what are these wonderful systems of ours going to tell us?' "

The systems would reveal for all to see, Arthur was saying, who the good workers were, and the trust that developed between workers and managers would stand on an objective basis, where it would be more likely to last.

"So after about two hours of this—I really know how to do this stuff on my feet—I said, 'Look, I'm a very good salesman. Don't believe anything I said for now. I've brought fourteen guys up here.' I introduced them. I said, 'We got some that are great, we got some old ballbusters ["ballbusters" is labor parlance for militants], we got some mechanics, we got some dockmen, some of the best employees in the company and some of the worst, some of the most militant.' I brought a cross-section. I said, 'Now I'm clearing out of the room, and I'm gonna let you ask these fellas what kind of an outfit we are, what kind of a company we run, what kind of people we are, what kind of a man I am, whether you can trust me, and you tell me when I come back in here whether you want us. You don't want us, we're clearing the hell out. We got no deal. You want us, you buy us on this basis. Right?' We left them in there for an hour or so, and that was it. 'Okay, we'll take you.' So we made the deal."

"What if they'd said no?"

Arthur shakes his head with absolute negation. "I would have walked. I would not have done the deal. Because I know working people. I knew by then, that they've got to like you. They got to want you. They got to want to work. They got to believe in you to some degree. Now they're very cynical, they're very suspicious, y'know, and they can't be fooled easily. You can fool them once. Even the perception of injustice is remembered for decades. You screw them once and they never forget it. But if you can reach them—I always could reach them.

"So, after that meeting—we'd bused them all in, or paid their way if they drove, I forget how the hell we did it, but they all got there—we had a party, a dinner, for something like 400 or 450 people, before they were our employees, boozing it up with the guys at the bar. I spotted a couple of guys that night, a couple of real wild men, political operatives, in the local union. I forget the names. They were two Irishmen. One was a big heavyset guy, he was a sergeant-at-arms at Local 25. He got drunk. There was another guy, a real wily Irishman, and he was running for trusteeship or something like that in the local. I knew they were Billy McCarthy's henchmen, because that's the way McCarthy ran the local.

"So we do the deal. That first meeting took place in June, and it took six, eight, ten weeks to get the papers filed and get the temporary authority to begin to operate from the ICC. We took over the operation on a Monday morning in September. We went crazy with the volume. We didn't have the capacity or the capability in North Bergen. The freight backed up, customers were unhappy, and we lost a lot of business. We had to build a big addition to the dock. Three months went by. We'd finally got control of it. We were operating out of the old Braintree, Mass., terminal. And in December I got a call late at night to tell me that the big heavyset guy I'd spotted at the party at 1200 Beacon Street had left the property, got drunk, came back to the property in his own car, got caught stealing gas; a dispatcher who saw him challenged him, fired him, and he was going to kill this guy with a two-by-four. He committed four cardinal sins."

Cardinal sins, in labor parlance, are work-rule violations meriting immediate dismissal: in this case, abandonment of work, drunkenness, theft, and assault.

"He took a twobie, y'know? This was the way that business was run, the whole industry up there. The Teamsters ran the various companies. Next morning I called Billy McCarthy up. I said, 'Billy, your man'—I forget his name." Arthur frowns. Forgetting even one of the myriad names in his mental file bugs him. He lets it go. "Well, it was twenty-five years ago. I said, 'Billy, your man did the following. You know who I'm talking about, right? I know he's one of your henchmen. Well, he did one, two, three, four.'

"Billy said, 'What'd you do to him?'

"I said, 'We fired him.' I said, 'I'll tell you what, Billy, do you remember what I told you about militating? Billy, I'm just telling you that what I told you still goes. That man will never set foot on. . . .'

"He said, 'You'll have to arbitrate it.'

"I said, 'We'll arbitrate it, that's part of the agreement. But he'll never set foot on our property again.' I said, 'You get it, Billy?' So he got fired, it was upheld in arbitration, and that was it. But otherwise, if you weren't that tough, they'd foist him back on you, and then you'd have the the beginning of a real den of iniquity."

A single confrontation with the union local could only mark a beginning. Truly absorbing Henry Jenkins Transportation into A-P-A would involve teaching its employees to work, walk, and think like A-P-A employees. That, Arthur says, took seven years. Converting unbelievers at Sanborn's Motor Express, a Maine-based company which A-P-A bought in 1986, has taken almost as long. It is still possible to identify a few unreconstructed Sanborn's road drivers by their slowness of amble across the North Bergen yard.

In the spring of 1992, A-P-A's most ambitious missionary campaign began with the purchase of two wholesale newspaper delivery companies, Westfair Newspaper Distributors in Westchester and Newspaper Distributors Company on Long Island. The purchase was made at the suggestion of *The New York Times* Company. The wholesalers, which were responsible for delivery of the *Times* and other newspapers in their areas, had lost control of their labor. As an indirect result, the *Times* had not been able to open a new, automated printing plant in Edison, New Jersey because the newspaper's printers had threatened to strike over lost jobs, and the delivery drivers had pledged to honor the picket lines. Newspaper publishers can bargain with their printers, but they have long been afraid to bargain with their delivery drivers. As an item of value, newspapers are even more perishable than fresh fruit, and so the delivery drivers hold the trump cards.

Newspaper drivers in New York are organized by the Newspaper and Mail Deliverers' Union of New York and Vicinity, an independent local with no ties to the Teamsters, but with their own connection to the Bonanno Mafia family. The old labor agreement with the newspaper wholesalers was a corrupt union's dream. No management representatives, not even the owner, were allowed on the shop floor, and if any appeared, the work would stop. The foremen, who were union members, did the hiring and the nightly manning, and it was standard practice to send trucks out only one-fourth full, so that more men could work. It was also standard practice, if illegal, for drivers to pay friends and relatives to sign in and drive their runs for them. The legitimate drivers had room to make money off their substitutes, because the contract specified work for eight hours, at twenty-four dollars an hour, plus a guarantee of overtime, even though most runs took even less than eight hours to drive. Some runs took six hours and paid for twelve. The senior drivers worked three and a half hours a night and earned $80,000 a year. They treated their jobs as moonlighting and held other jobs or ran small businesses. The no-management-allowed contract was also an unspoken green light for pilfering of newspapers for resale. (In November, 1992, the Manhattan District Attorney issued indictments on state racketeering charges to twenty-nine people connected with the Newspaper Deliverers' Union, including three men identified as members of the Mafia. The union itself was indicted on charges of racketeering, stealing newspapers, bribery, belonging to a criminal enterprise, and criminal contempt.)

In February, 1992, when A-P-A, through its subsidiary, Imperial Delivery Service, agreed to purchase the two wholesalers, Arthur, Armand, and their vice-president for labor, Burt Trebour, offered the newspaper drivers a new contract. According to its terms, the drivers would be paid the same wages as before, but management supervisors would be allowed on the floor, the delivery routes would be manned according to need, wages would be paid according to hours actually worked, and the union would agree not to support strikes by other unions when the *Times* opened its new printing plant. When the sale closed in May and the drivers became Imperial Delivery Service employees, they struck. Burt had scab drivers ready. In the worst of the ensuing violence, one of the strikebreakers was critically injured by a rock thrown at his head. Pete Leota, who had left City Dispatch to supervise the newspaper wholesaler's terminal in Long Island, went nowhere without a bodyguard. After three weeks, the union ended its strike and ratified the new contract. Two months after the settlement, more than half of the drivers, unaccustomed to delivering papers for eight hours, five nights a week, had accepted A-P-A's offer of a severance package and had quit.

A-P-A's dispute with the newspaper drivers' union was closely reported in the New York metropolitan press—although the corrupting excesses of the old labor agreement went largely unmentioned, whether in deference to the union's power or because of an embarrassed reluctance to admit how thoroughly the newspapers had capitulated in the past. In the press reports, A-P-A sometimes appeared in an anti-union light, especially because it had hired scab replacements to force a settlement. Nevertheless, A-P-A's goal in the dispute was not expulsion of the union but an evenhanded agreement. The use of scabs was a feint in a sharp-weaponed game that the newspapers themselves had never dared to play. In truth—like many American corporations that have, since World War II, established a *modus vivendi* with craft unions—A-P-A is in effect pro-union. The labor agreements in established industries are stabilizers and regulators, particularly in regard to work rules and discipline. For the maintenance of labor peace, consistent operations, and a predictable level of productivity, the honest employer is as dependent on dispassionate enforcement of the labor contract as are the employees and the honest union. In Arthur's standoff of wills with Billy McCarthy, it was Arthur, not Billy, who was demanding that the labor agreement be honored.

The chief duties of a union official, as Bill McKernan of Local 617 expounded them to me, are negotiating agreements, organizing nonunion workplaces, and resolving disputes that arise when an agreement has been violated. The last duty consumes by far the most time. When I called on Bill in his Jersey City office—a mostly bare floor, with a bookcase stacked with Teamster magazines, a free-standing coat-and-hat rack, two visitors' chairs and his own desk—Bill was on the phone with an employer concerning five missing cartons of fruit juice. The worker in question, a food-delivery driver and Local 617 member, had unloaded the cartons into a car parked on the street, evidently a case of pilfering. I remembered Harold Petsch saying (Harold now works for Bill as Local 617's business agent) "The hardest thing is when the employee is wrong." Bill hung up after making an appointment for a hearing on the employee's dismissal. "It's a weird case," Bill commented, because when food-delivery drivers pilfer, it's usually something expensive, like coffee or lobster tails. Bill shook his boyish white bangs in bemusement. Why fruit juice?

But, he explained, "You got to go to bat for them. You kiss ass trying to get them back in the door. Defending workers is a big part of our job. The average worker doesn't need a union to defend him. I spend ninety percent of my time defending stiffs, who are ten percent of the workforce. Ninety percent of my calls are for workers who have done something wrong, or else their bosses allege they've done something wrong.

"The bosses are stiffs, too," Bill continued. "For example, we have members at a cold-storage firm, which was bought by a European company, and the new management drives them with a whip. The contract gives men twenty minutes in the warm-up room, and they were taking thirty minutes, so the company shut the room down. I got it open again and then they closed it again. So now it's a contract dispute and it'll go before the National Labor Relations Board. That company's had five managers in five years. We've never had a chance to build up a relationship with management. There's a constant turmoil in their supervision and no consistency in their work rules. New supervisors come in very arrogant and abusive, calling men older than them 'You so-and-so snails.' " (Bill has a mild tongue and edits.)

Sometimes it's not clear who's wrong. "Harold's up at A-P-A once a week for a grievance. He's up there today for a guy who got a warning for leaving the motor running at a stop. Other companies don't care about that." He added, "Other companies' drivers could be standing around smoking, kicking tires, and bullshitting till 10:30 in the morning."

"For discipline there's a script," John Occhiogrosso told me, when I asked him about contract enforcement at A-P-A. "First it's a warning, then a one-day suspension, then three days which you fight down to one, then one week, two weeks, et cetera." (John has never been suspended.) By "et cetera" he meant dismissal, which the union will almost always take to arbitration. Dismissal will be upheld for a cardinal sin such as drunkenness or theft or failure to report an accident, or for accumulated lesser infractions. The accumulation must be proximate; warnings are expunged after six months if there are no further difficulties.

Warnings at first are merely spoken and come from the supervisor, or from the line manager, like Vinny Carnavale for city drivers or Sam Chominksy for night dockmen. The next step is a written warning from the Personnel Department, signed by the line manager. Here are examples of the admonitory prose of Joe Whelan, the personnel director, with all the wordprocessor boilerplate intact, but with the names, addresses, and dates changed.

First, a warning for laxness:

Mr. Jack Camp
1320 16th Street
Hoboken, NJ

Dear Mr. Camp:

On August 11, 1990, you were observed starting your ten (10) minute coffee break at 8:00 A.M. At 8:15 A.M. you were observed again and found to still be on your coffee break which extended your break by five (5) minutes.

You have been warned verbally in the past that extending your coffee break constitutes theft of time. As you are aware, theft of time is a serious violation.

This letter will serve to warn you that any recurrence of this type on your part will result in more severe disciplinary action.

Sincerely,

Vincent Carnavale
City Operations Manager

Second, a warning for the more serious lapse of not being good at the minutiae:

Mr. Sylvio Contini
213 Central Avenue, Apt. 114
Jersey City, NJ

Dear Mr. Contini:

On May 13, 1991 a review of your work assignment for the previous day reveals that you signed for a 21 lot on unit #4438 moving from Calibrated Associates in Teaneck, NJ consigned to

Dennison Industries, King of Prussia, PA. Our records indicate that at the time of unloading 20 pieces were checked off your unit, leaving this shipment 1 piece short. In contacting the shipper, we were advised that the freight was left behind. It is quite obvious that you are not checking your freight properly at the time of pick-up.

This letter will serve as warning that repetition of the above will result in disciplinary action.

Sincerely,

Vincent Carnavale
City Operations Manager

Third, for discourtesy to a customer, a three-day suspension, presumably to be fought down to one:

Mr. Dave Panacek
22 Rolling Hills Lane
Toms River, NJ

Dear Mr. Panacek:

On February 12, 1992, you were dispatched on a delivery with unit #5492, a trailerload consigned to Vineburg Corporation, in Cranbury, New Jersey. You arrived at Vineburg just prior to 8:00 A.M. and were backed into door #13. You were observed by the receiving supervisor at Vineburg at around 8:15 A.M. standing on their dock reading a paperback book. You were confronted by the supervisor and told that you were not permitted to be reading a book on their platform and you were instructed to return the book back to your tractor. You responded, "I can read this book in the back of my trailer," displaying a discourteous, unprofessional, and lackadaisical attitude. Since you failed to follow the instructions given to you from our customer and projected such a poor and negative attitude, the load was refused and had to be returned to the North Bergen terminal.

We have received a letter from this valued customer, who we deliver to on a weekly basis, advising us that since this was not the first incident and that there have been previous problems with your attitude at this customer, you have been banned perma-nently from this location.

I need not remind you, Mr. Panacek, that we are in the business of servicing customers who are the life-blood of our organization and quite frankly are directly responsible for seeing that you get a paycheck on a weekly basis. You actions and attitude are deplorable and cannot and will not be tolerated. It is attitudes such as yours that have put many fine organziation out of business and we will not let that happen to A-P-A Transport Corp.

In light of the above, be advised that you are hereby suspended for a period of three days. You will serve your suspension on March 10, 11, and 12, 1992. You are also warned that if there is not an immediate improvement in your attitude and if there is ever a recurrence of the above, you will be subject to more severe disciplinary action up to and including discharge.

Mr. Panacek, I strongly suggest that if you intend to remain in the employ of this company, you had best heed the warning and report to work with a changed attitude.

Vincent Carnavale
City Operations Manager

Last, a dismissal for abandonment of work:

Mr. Howard Smythe
27 Inverness Court
Highland Hills, NJ

Dear Mr. Smythe:

On June 2, 1991, you were issued a warning letter advising you of a three-day suspension for your involvement in a theft of time. You served this suspension on July 6, 7, and 8, 1991.

On June 7, you were issued a warning letter regarding your insubordination.

On July 9 you called the city dispatch office and stated the following: "Since you didn't need me the last three days, I'm not coming in today." You were given a direct work order that since you were not sick you were to report for work.

Since you failed to follow a direct work order and never showed for work as instructed, your actions are considered job abandonment. As such, be advised that your name has been removed from the seniority list of the North Bergen terminal. You are no longer in the employ of this company.

All monies due you will be released upon your returning company property.

Vincent Carnavale
City Operations Manager

"Every day of my working life," Burt Trebour told me, "one employee gets a warning." (In 1992, there were 1,800 people on the truckline's payroll.)

Sometimes a warning is accompanied by testing and retraining by one of Augie Pagnozzi's engineers. When I rode with Tony DeRosa, some of the men on the shippers' docks thought at first that I was a time-study man, and I cost Tony some ribbing. (Arm around Tony's shoulder: "Lemme tell you, this guy's terrible."— Serious, deadpan: "This DeRosa is the worst driver who picks up here.") But that was joking about a popular driver; in reality, retraining can be a humiliation. "Like one dockman," Augie told me, "his supervisor told me he had requested an engineer to watch the man work on the dock. The man said to his supervisor, 'Don't embarrass me. I don't want to be embarrassed. I'll improve my productivity.' The supervisor said, 'Okay, I'll give you two weeks to show me.' And the guy performed. We never sent the engineer. Usually a warning letter, a confrontation is enough. But sometimes you have to have a sacrificial lamb."

The cold tone of the warning letters, the ubiquity and exhaustiveness of the work rules, the monitoring clocks under the seat, the long hours, the flinty voice from dispatch over the radio— "All day long you did diddly. Let's have a change of attitude and then you'll get home early"—in short, the hard side of Arthur's personality, which, over the years, has translated itself into the hard side of the institution he built: how can that exist in a company that calls itself a family, that inspires loyalty and devotion, that union officials say is the hardest truckline to work for and also the best? "Sometimes they seem to be talking out of both sides of their mouth," George Cashman, the new president of Local 25 in Boston, told me. "On the one hand they're loving and compassionate, on the other hand they're hard and vindictive."

The paradox exists in schools, in monasteries, in the military, in sports teams, in any institution where rules of behavior can be strict and comprehensive. People can be content and can flourish in such settings, but only under certain conditions which ensure that the conditions of membership are humane. In the first place, the insitution must have a clear purpose, and the rules must manifestly further the purpose: in A-P-A's case, to move freight and make a living. The rules must be clearly stated, not impractically numerous, and not subject to arbitrary change;

in A-P-A's case, that is the function of the labor agreement. Finally, enforcement must be public, consistent, fair, and allow for appeal and for exception; in other words, there must be due process: a grievance procedure. All this requires restraints upon the rules, upon the rule-makers, and upon the rule-enforcers. In other words, there must be regulation of the regulators. This is the union's role. Without such an external, even adversarial, regulator, a zealous company—indeed a goal-driven community of any kind—can become oppressive and even destructive of its individual members. It is no accident that some of the bitterest strikes in nineteenth-century Britain and America took place in company towns that had been founded in the utopian tradition of Robert Owen and Francis Cabot Lowell. Without external restraints, utopias can become tyrannies.

I heard this view expressed best by George Cashman, the reformer who in 1991 unseated Billy McCarthy as president of Teamsters Local 25. The local is headquartered in Charlestown, the old Irish and Italian working-class enclave in North Boston, in a two-story pre-World-War-I red-brick across the street from an enormous defunct candy factory. I spoke with George at the conference table in the dark-paneled, leather-armchaired office from which Billy McCarthy had reigned for thirty-five years. A burly, dark-bearded working-class idealist, George had been a business agent for Local 25 before becoming its president, and he had been in charge of the union's relations with A-P-A's second-largest terminal, in Canton, south of Boston. He outlined for me his understanding of the soft and the hard, the light and the dark of a rule-based community like A-P-A. He took notes on my questions and his answers on a yellow legal pad as we spoke.

"Arthur's presence is still in the company," George said. "He's like a very strict, distant, hardworking father. He has managed a tremendous psychological thing. He treats it as a family. He has his employees in this psychological mode that if they didn't take that extra step, that extra inch, they'd fail him *and* themselves. You have to fit that psychological mold to be hired. Like the Marines: they're looking for a few good men. They're told they get respect. I don't know that they get it, but it's understood that there's a distinction. Those guys!" Here George put down his pen and shook his head. "They won't even stop for coffee. So they never get too close to others in the industry. They lack a craft solidarity. They have an A-P-A solidarity, but it's not horizontal, it's vertical.

"But it's been beneficial to him and to them," George continued, "because it has provided security, and the business has grown. They've managed to survive in a market that has devoured itself. It's due to Arthur's style. But there's a psychological toll. Keep them whipped, keep their nose to the ground, and just when they're about down, he sends them a box of chocolates, and that keeps them going. But in this difficult economic environment, especially for trucking, it may be the only thing that works."

George is not a believer. On the one hand, he understands A-P-A's zeal. "I have a similar ethic," he told me. "I'm a strict father, and my kids know I'm on a mission. If you reach one level in this business, you have to strive for the next level. You never sleep in this business if you're a leader. I don't stop. You rest thinking all the time." Yet, in A-P-A's case, he sees the dangers of too much zeal, and is uncomfortable when he sees it imposed on workers who are not leaders. To keep the zeal within bounds is the union's charge. "I see our role as keeping them in check," George said, when I asked him what the union could do in a company where the vectors of loyalty are vertical. "And I think they respect the fact that we keep them in check. There's a chess game going on. Their hard side is too much compared to their soft, and in their desire to win every game, sometimes they miss what people are trying to say. So we've had some heated debates. The fight goes on. But friendly relations continue. It's like two brothers, one Democratic, one Republican."

In fact, George told me that if it had not been for his respect for A-P-A, and in particular for Burt Trebour, who telephoned George on my behalf, he would not have granted my request for an interview. (Bill McKernan was equally reluctant.) Thus George's yellow legal pad. Both men are well aware that American journalists, publishers, and broadcasters confine their attention to the interests and values of the professional classes, and that stories about craft unions appear rarely, except when white collar interests are challenged or titillated by a strike or a scandal. Little good is reported about the Teamsters. Bill McKernan was ready to talk with me only after I attended a pension fund meeting that he chaired. When he saw that Burt and Armand had accepted my presence and my clipboard, he said, when I asked for an appointment, "Sure. You're a friend of friends, right?"

For union officials, A-P-A's zeal requires attentiveness and vigor in their own role of regulator. Harold Petsch told me: "At first Arthur had his bouts with the union, but later he learned to use the contract to his advantage. He goes by the book, which is not to say it's never exceeded, but most companies are very sloppy in following the book. A-P-A's going by the book has forced me to be strict, to know the book, and to be good at my work in my second career as a union official. My meetings with management over there always have a problem-solving approach, although sometimes you can't come to an agreement, especially on discharge questions, and then you go to state mediation."

For their own part, A-P-A executives justify the sternness of the management style on the grounds that it is based on honesty. In showing me the disciplinary letters, Joe Whelan said of their tough tone: "It's a question of credibility. We don't play games. When someone doesn't perform, they're confronted. When they're told something, it's fact. When we're wrong, we admit it. We don't come from left field."

Armand said: "You don't say yes to humor people and then deny you've said that. That's a style in many places, but not here. We've been successful here because our marching orders are very clear. No one says he didn't have to do something this way before."

The importance of straightforwardness and consistency is often overlooked by corporate managers. They themselves thrive on uncertainty and risk, or at least they accept uncertainty and risk as unavoidable in a business career. It is easy for them to forget, then, or to dismiss as unimportant, the opposite needs of working people, who want above all to know where they stand. In exchange for the remunerative uncertainties of a career in management, working people settle for security, and very often prefer it. They count not only on job security, which is entitlement to continued employment, but on the security of stable work rules. Thus management poisons its relations with labor most of all by the creation of doubt and distrust—agreeing to one thing and doing another, promising X and performing Y, whether out of greed, or indecisiveness and lack of courage, or simply ignorance of the psychological needs of their own workers. What employees respect about Arthur and his successors, probably more than anything else, therefore, is their honesty. Their strict and nitpicking enforcement by the book is preferable by far to laxness and favoritism, to smugness and deviousness. A-P-A line workers have told me: "You do your job, they leave you alone."

Nevertheless, rule-based conduct can flourish only if the rules can be set aside when they conflict with an individual's need. "You have to know how to bend," Armand said, and he offered this example: "There was a driver who wanted a personal day on the Monday after his vacation, to fly to the West Indies to visit his ill father. He got a waiver from Joe Whelan. In most companies, he'd have called in sick. But here we would check if someone called in sick after a vacation. If he was lying, we'd discipline him. But if you check like that, there has to be a human side, a possibility of exception. They don't want to break the rules. If you're going to enforce the rules, you have to be equally willing to relax the rules for a just cause."

The point is that the driver called in to ask. He expected to be trusted and expected to be granted the exception. Jim Gillespie, the city trailer driver who took me along on his run to the Conrail yard in South Kearny, told me of a friend and fellow driver who was repeatedly given leave to take his wife to chemotherapy. "The company gave him the time off. Your word is your bond in this place. If you lie, you're in trouble. If you call in, they trust you."

Ronnie Parham's battles with the dispatcher who wouldn't give him leave to take a personal day to be with his son or daughter contrasts with Jim's story. Like John Occhiogrosso's reports of workers who are hounded by dock supervisors because they've gained a reputation for poor work, Ronnie's experience indicates that A-P-A's system is imperfect and that it can succumb to personal animosities. Armand says that the dispatchers and supervisors, at the lowest level of management, are the least willing to bend, because they are proving themselves as managers and will have to defend any exception to their own superiors. Their exactitude is one reason that an appeals process is a necessity.

Despite its excesses, A-P-A's straight-arrow approach to the rules is, nevertheless, an island of respite from the deviousness and bullying of the bosses who are stiffs. As Bill McKernan expressed it: "If Arthur gave his word to something, you could sleep on it." Walter Shea, the Teamsters International vice-president, amplified: "With all due respect to the big nationals, other companies try to distort or expand what's been agreed upon, but we've never had that with A-P-A. With other companies, there are personalities, there's distrust, hatred, dislike. With A-P-A you work out a problem and you come to an agreement and it stays the same. I'm a great admirer of Arthur. I probably shouldn't say that in my position. But Hoffa liked Arthur and had a high respect for him. Billy McCarthy hates employers and won't socialize with them, but he has a great respect for Arthur, because what Arthur says doesn't change. He takes care of his workers. He gets the most of what he wants without subjecting them. He's the best of the trucking executives."

Walter continued, "I'd have to compare them with UPS, in the organizational sense, in terms of the work ethic, in terms of the workers' respect for the company and for the union. If ever a company didn't need a union, it'd be A-P-A."

I think Walter's compliment is, nevertheless, exaggerated, and that George Cashman is right: A-P-A does need a union—a good union. And every company does. To say so is, of course, to sound like a union partisan. But that is only because it is so difficult to see clearly amidst the smoke of class warfare. To be pro-union and pro-worker is not necessarily to be antiprofit and antimanagement. To champion workers can promote profit. This is precisely what Robert Owen, in the first two decades of the nineteenth century, could not get his partners at New Lanark to understand. They thought of productivity in terms of work performed per pound sterling paid; therefore, to earn higher profit one must exploit the workers. But Robert Owen thought of productivity, as Arthur and Armand do, in terms of work performed per hour worked. Therefore, to earn higher profit, one must inspire the workers to harder work, and one must meet their needs. For that, one needs a company that is a purposive community and a union that is an effective regulator.

In the last decade of the twentieth century, with the near-abandonment of trucking regulation and the decline of the Teamsters, A-P-A now competes directly with nonunion trucklines. On the average, nonunion companies pay drivers and dockworkers about seventy percent of the union wage. Yet A-P-A still moves freight more productively, at a net lower cost, than its nonunion competitors. Nonunion workers do not work even seventy percent as well. Employees of a few union companies, which, like UPS, are also intentional communities, do work as well. Armand says: "If the nonunion companies could ever run as well as us, we'd be out of business. But there's a serious doubt that that could ever be done."

We've arrived at the truckline now, and Arthur is Arthur, both the soft and the hard. He parks in the chairman's designated space, and as we cross the yard to the administration building, we pass a driver standing by a yard-tractor. He's chatting with the switcher, who's sitting in his cab. Both men turn, smile, and wave. "Hi Arthur!" Arthur doesn't smile, doesn't wave. He taps his wrist watch at them and calls out coldly, "The freight won't walk." But then, upstairs in the office pool, he winds through the rows of desks, slapping backs, touching shoulders, shaking hands, asking after daughters, sons, kid sisters, fathers, remembering all the veterans. To some he is Mr. Arthur, to others Mr. Imperatore, to others Arthur; a number of the younger people clearly don't know him except by sight, nor he them. Everybody smiles.

Now Armand appears with two real-estate developers. There's a meeting concerning the purchase and possible development of a vacant lot in Manhattan. Hardly past thirty, the real-estate men have already grown confidently into their stereotypes: sleek bodies under gray-black suits a shade too shiny, dark hair coiffed back a shade too slick, faces at once sharp with avarice and flush with indulgence. I excuse myself to give Arthur a break from the tape recorder and to gain time to catch up on my notes. Arthur shepherds the developers into the Florentine office.

No doubt the ice will be broken by the young men's warm admiration of the office's luxurious appointments. But as I wait outside the door in an alcove for visitors, something about Arthur's office strikes me that had been too obvious to recognize before: its location. I remember discussing with him the problems and advantages of concentrating so much traffic in a single terminal, instead of scattering it among smaller ones, as most trucklines do. But it's equally unusual, it occurs to me now, for a truckline's corporate offices to be located at a terminal at all. The general offices are more likely to be in a downtown highrise or a suburban industrial park, where the architecture, furniture, noise level, view, dress, and conversation are all white-collar. For Arthur, though, it would have been unthinkable to sequester himself in a downtown office. Later, leafing though my tape transcripts, I find Arthur saying about the repeated expansions of the North Bergen terminal:

"I found it was better to operate a big, centralized facility and to concentrate the energy, the managerial energy, here. We had the horsepower, the economic firepower to hire the right people. We had good control. We ran a quite monolithic kind of company, in the sense that it was a whole. It was not many parts. The thinking, the philosophy, the habits, the practices, the routines were all coined here. And then they were in effect exported, displaced into the other terminals."

In order to exert good control, it was necessary to stay close to the men. Arthur could not afford, nor was he inclined, to create in the company, as most companies do, a physical distance between management and labor. In the larger society, the rough social distinctions of class are expressed and enforced by a partly voluntary physical distance: different neighborhoods, different workplaces, different schools, different places of leisure. In corporations, where hierarchical and organizational distinctions are much clearer and much more rigid than they are in society in general, physical and social distances are exaggerated as well. The factory, where blue-collar labor uses its hands, is noisy, hot, dirty, smelly, and dangerous; the office across town, where white-collar management uses its head, is quiet, cooled, clean, placid, and safe. That A-P-A's corporate offices share a wall with the dock, that an inside stairway leads from one to the other, that Arthur's own office sits above the freight dock like a chairman's docktower—this is Arthur's statement in poured concrete that he does not want a caste system as a byproduct of an organizational chain of command. He, and now Armand, can be the boss, the vice-presidents can be the brass, and the supervisors and dispatchers can have authority on the dock and on the radio, without any of them thinking of themselves as socially above the men, as requiring a protected and prettified place to work.

Arthur emerges from his Florentine docktower with the real-estate developers in tow. Armand extricates himself, while Arthur leads me and the visitors downstairs and across the lane for a tour of the recreation center. He shepherds us past the swimming pool, through the weight room, the men's locker room, the ceramics studio, and the basketball court, past the lounge with pool table, ping-pong table, heavy sofas, and TV. "We've done a lot about health, about smoking and obesity," Arthur says, perhaps thinking of the sleekness pressing outward upon the developers' suits. "My brother Arnold loved to eat, so I built him this kitchen."

The two developers are suitably amazed, as visitors always are, by Arthur's enthusiasm and his largesse. But my present line of thought suggests to me that the real focus of their amazement is unspoken, perhaps unapparent to themselves: that Arthur would have built all this *here*. This recreation center is not a management privilege, not the usual executive perquisite of membership in a suburban country club, but a gym and pool on the terminal grounds, across the lane from the office and the dock. Dock and office lunch-hours fall at the same time. Contact sports are social levelers; going up for the rebound, the bosses' armpits stink, too. As segregators have always understood, you cannot maintain social superiority in the shower. Nakedness is no respecter of persons.

One might suppose that middle and senior managers at A-P-A would be restive under Arthur's radical lessening of that social and physical distance from blue-collar life which, together with a good salary, is a manager's chief privilege and reward. But these managers have all risen from the ranks of drivers, dockmen, and clerks, and it is a focus of camaraderie and a point of pride for them that they have not abandoned their working-class identity. Even their salaries are modest by executive standards: the vice-presidents earn about three times what the drivers do. Yet, though they are occasionally wooed by other, higher-paying companies, they don't go elsewhere, because then they would be under pressure to abandon the identity they have chosen to keep.

Burt Trebour, for example, vice-president for labor relations and administration, began at A-P-A as a rating clerk, at the age of seventeen. Behind his broad and generous face and his frequent, delighted laugh that punctuates his flow of ironic stories, behind his gentle-natured mastery of social courtesies, Burt hides a swift and encyclopedic mind. He can flip mentally through the small-printed pages of the National Master Freight Agreement and place a mental finger on a clause faster, probably, than any union official or labor lawyer that he's ever argued a grievance with. He's secretly a bit of a sly one, I suspect, and doesn't mind if his appearance and soft manner lull the expectations of an adversary. But though his role is adversarial, in defense of his company's interests, he doesn't think of the Teamsters and A-P-A's other employee unions as enemies from another social class. Rather, he's a diplomat whose work is to resolve disputes and build agreements between competing, yet interdependent forces that are roughly equal.

Burt told me one day, "I think blue-collar, and I think Armand does, too. I live in Cateret, a blue-collar town. I like living there. I don't have the nicest house on my block. I don't have to worry about keeping up with the Joneses. The first five years I was there, my neighbors used to think I was a truck driver, and I like that. I don't have a big ego. I like people to say 'Hi, Burt,' not 'Hi, Mr. Trebour.' A former A-P-A executive calls me up about once a year, and he always asks: 'You still living in Carteret?'—'Yes.'—'Good,' he always says. 'Don't forget where you came from.' "

Even Arthur's wealth has not separated him from his background, because he doesn't keep his wealth separate. He doesn't hoard it or build a villa in Provence with it. He spends it in the midst of the workplace, on his Florentine docktower and his waterfront, on the recreation center, the anniversary trips, and the college scholarships, on the best tractors, the best diesel engines, the best truck maintenance: "everything first class," as A-P-A people say. He bought a yacht, outfitted it with Pisarros and a gourmet galley, and takes out his employees and customers for cruises on it. The British, who treasure and agonize over their class system as fervently as we ignore and deny ours, understand Arthur's sort of choice very well and approve of it. In Britain, one doesn't mind if one's schoolmates get rich, so long as they don't attempt to enter a higher social class. That would be contemptible: "putting on airs," "lording it over your mates," "getting above your station." The immediate marker of a class apostate is speech. To abandon the dialect of one's childhood neighborhood is to announce that one has forgotten where one came from. As for Arthur, his regional accent survives: he still rhymes "because" with "boss," says "beauty-full" for "beautiful," and uses the glottal stop for the medial "t" in "bottle" and "totally." While some workers at A-P-A, especially new employees who don't know him personally, are irritated by Arthur's wealth, most are gratified that he hasn't forgotten who he was and is, and that he clearly prefers to spend his time and his money in their company than with the fancy people in the glittering high-rises across the water. That can buy forgiveness for a lot of millions.

It has taken me some time to understand the importance of what Bob Reichenberg, A-P-A's regional manager for the Eastern terminals, said to me during my first round of interviews at A-P-A in 1990. "I don't think there is a very strong caste system in this company," Bob said. "The vice-presidents (his immediate bosses) aren't country club types. They're human beings, and they let their guard down often enough to let you see that." That Bob should think of "country club types" and "human beings" as opposites speaks volumes about the American class system as perceived by people with working-class backgrounds. It informs us, in a few words, why American corporate managers have "lost touch with their people," as Arthur says—a loss that he identifies as the real cause of the decline of manufacturing in this country. In pursuit of class superiority, the managers have set themselves apart. The price of their pursuit of privilege is their deliberate ignorance of working people and, as a result, their floundering when the world economy calls upon them to increase productivity and quality. This is what Arthur means when he says the failures of American industry are moral failures.

In March, 1975, A-P-A's company helicopter crashed in Shelton, Connecticut. The pilot and Arnold Imperatore were killed. The company was stunned. As vice-president for operations, Arnold had managed the daily business of the company; together with Arthur, he had been the focus of the employees' loyalty, and more than Arthur, a focus of their affection. Two weeks later, Teresa Imperatore, mother of the Imperatore brothers and, like Arnold, a binding force among them, also died. (Their father and nemesis, Eugene Imperatore, had died in 1952.) "I was in a terrible depression because of my brother Arnold's death," Arthur told me in an earlier interview. He had leaned on his brother to help translate his ideas into action at the truckline and to balance the hard side of his personality. During the ensuing year, Arthur's discouragement turned to restiveness, as it had twenty years earlier after the wildcat strikes of the 1950s. He was now fifty-one; the creative work of building the truckline was complete; filling Arnold's shoes as a day-to-day manager didn't interest him. Further, in 1976, he separated from his wife, Helen Imperatore, who is Armand's mother (the couple has not divorced). "When I left home," he recalls, "I was restless, looking for things to do." He began to contemplate selling his share of A-P-A to his surviving brothers or to an outsider.

At this point, Armand stepped in. During his twenties, he had kept his distance from the truckline, but by 1976, when he was thirty-two, he had established the independence he felt he needed to balance an entry into the family business. He had married, and he had made partner in New Jersey's largest law firm, McCarter and English, in Newark. Armand said later, "I felt very strongly that there's a structure at A-P-A that has value. Irrespective of whether it's making money, it's worth preserving, which is why I came in." (As I have mentioned, I myself, at the time, found Armand's move mystifying, given the breadth of his intellectual gifts. I don't find it mystifying now.) Arthur, realizing, as he expressed it to me, that he could have a second generation, bought out his brothers instead of selling to them. In 1977, Armand left his law practice and entered the company.

While Armand learned the business, Arthur began looking for something else. During Armand's apprenticeship, the daily running of A-P-A was entrusted to Dick Melosh, as executive vice-president, while George Imperatore continued as vice-president for sales. Meanwhile, Arthur vetted several national trucklines, including Associated Transport and Railway Express, with the thought of buying them and reviving them before they went bankrupt. He ended by keeping his distance. To avoid, as he told a trade journal at the time, being awash in cash, he bought two coal mines in Virginia, financed a low-rise condominium on the edge of the Palisades, and acquired a professional hockey team in Denver, which Armand oversaw as part-time president until it was sold. Then, in 1981, Arthur went to Washington.

The real-estate men have departed now, and Arthur and I are sitting in the Florentine docktower again, with Arthur at his writing desk, his back to the sliding doors that open to the balcony over the yard. I ask Arthur about his stint in the Reagan Administration. He cocks his weary eye at me and smiles sardonically, tipping his head to the right and raising the left corner of his smile. He says:

"It was through a guy named Sonny Werblin, whom I'd known from the sports world when we owned the hockey team." (Werblin was the developer of the Meadowlands Sports Complex, a few miles southeast of A-P-A. Before coming East, he was a theatrical agent for, among others, a Grade B movie actor named Ronald Reagan.) "I forget what the hell Werblin did," Arthur continues. "I guess he used to sell big shows. I liked him, and I'd socialize with him over at the Garden. He knew Reagan very well. This was 1981. We'd made a lot of money, I was fifty-six, Helen and I had been separated for five years, and I really figured, 'Oh, shit. I've made enough money.' Armand was coming along, by then he'd been in the company five or six years, and I knew I had to leave in order to give him room.

"So I told Werblin I would like to meet someone in Washington to become a volunteer. I wasn't looking for glory or anything. I figured I'd made a fortune in this country and I loved the country, and I'd go to Washington and volunteer. I said I had very few criteria, but one of them was I had to do something meaningful. About that same time, Charlie Wick had been looking around. I'd met Wick, I was in several meetings with him and other people, and he knew I was articulate, and he'd asked me to send him a lot of stuff, and I sent him some material on the companies and on myself."

Charles Z. Wick, né Charles Zwick, was another White House recruit from the Grade B movie industry; he was the producer of the "Three Stooges" series. As a player at Ronald Reagan's evening poker table, he'd been rewarded with the directorship of the United States Information Agency.

"In fact," Arthur recalls now as he tells the story, "I'd offered Reagan my yacht. Carter had gotten rid of both presidential yachts, since he had decided he was going to cut costs. I mean of all the stupidity, the one thing Carter could have used was some detachment from the White House. So now Reagan comes in, and I figured, my god, these killer jobs—I mean, I've worked like a maniac all my life. I figured this poor old guy, in his early seventies by then, y'know, he's going to have this terrible job. I said to Werblin, 'Jesus, send word, I got this great yacht, it'd be wonderful.' I felt very patriotic." Arthur chuckles ironically at his own expense now, remembering. "Of course, I found out Reagan knew how to live. He didn't need to have any help to relax. He did plenty of relaxing even while he was in the White House.

"Well, they didn't take the yacht. But that was my introduction. Meanwhile, at the same time, I had the opportunity to buy the railroad yard on the waterfront. Now I'm torn. So I figured, 'Jesus, this would give me a lot of chance to detach myself away from Armand,' give him a chance, y'know. I'd be down at the waterfront, which is what ultimately happened, or I'd go to Washington as a volunteer, spend four years there, do something. Wick finally called me about the third week in September, 1981, and said, 'Listen, come on down,' and he made me an ombudsman in his agency. It was then the ICA, the International Communications Agency; it was a stupid name because it sounded like a commercial enterprise. They'd changed it from the USIA, and later they changed it back. Well, I was the ombudsman. The only expense I created for the government was two phone lines to my office. I paid my own rent, I paid for my secretary (Kathleen Husoskey, who later followed Arthur back to New Jersey). I paid my own travel expenses, I didn't use a dime of the government's money. But I wanted to do something. And I found out that the worst guy in the whole goddam agency was Wick. He was the worst man that I had ever met."

Arthur was appalled by the ignorance and venality of the Reagan Administration, and above all by its hostility to its own civil service employees. During the 1980 presidential campaign, he had heard the rhetoric about bringing the expertise and efficiencies of business to government, and, agreeing, he had contributed money to the campaign; but he soon found that his own concept of business and his understanding of efficiency were not the same as what the Californians had brought east with them. Arthur wanted to offer his ability to inspire a workforce through discipline, generosity, respect, and a closely organized cooperative effort. His offering was valueless, indeed an irritant, to political appointees whose express purpose was to weaken or dismantle the agencies they headed, or else milk them for the enrichment of themselves and their friends. Even those whose intents were money-honest and who were sincere in their rhetoric believed that government should resemble business because the purpose of business, to advance the private ends of its owners, should parallel the purpose of the state—to advance the private ends of its citizens. Arthur believed the opposite: that the purpose of business, and of the state, should be to provide a vehicle for individual fulfillment through service to a community.

"Wick," Arthur says now, pounding his fist on his writing desk, "was the most destructive, antihuman person I've ever met. A close friend of the President of the United States, a confidant—Jesus Christ, I couldn't believe it. Ultimately I found him destroying these foreign service people, and if there is a group that is deserving of great, great credit, it is the foreign service. The professional people, they are brilliant people. They're in the State Department, they're in the USIA, they're in AID, four or five different agencies. These guys are great people, and I got to love the agency. I eventually resigned. I wasn't disillusioned with the job, I was disillusioned with Wick. I tried to force *him* to resign."

As the agency ombudsman, he had been funneling to Wick's office complaints from foreign service officers that the agency under Wick was being degraded by nepotism, cronyism, hiring abuses, and sexual misconduct. Wick ignored him. Arthur told *The New York Times* after his resignation from the agency in April, 1982: "I left because it became clear to me that I was party to a sham." In his letter of resignation to Wick, he wrote: "After many serious efforts to assist the agency and to persuade you of the seriousness of agency problems, I have concluded that I can no longer be associated with the mismanagement, waste, inefficiency, and concern about the possibility of corruption and fraud which remain unaddressed and unabated." His letter was followed by a brief internal investigation that found no fault and that Arthur called a sham as well. He went home to New Jersey in disgust.

Arthur moved his workplace to the waterfront and plunged into the design of Port Imperial. In 1983, in a suprise announcement at a sales meeting, he named Armand president of A-P-A. "I didn't know he was going to do it," Armand recalled on another day. "But at that point it really wasn't that important, it didn't really change anything to say that now I was to be the president of the truckline, because, in effect, I had already been running it day-to-day for two years, and so *de facto* I already was the president, and he was still *de facto* whatever he was, the spiritual leader, the force."

"I tried to persuade Armand to take this opulent office," Arthur says now, waving to the hand-carved conference table, the marble mantle, the trompe-l'oeil mirror and murals in the Florentine docktower. "But he wouldn't take it. Armand was never one for show." (Armand instead chose a much smaller office near the stairs, with a plain executive desk, one sofa and an armchair for visitors, a shelf laden with a computer beneath a single bank of windows overlooking the terminal, and a wall packed to the ceiling with the *New Jersey Statutes Annotated.*) Arthur continues to be chairman of A-P-A, and he still owns the large majority of all the companies, with minority interests held by Armand and by Arthur's and Helen's two children, India, a Pennsylvania veterinarian, and Arthur Jr., a Manhattan lawyer. But in practice, Arthur's role remains, as it always has been, undefined.

At first, in the early and mid-eighties, when the ferry was being established and planning for Port Imperial was still intense, Arthur had more to do at the waterfront, but when development was stalled by height limits and by the crash in the real-estate market, Arthur was idle. He found himself wading upstream against a constant temptation to involve himself in the running of the truckline again. "It would drive me crazy," he tells me now. "But to come back here would have been to intrude upon Armand. This has taken one hell of a lot of discipline on my part, frankly, because I love this business. I could spend my whole life here. So I'd have a few bucks more. What the hell's the difference."

In the fall of 1990, Arthur experimented with retirement at his farm in eastern Pennsylvania, "riding horses, observing the flowers, and planning new developments with my gardens and whatever, to refine nature." But the retirement didn't last beyond the spring. Idleness bored him. He came back to the waterfront.

This time, though, he found an exit from his dilemma. On the one hand, the planning, waiting, schmoozing, and scheming that are the daily tasks of real-estate developers had tried his patience, and had, besides, come to nothing. On the other hand, returning to the truckline and jostling Armand was out of the question, and would anyway have meant a move backwards. Instead, he threw himself into new activities that called upon his old skills as a creator and manager of operations. He fired an unsatisfactory ferry-terminal manager and took the job himself, assuming possession of a third office, the ten-square-foot captain's cubicle on the *Jamestown*, with its nautical-blue walls and porthole window. He reigns and teaches there in the mornings now, wearing a three-piece suit and an Irish workingman's cap. He exercised his old strengths even more directly with the purchase of the two newspaper delivery wholesalers and with the campaign to inculcate his corporate Torah, as he calls it, into the heathen routines of the Newspaper and Mail Deliverers Union. As for the waterfront, he and Armand are now planning ways to turn the property into an active revenue-earning enterprise. In addition to rental housing at the center of the property, the two men are thinking of an upscale water-park at the northern end, with wavepools and waterslides, and an indoor entertainment complex, to be housed in the banana pier, at the southern end.

Musing now about his abandoned plans to build a city, Arthur acknowledges that he was moving away from his own gifts. "It's been my belief for so long—I've known it since I was a kid—that there was so much opportunity right around me that could really generate good, whether it be profits, learning, growth, or knowledge. I always say that I want to build a piece of the world. God needs help, and he picks guys like me. And here I've sat on that land down there, full of greed—if you quote me this way, I'm going to look like a really terrible man—but it's the truth. It was a typical developer mentality. But I didn't know how to develop. And I bought the land originally to have something to do, something geographically close to the company, which I wanted, because I grew up here. I grew up in this company, so I didn't want to go far afield. It was like a providential experience to be able to buy that wonderful piece.

"So I bought the land, and then I got these great ideas and I'm dreaming of grandiose development and grandiose profits, y'know, a great monument to my life and to my family and all that, and I've been striving to do that all my life. To put my family on the map and so on. Meanwhile it takes years and years, and we're spending tons of money with architects and plans and doing all the regulatory crap, and the market crashes. At one time, before it crashed, we were on the brink of doing something enormous and enormously risky"—the $6-billion, 16-million-square-foot, thirty-year development that was to be called Port Imperial—"which I didn't finally do. We could have been broken by it, because I don't believe it would have sold. But here we had all these great ideas, and meanwhile we're sitting on land that has such potential for operations. And if there's one thing I always knew how to do, it's how to run an operation on a piece of land. It was a laugh.

"The whole point of the story was in a book called *Acres of Diamonds*. It was a legend from India, I think, about a man who had a great farm, but he was always dreaming about acres of diamonds, about another farm where he might find them. So he left his own farm to find this other farm where there would be diamonds. And he was broken in spirit and wealth. The man to whom he sold his first farm *worked* the farm and found"—Arthur pauses for the drama—"the diamonds. And that's really the story of my own life. Here I was sitting on that land. That's why I'm back at the waterfront. We have all these opportunities to work the land"—opportunities such as the waterpark and the entertainment center he now plans—"and I never did it. I never made it happen. And I know how to *do* all this stuff."

I'm thinking again of Robert Owen. After selling out to his partners at New Lanark, Owen founded a utopian community called New Harmony, in Indiana, a kind of frontier Port Imperial. He tried to manage it in absentia while he labored in union-socialist politics in England. New Harmony failed after two years, and Owen lost two thirds of his fortune. Although he continued to be an influential voice for reform in labor legislation, the workingmen's federation that he led disintegrated. He never again made use of his genuis for organizing an industrial operation into a community. He spent his old age studying spiritualism. In the long run, Arthur has avoided Owen's mistakes. He flirted with Owen's forays into city building and politics, but he was rescued by his workingman's preference for security on his home ground, doing what he knows. He has returned to where he came from.

Fred Astle, a lean, black-goateed Mainer who joined A-P-A in 1986, is vice-president for finance at the truckline and also at the waterfront. Over dinner in February, 1992, he told me he had often wondered which was the prime mover among the causes for A-P-A's success. Was it the company's special mastery of the unique New York–New Jersey freight market, or was it the excellence of the company's employees at all levels, or was it, simply, Arthur? Which one was the chicken, Fred would ask himself, and which two the eggs? That day, returning from Manhattan on the ferry, Fred had noticed for the first time a taxicab waiting outside the *Jamestown*. Delighted, he took the cab to the truckline, thinking: "Now the ferry has really arrived. Taxis are meeting it." At A-P-A, he ran into Arthur Jr., and Fred told him about the cab. Young Arthur, as everyone calls him at the truckline, laughed and said that his father had noticed the same taxicab. And Arthur Sr. had been furious. The cab, he had raged, was making money *off his property.* The cabbie should be paying a percentage. Besides, if money was to be made off a cab service to the waterfront, then he, Arthur, should be making it.

"Arthur saw the same cab I saw," Fred told me, "but he saw something different. I saw that the ferry was doing well. He saw that someone was making money off of him, and, by the same token, he saw an opportunity to start a new business. This is the true entrepreneur. He sees opportunities where others see just a taxicab. When I think this way, I think Arthur is the chicken and the other factors are the eggs."

When I retell this story to Arthur today, he chuckles throughout, confirming, nodding, saying, "Yeah, right, sure, absolutely," until we are both laughing. In his mid-sixties, he's enthusiastic once again about creating new works of entrepreneurial art, about carving the images that only he sees in the formless stone.

"Oh, we're going to be able to run that whole operation now," he tells me. "Within about two to two-and-a-half years—it's a nervous time, with this recession, and the carry on the property is enormous. But the opportunities for enrichment are also enormous. It's such a great parcel of land. *Taxis,* y'know." (Arthur's voice is contemptuous.) "I'm not looking for piddling stuff. But," he speculates, "I could run a taxi operation, I'll bet, and do a million bucks a year and make a couple hundred thousand profit. We can run the cabs, we could run a newsstand, we're going to open another restaurant, we may open a golf school, I mean we pick up fifty thousand here, a hundred thousand there, and the rest is starting to generate some decent money."

We rise and look out through the sliding glass doors and down onto the North Bergen yard. It's 5:30 P.M. and the earliest straight trucks are arriving from their pickups. Below us on the dock, the day operation is clanking towards a close. "I don't know, David. I guess I'll go out with my boots on. What else is there to do? I see my buddy in his villa, he says there's always something else to do in downtown Antibes. He can go to the post office. He can do things his maid did, his chauffeur did, his housekeeper did. But I don't choose to do that. I mean, what would I do with my life? I love to take something and I love to create. I love to take people, first of all myself, if it's my own idea, if I have to build it around myself to start with, and conceptualize, then organize, then equip something, build a new company. I want to build a little car-leasing company. Why? Because the needs are here."

6. The *Nancy* Brig

Truckers like to assert that, whatever else people may think of them, they are indispensable. It would be hard to dispute their claim. Without the wheels of trucks, the national economic engine is next to useless. The fundamental importance of trucking and indeed of all forms of transportation has led, during the last hundred years, to governmental protectiveness and to labor power. Transporation strikes immediately slow down many other industries, and the federal government has traditionally responded with intervention. (The Reagan Administration chose advisedly when, in initiating its successful drive to weaken the American labor movement, it began by destroying a transportation union: the Professional Air Traffic Controllers' Organization.) For many years, also, Washington protected transportation industries not only from long strikes but from the self-inflicted damage of price wars. Until the late 1970s, all public forms of freight and passenger transportation were thought to be too vulnerable and too essential to be exposed to the challenges of the free market. They were treated, to some extent, as utilities.

During the last fifteen years, some of these protections have been dismantled. The airlines, the railroads, the interstate trucklines, and the oil pipeline industry have been deregulated; only maritime shipping remains under federal controls. Nevertheless, the indispensability of transportation to economic life is such that many of its elements remain not merely regulated, but publicly owned and operated. Waterways and piers, airways and airports, roads and streets, and almost all of the intracity passenger-transport system are public property in the United States. In most countries, virtually all public transportation, with the exception of the trucklines, some shipping lines, and a few airlines, is an arm of the government.

The inconsistency, not to say haphazardness, in public control of transportation in America has a long history. The National Road, predecessor of U.S. Route 40 and Interstate 70, was one of Thomas Jefferson's many inspirations, and the route was first approved by Congress in 1806. The Erie Canal, completed in 1825, was built by New York State. On the other hand, many early canals and toll-roads were private. The airlines, like the railroads, have been private from the first, but the airports, unlike the railroad stations, have always been public. The railroads are unique in that the public has owned neither the industry's roadways (the rails), nor its transshipment points (the depots), nor its operators (the railroad companies). This independence gave the railroad corporations so much power to control public economic life through price fixing that the government intervened with regulation a century ago, through the creation of the Interstate Commerce Commission in 1887. Similar interventions followed: municipal governments began acquiring privately owned subway lines and bus lines, as well as refuse haulers, electric utilities, gas companies, waterworks, and steam heat companies. The Interstate Commerce Commission's control of railroads was extended to oil pipelines in 1906 and to telephone and telegraph companies in 1910. By the 1920s, when private trucking began filling the public roads, precedents for governmental control through regulation were already in place.

The regulation of interstate trucking was established within the Interstate Commerce Commission by the Motor Carrier Act of 1935. This legislation grew out of the National Industrial Recovery Act of 1933, which established the National Recovery Administration. Through it, the Roosevelt White House attempted to prescribe business conduct, in order to limit exploitation of labor and to restrict what in those days was judged to be the destructiveness of competition. The National Recovery Administration did not survive the attacks of its enemies, who denounced it as communist and also, more accurately, as fascist.

The Motor Carrier Act outlived its parent, however, because trucking was recognized as a part of economic infrastructure, and because the trucking industry itself desperately wanted it. The dominant industry trade group, the American Trucking Associations, was formed in the early 1930s expressly to promote trucking regulation, because the trucklines had exhausted each other with ceaseless price wars.

From 1935 to 1980, the Interstate Commerce Commission, acting under the Motor Carrier Act, restricted trucking at three gates: routes, rates, and entry. In the case of utilities such as electric power companies, which usually operate as monopolies, the work of government regulators has been to restrain the utilities' eagerness to raise their rates. But the trucklines were in the opposite situation: competing for the same freight, they had been killing each other off by lowering their prices below cost. The ICC's aim was to keep freight rates consistent among competing trucklines and high enough so that no one was driven out of business. With the ICC's blessing, and with antitrust immunity granted by Congress, the trucklines formed regional trade associations called "rate bureaus." The bureaus determined a "just price," according to weight, distance, and the classification of the freight. These rates, to be charged by all truckers to all shippers, were submitted to the ICC for approval. A Byzantine complexity of exceptions and variations developed, but, in general, the ICC approved rates that the bureaus could show were seven percent above cost. Once a rate had been filed and approved, undercutting it was illegal. Attracting customers by promising a rebate was a crime. This was the "filed rate doctrine," which has been a feature of transportation law since the nineteenth century.

Restraints on price competition were complemented by controls on routes and entry. In the belief that too many competitors would create chaos, the ICC allowed new companies to enter the trucking industry only where they were replacing an existing carrier or where they could show they would not be competing with one. In most cases, an established truckline could expand its routes only by absorbing another carrier. Thus a small truckline's most valuable asset was often its permission to operate; truckers called it their certificate or their medallion. Aggressive operators like Arthur Imperatore expanded by buying the me-dallions of weak competitors. Before deregulation in 1980, there was no other way to grow.

"There were a finite number of certificates to move freight from Philadelphia to New York, for example," Armand told me in his office one afternoon when we discussed the era before deregu-lation. "One guy could only move it through New Brunswick via Route 1; another guy could only move it via Route 206, through Somerville. It was even that particular. It was medieval. It was really the guild system. The idea was that competition is bad, competition is ruining us here in this depressed time, let's get all of the players that are left, and have them stop cutting each other's throats and have them work together for the good of the country."

The system of trucking regulation that emerged was flawed, and its imperfections were well known to the trucklines long before the 1970s, when the movement to abolish regulation be-came a public and political force. In a word, regulation protected inefficiency. Truckers themselves disliked route regulation, which often forced them to drive the long way around. Another un-popular restriction forbade private carriers who moved their own freight—chain stores and supermarkets, for example—from hir-ing themselves out to other carriers on the return trip; they were thus saddled with the cost of empty backhauls. In general, price regulation discouraged trucklines from aggressive cost control. Assured of prices that were seven percent above the industry's average operating costs, a sloppily managed company whose operating costs were well above average could still limp along. (Meanwhile, managers like Arthur who watched the store could make twenty and more cents on the dollar by pushing costs down farther and farther below the price ceiling.) Most visibly, truck-lines had little incentive to face down the Teamsters when the union demanded more generous fringe benefits and higher pay. The ICC could be counted upon to approve higher rates that would pass the cost of labor settlements onto the shippers. The shippers, in turn, had no choice but to pay, because there were no trucklines outside the guild.

Yet the costs and inefficiencies of regulated trucking were accompanied by benefits that are often overlooked today, when competition has a nobler reputation than it did in 1935, or, for that matter, in 1887. The greatest beneficiary of regulation was labor. By sanctioning costly labor agreements, regulation promoted an entire generation of truck drivers, dockworkers, and mechanics into the financial prosperity of the middle class. Price regulation protected another vulnerable group: small shippers. Start-up manufacturers, specialists supplying economic niches, family-owned companies of every sort, and manufacturers in rural areas were each assured of shipping rates equal to the rates charged to their larger competitors, in the same way that they were assured of equal access to the public roads. Freight-rate regulation amounted to a partial denial of bargaining advantage to large shippers like national retailers and manufacturing conglomerates, because volume discounts on freight rates were illegal.

With price competition forbidden, trucklines competed on service. This was the opportunity, the uncarved block, that Arthur discerned with his entrepreneurial eye. He saw that while regulation allowed sloppy truckers to survive, the companies that would grow rich were those that would concentrate on excellence. His epiphany in the snowstorm in 1960 would probably have meant less in an industry in which winners were created more by high-pressure marketing and aggressive price competition than by quality of product or of service. But successful competition on quality, instead of on price, required a focus on *esprit de corps*, on standards of performance, on "pride in the freight." With the prescience that is part of his gift, Arthur saw that the more A-P-A attended to quality instead of money—because price was already decided—the more money it would make.

During the last two decades, management consultants and industry innovators who have championed worker decision making and product quality as corporate goals have cited the Japanese model. But trucking regulators who narrowed the industry's focus to competition through quality of service were not drawing on the Japanese experience, which had not yet come into vogue in this country, but, as Armand pointed out, on the nearer European tradition of the craft guild. The medieval and Renaissance guild was an artisan's cartel. The artisan's prestige, his place in society, and his livelihood derived from his ability to provide a service or product that no one else could provide. Distinction among his peers was earned by what would now be called operating excellence. Arthur's success in inspiring an intense drive in his employees to become and remain "the best," as they still say, is founded on this tradition of craft pride.

Before deregulation, all truckers, not just A-P-A, shared in the craft tradition—not that they all practiced it; but they all recognized excellence in terms of it. This was the basis of A-P-A's reputation in the industry, both among line workers like Tony DeRosa's friend who drove for ABF, and among trucking managers and customers. "When I traveled back then," Dan Solazzo, A-P-A's vice-president for sales, recalled when I interviewed him, "people had read about A-P-A in the industry press and always wanted to see me even if they had no business in our operating area. A-P-A was on a pedestal. I had an open door."

The guild tradition also informed truckers' acceptance of regulation and their willingness to forgo direct competition, even when that meant inefficiency. Most truckers saw their companies as members of a larger community, which was the trucking industry as a whole, and which claimed part of their allegiance. The American Trucking Associations and the rate bureaus were, and to some extent still are, institutional expressions of that guild loyalty. For Arthur, certainly, and for Armand after him, protecting the health of their guild has been an important professional responsibility. Armand and his top managers continue to devote time to the American Trucking Associations, to the rate bureaus, and to Trucking Management, Inc., the consortium for negotiations with labor. In the same spirit, Arthur underwrote Augie Pagnozzi's role as tour guide to visiting truckline executives and as a logistics expert to be loaned free to other companies.

The vicious price wars that followed deregulation in 1980 have destroyed much of the craft collegiality in trucking. A-P-A recently stopped the tours (although an exception was made in

1992 for a delegation of truckers from Russia), and the company's newer logistics programs are kept secret. Still, in a telephone interview in 1990, after ten years of price war, William Clifford, president of St. Johnsbury Trucking, A-P-A's largest competitor in the New England freight market, could speak of A-P-A in the friendliest tones: "I can go way back with Arthur Imperatore, because I've been with St. Johnsbury since 1968," he told me. "I strongly admire Arthur, and Armand has stepped right in. Arthur is one of the pioneers and has dedicated a lot of personal time to the industry. He's still very much industry-oriented. A-P-A continues to get tremendous respect."

The trucking guild, with its collegial coziness and its craft ethos, its cost inefficiencies and its esteem for excellence, was broken by political change. Arthur places much of the blame on the Teamsters. Of course, the trucklines' sloppiness in controlling costs was as much to blame as the Teamsters' corruption and fumbling. But Arthur is right in pointing in particular to the disastrous role played by Frank Fitzsimmons, who replaced Jimmy Hoffa as president of the Teamsters International when Hoffa was imprisoned in 1967.

By all accounts a stupid man, Fitzsimmons was afraid of losing the presidency, a position he was unequal to; he was also afraid of being murdered. (Hoffa himself was kidnapped in 1975 and almost certainly killed. His body was never recovered.) In order to secure support and power in the International, Fitzsimmons insisted on wage and benefit settlements of unprecedented size. In the National Master Freight Agreement negotiations in 1970, 1973, 1976, and 1979, Teamster wages and benefits (in the New York–New Jersey area, for example) rose respectively 39.5 percent, 34.5 percent, 33 percent, and 30 percent, each over three years. The trucklines gave in, because so many of them operated on thin profit margins and thus feared bankruptcy from the nationwide strikes that Fitzsimmons threatened. Besides, they knew the Interstate Commerce Commission would let them pass along the expense of the settlements to the shippers. Meanwhile, the Nixon and Ford Administrations were breathing down the necks of the trucking company negotiators, making it clear that a strike of any length would not be tolerated. (Both Republican administrations were supported financially and politically by the Teamsters International. Fitzsimmons liked to brag of his friendship with Richard Nixon, whom he called "His Nibs.")

With each costly settlement, the ICC approved steep increases in freight rates. In response, the national retailers and manufacturers sent their lobbyists howling to the Capitol—although they themselves, especially the manufacturers, were also granting large wage settlements during an inflationary decade. In trucking, though, corruption was added to inflation. Everyone knew Fitzsimmons was allowing the Mafia to feed at the troughs of the pension funds, which were heaped with unsupervised cash. Arthur, who was an angry dissenter among the industry negotiators, summed up his view of Fitzsimmons for me: "A lazy, egotistical nincompoop, the guy who destroyed the industry singlehandedly, an insect of a man."

The Fitzsimmons settlements and the Mafia excesses brought together an insuperable coalition for deregulation. On the left were, first, opponents of the Mafia, led by Senator Ted Kennedy and others wishing to carry on Robert Kennedy's legacy of enmity against organized crime, and, second, consumer advocates, led by Ralph Nader, who argued that reduced freight rates would eventually be passed on to the public. On the right were enemies of labor, who were outraged that mere truck drivers should be earning a middle-class income, and also free-market ideologues, who opposed regulation on principle, just as they had opposed it in the 1930s and in the 1880s. Joining them all were the large retailers and manufacturers, who wanted power in the freight marketplace.

Railroad and airline deregulation in the late 1970s had laid the groundwork. In 1980, a new Motor Carrier Act replaced the old Act of 1935 as the basis of trucking regulation. The 1980 law was actually a cautious compromise. It left in place the rate bureaus and the medallions, but directed the ICC to rationalize route restrictions, to greatly increase flexibility in price regulation, and to permit any qualified trucking company to enter the industry, whether or not it threatened to compete with an established line.

The compromise did not hold. Under the Reagan and Bush Administrations, the ICC was governed by a majority of laissez-

faire partisans, and trucking regulation, instead of being rationalized, as Congress directed, was largely abandoned. Route
restrictions and entry became a formality, and rate regulation
with its filed-rate doctrine now exists more as a name than as a
reality. The Commission has reduced its staff—to fewer than 600
in 1992, as opposed to more than 2,000 in 1980—such that there
are not enough employees to review all the rate applications.
After forty-five years of preventing cut-throat competition by
prosecuting low-ball pricing, the ICC reversed its policy and in
effect has been encouraging trucklines to drive each other out of
business, as they had been doing before the advent of regulation
in 1935.

After 1980, as the trucking guild awoke painfully to the new
regime of deregulation, A-P-A Transport Corp. was itself
undergoing a change of governance. Arthur, who had shaped
the company in the image of his own personality, had withdrawn to Washington and then to the waterfront, and Armand
was gradually establishing himself as the new leader. He moved
slowly, because Arthur was releasing his hold slowly, and because even as Arthur retreated, his old colleagues remained: Dick
Melosh, executive vice-president until his retirement in 1985, and
George Imperatore, vice-president for sales until 1986. Until the
mid-eighties, then, Armand was the only member of the new
generation on the management team. In any case, conservation
of the community that Arthur had built was Armand's primary
mission. He had entered the company because he had sensed
that this family business, like so many others, might not survive
intact if the founding family departed. It was a general fear, which
Augie Pagnozzi expressed to me this way: "When Arnold Imperatore died and Arthur started withdrawing, there was uncertainty in the company, until Armand made the decision to stay
for life."

Change, therefore, was at first the opposite of Armand's intent. The role of conservator suited his temperament, which tends
to loyalty, caution, and rootedness. (I remember my puzzlement
when, after earning his law degree in 1967, he returned to New
Jersey to practice. It had never entered my own thoughts to
return to Connecticut. When I asked Armand then why he'd

chosen New Jersey, he said merely, "Because it's home.") In the 1980s, during my years at a Buddhist monastery, I worked and studied among dozens of Chinese colleagues; but later I came to recognize Armand as the most intensely Confucian person I know. His subsequent move from law to trucking was a classical act of filial piety. The *Confucian Analects* describe it this way:

> The Master said, 'When his parents are alive, the son may not travel far. . . . If after their death the son does not stray from his father's path for three years [the traditional period of mourning], he may be called filial.'

No one at A-P-A had anticipated how violently the landscape of trucking, upon which Armand's stepfather had marked A-P-A's path, would be altered by deregulation. The entire industry was slow to understand that the Interstate Commerce Commission was undermining the compromise that had been expressed in the Motor Carrier Act of 1980. They realized only gradually that financial stability and quality of service were no longer to be in fashion, and that the new orthodoxy was to be market share. Cautiously, the major trucklines—led by Yellow Freight System, in 1992 the largest single truckline, and by Overnite Transportation, the only national nonunion less-than-truckload carrier—began introducing price cuts for large shippers in the form of discounts off their filed rates. The first discounts were ten percent. The ICC said nothing. Discounts increased, and the large retailers and manufacturers discovered that as customers they could demand the discounts and call for bids. No longer were they at the mercy of the one or two trucklines that owned a medallion for their area. By 1992, a decade later, discounts reached an average of about fifty percent in the less-than-truckload sector, with seventy-five percent discounts not uncommon. To stay in busines, many trucklines have balanced the below-cost rates granted to large shippers with much higher rates charged to small shippers. They have also reduced their workforce, skimped on maintenance, let their equipment age, and sunk into debt. More often than not, the eventual result has been bankruptcy.

The shakeout that deregulation imposed upon the trucking industry occurred in two separate patterns. For the first time, the truckload and less-than-truckload markets divided and became two distinct industries. Large carriers that had moved both truckload and less-than-truckload shipments lost their truckload freight to owner-operators and small new trucklines that undercut established prices. The truckload sector blew into fragments. Between 1980 and 1991, the number of trucklines holding ICC medallions rose from 18,000 to 47,900—all but about 500 of them independent truckload carriers operating with a single vehicle. The market was overrun with trucks, and freight rates crashed. As intended by deregulators, the governmental protection afforded to trucklines and drivers was removed in favor of protection of shippers and, when the shippers passed the savings onto them, consumers.

Commuters and other automobile drivers, however, were suddenly unprotected. Many of the independent truckers who swarmed onto the interstates could not attract enough freight to pay for maintenance of their trucks, as Ronnie Parham explained to me from his own vulnerable position in his tractor cab. Truck accidents reported to the United States Bureau of Motor Carrier Safety (those involving more than $2,000 in property damage) increased by twenty-five percent during the first five years after deregulation, from 31,500 in 1980 to 39,500 in 1985. The accident rate for trucks in interstate commerce, expressed in incidents per million miles traveled, rose by twenty-eight percent in two years, from 1983 to 1985. Government responded with another form of regulation: roadside inspections by highway police. By "getting the junk off the road," as Ronnie put it, the inspections have helped reduce accident rates. But there has been no lessening of the economic pressures on trucklines and shippers to force drivers to haul overweight loads for long hours.

As soon as the ICC relinquished control of the truckload sector, the Teamsters lost control of it also. Tens of thousands of new entrants owning one or a handful of trucks could hardly be organized as union workers or employers. Meanwhile, as prices crashed, the existing unionized carriers abandoned the truckload market and concentrated on less-than-truckload carriage; if they failed to command a share of that, they went bankrupt. As a result of the expulsion of the Teamsters from truckload hauling, together with the numerous failures among less-than-truckload lines, the number of Teamsters among trucking employees has shrunk by fifty-four percent since 1980, to 140,000. The average real earnings of all trucking employees has declined by twenty percent.

At the same time, the loss of union protection for truckload drivers has allowed their employers to force them into a brutal and unsustainable way of life. Although the humbling of the Teamsters has been a source of joy to many, the larger truckload operators now realize that they must pay higher mileage rates, and must moderate hours and layovers, in order to reduce the extremes of turnover among drivers. But they are prevented from doing so by price competition. It is likely, therefore, that the longhaul truckload business, especially cross-country hauling, will continue to fall more and more into the hands of the railroads. Considering the highway dangers of longhaul trucking and its inefficient consumption of fossil fuels, the resurgence of the railroads may prove to be the greatest public benefit of trucking deregulation.

The less-than-truckload industry proved to be another matter altogether. Instead of exploding with thousands of new, small entrants, it has imploded. Before 1980, new trucklines could buy existing medallions and be assured of membership in the guild. Now, no one at all can enter, except on the local level, because no one new can compete with the established lines, a situation exactly the opposite of the truckload business. Little expertise and less capital is needed to haul truckloads, but a trained workforce, a computerized logistics system, and a network of terminals are needed to compete for less-than-truckload freight. Since 1980, not a single large, new, less-than-truckload operation has been successfully established by a company new to the industry. Instead, a murderous consolidation has raged for twelve years. Of the 518 less-than-truckload carriers that earned ninety-nine percent of domestic less-than-truckload revenues in 1978, 112 remained in 1990.

The shakeout has been harshest in the Northeastern regional market, where the pool of customers among manufacturers continues to shrink. A-P-A has watched the guild membership dwindle until A-P-A itself now survives as one of only five large less-than-truckload lines in its region. (These are Preston Trucking Co., with $408 million in revenues in 1992; St. Johnsbury Trucking Co., with $290 million; TNT Red Star Express, with $178 million; A-P-A, with $137 million; and New Penn Motor Express, with $138 million.) Preston and St. Johnsbury lost money in 1991 and 1992, and at the end of 1992, St. Johnsbury underwent the latest of several financial restructurings, while Preston, facing bankruptcy, was rescued and bought out by Yellow Freight System, the largest of the nationals. A-P-A has continued to make money; it has never had an unprofitable year.

Among nationwide less-than-truckload carriers, meanwhile, only Yellow and five other lines are still in business. Together with the regional subsidiaries that they have been acquiring at an accelerating pace, the six nationals now control nearly seventy percent of the domestic less-than-truckload market. In a similar shakeout that has followed airline deregulation, the five largest passenger airlines have consolidated control of seventy-five percent of domestic air travel. It is likely that, after further bankruptcies, both industries will move again toward operating inefficiences and price-fixing, this time through the formation of loose private cartels, rather than through public regulation.

Armand offered an analogy for the trucking shakeout when we were discussing the demise of North Penn Transfer, a smaller rival, in 1992:

> "Oh, I am a cook and a captain bold,
>   And the mate of the *Nancy* brig
> And a bo'sun tight, and midshipmite,
>   And the crew of the captain's gig.

Have you ever heard that?" he asked me.

"No. What's that?"

"It's a poem by William S. Gilbert of Gilbert and Sullivan, which caused quite a furor back when he published it in the 1860s. It's a kind of a variation on the story of the ancient mariner. A man's going down the street and he meets this crazed sailor, who starts reciting, 'Oh, I am a cook and a captain bold . . . ' And the story of the poem is that there's a brig called the *Nancy*, which founders on a reef, and the crew is stranded, and everybody gradually eats one another till the sailor who tells the story is the last one left."

"The Yarn of the *Nancy Bell*," as I discovered later, continues:

Twas in the good ship *Nancy Bell*
    That we sailed to the Indian Sea,
And there on a reef we come to grief
    Which has often occurred to me.

And pretty nigh all the crew was drowned
    (There was seventy-seven o' soul;)
And only ten on the *Nancy's* men
    Said 'Here!' to the muster-roll.

There was me and the cook and the captain bold
    And the mate of the *Nancy* brig
And the bo'sun tight, and a midshipmite,
    And the crew of the captain's gig.

For a month we'd neither wittles nor drink
    Till a-hungry we did feel,
So we drawed a lot, and, accordin' shot
    The captain for our meal.

The next lot fell to the *Nancy's* mate,
    And a delicate dish he made;
Then our appetite with the midshipmite
    We seven survivors stayed.

And then we murdered the bo'sun tight
    And he much resembled pig;
Then we wittled free, did the cook and me,
    On the crew of the captain's gig.

Then only the cook and me was left,
    And the delicate question, 'Which
Of us two goes to the kettle?' arose,
    And we argued it out as sich.

For I loved that cook as a brother, I did,
    And the cook he worshiped me;
But we'd both be blowed if we'd either be stowed
    In the other chap's hold, you see.

'I'll be eat if you dines of me,' says Tom;
  'Yes that,' says I, 'you'll be—'
'I'm boiled if I die, my friend,' quoth I;
  And 'Exactly so,' quoth he.

Says he, 'Dear James, to murder me
  Were a foolish thing to do,
For don't you see that you can't cook *me*,
  While I can—and will—cook *you!*'

So he boils the water, and takes the salt
  And the pepper in portions true
(Which he never forgot) and some chopped shalot,
  And some sage and parsley too.

'Come here,' says he, with a proper pride
  Which his smiling features teli,
'Twill soothing be if I let you see
  How extremely nice you'll smell.'

And he stirred it round and round and round,
  And he sniffed at the foaming froth;
When I ups with his heels, and smothers his squeals
  In the scum of the boiling broth.

And I eat that cook in a week or less,
  And—as I eating be
The last of his chops, why, I almost drops,
  For a wessel in sight I see!

And I never larf, and I never smile,
  And I never lark nor play,
But sit and croak, and a single joke
  I have—which is to say:

'Oh, I am a cook and a captain bold,
  And the mate of the *Nancy* brig,
And a bo'sun tight, and a midshipmite,
  And the crew of the captain's gig!'

"He's all these people he's ingested," Armand glossed for me, "all these failed players, so it's sort of like what we are in trucking, we're all in a lifeboat and we're running out of market, so we're going to have eat each other."

Old habits die hard, and they die hardest in strong communities. So it was with A-P-A. Trained as a guild member, it couldn't bring itself to attack and devour its colleagues in defiance of guild loyalties. "It wasn't till 1985 that the company realized the necessity of discounting and marketing," Dan Solazzo, vice-president for sales, recalled. "The old guard wouldn't change. We lost the 3M account for a while, $1 million a year, until we finally agreed to discount their rates." The old guard was George Imperatore, Dan's predecessor; Marty Marino, director of traffic until his retirement in 1984; and, from his distance in Washington and then at the waterfront, Arthur himself. Armand amplified: "We may not have been the last holdout in the industry in giving discounts, but we trailed the pack. When others gave fifteen percent, we grudgingly gave five. When others went to twenty, we were giving ten. Not till 1987, 1988, did we start reaching the realization that we had to match or beat competitors."

"Why were you so slow?" I asked him.

"There were several reasons. First, we'd been the most successful carrier by the old set of rules, and there was a great reluctance to change. It was the 'if-it-ain't-broke-don't-fix-it' mentality. George and Marty had lived and died by the classification system and saw, correctly, that the eroding of it would work to the detriment of A-P-A and the other carriers." Although Armand was aware of the anomalies and shortcomings of the old rules, he was still a newcomer, and he was neither then nor is now, any more than his stepfather had been, an autocratic leader who forced his view. Further, he himself was not yet convinced that the Interstate Commerce Commission would carry deregulation to an extreme unintended by the Congressional compromise.

"No one really saw further deregulation as inevitable," Armand said. "And all through this period of time, Arthur had positioned himself as a leading spokesman in the industry against deregulation and for the maintenance of collective rate-making and the classification system and all the trappings of regulation. He testified before Congress, he lobbied with senators and congressmen, he was very vocal on the executive committee of the

American Trucking Associations in urging them to fight harder. So it was a public statement. How can you condemn predatory pricing and then do it yourselves? It wasn't written policy, and it wasn't a directive from Arthur Imperatore, but there was a sense that the company had to support in practice what Arthur was saying in theory."

But A-P-A's stubbornness was more than simply a loyalty to virtues that were suddenly out of fashion. Its company culture, perfectly suited to an era where price competition was irrelevant and efficiency in operations was the vehicle for success, did not suit the new times, which rewarded aggressive marketing. Because of its reputation, A-P-A had never needed to beat the bushes for new business; now that it did need to, it didn't know how. It had taught everyone else how to monitor productivity of its operations people, but sales productivity was hardly supervised at all. No one else had the system of rewards A-P-A had for its operations people; for salespeople, though, it had no such system. A-P-A had helped invent computerized logistics, but that was for operations; it had no electronic database for locating customers to fit its marketing plan; it did not even have a real marketing plan. As the eighties drew on, salespeople became frustrated and disaffected. On the one hand, their old customers were deserting them for price-cutting rivals; on the other, A-P-A was refusing to bend. Thus arose the paradox of a company that for twenty-five years had led the vanguard of its industry, suddenly lagging behind. An operations man who moved to A-P-A a few years ago from a defunct rival, and who is still dazzled by A-P-A's operational mastery and *esprit de corps*, told me, in a still-incredulous half-whisper, that upon his arrival he had found A-P-A's marketing system "antiquated"—for this company, a jarring word.

During Armand's early years, the company's response to the competitive pressures of deregulation was not the marketing response of its rivals, but an operations response: it expanded. Geographical growth could now be accomplished quickly, because there was no need to buy other people's medallions. In 1981 alone, A-P-A opened terminals in Baltimore, Pittsburgh, Buffalo, Richmond, and Lewiston, Maine. Interline connections—freight sharing between carriers operating in adjacent areas—were established with carriers in the Southwest, the Southeast, and later the Northern Plains. A partnership was established with a local carrier in Chicago, and three terminals were opened in Ohio and another across the water in Toronto. A-P-A's overseas operation, which began in Puerto Rico, grew to include Europe, the Pacific, and eventually Africa. Taking advantage of other new operating freedoms, A-P-A rationalized its routes, began shipping freight long distance by private carriers that would otherwise be returning home empty, and started moving its own empties by railroad.

Meanwhile, the beleaguered Teamsters, who had won no raise in wages at all under the 1982 National Master Freight Agreement, succeeded in winning raises in 1985 only at the price of acceding to a "tiered" wage, in some areas: new hires would be paid seventy percent of the standard wage during their first year, then eighty percent and ninety percent in their second and third years. Some regions had begun the tiered system in 1982. The result was a labor-cost advantage to companies like A-P-A that were expanding and hiring.

"From 1982 to 1985 we made the most profits ever," Armand said, "because of our growth in new terminals that were covered by agreements with tiered wages." (The new men were paid less.) "But we kept the profits instead of using them for aggressive pricing to get new business in our established areas. Yellow and St. Johnsbury saw the same situation as an opportunity to be more aggressive in pricing new business, but no one here, including myself at the time, was making an aggressive case for that. This was an error on our part. We could have cleaned up. You pay a price for success." Andy Park, who became vice-president for operations after Dick Melosh retired, summed up A-P-A's slowness to change: "I guess we thought we were already good enough."

In 1986, at Arthur's urging, in a final effort to win new market by old methods, A-P-A acquired Sanborn's Motor Express, a Maine-based company half A-P-A's size. For three years, absorption of the new workforce and new freight at new terminals further diverted A-P-A's attention from the price-cutting battlefield.

For a while, the task of merging the two operations was made more difficult because the culture of Sanborn's had been market-oriented—A-P-A's opposite. At Sanborn's, people involved in operations had reported to marketing people, and the company was always ready to dispatch another truck to land a new customer, even if that would make a hash of elegant routes and drop a driver's productivity below standard—something A-P-A had never been willing to do.

Unexpectedly, an influx into A-P-A of sales-driven executives from Sanborn's management turned out to be, perhaps, the most valuable result of A-P-A's acquisition. Encouraged by Dan Solazzo, who was relieved to have at last the backing of knowledgeable allies, and led by Clark Shaw, who had been Sanborn's vice-president for sales, the marketing executives from Sanborn's undertook the task of persuading an operations-driven company to think in terms of marketing. Armand was prepared to listen, acknowledging that "marketing is the area I'm dissatisfied with about my management of things around here." Arthur acquiesced, acknowledging, for his part, that Armand's job had become harder than his had ever been. The company developed a marketing plan, revamped and retrained its salesforce, set sales budgets for each terminal, and entered the price wars in earnest.

But A-P-A is still unwilling to land accounts with no regard whatever to price. It won't follow the practice, now common in the industry, of not assigning overhead to the costs of moving the freight of large national shippers, and "letting the little guy pay the fixed costs." During the past three years, extremes of this sort of aggressive pricing have pushed many trucklines, including A-P-A's large regional rivals, into financial weakness, low or nonexistent profits, increased debt, and financial restructuring. Armand is unwilling to push A-P-A this far. "One key to profit is volume," he says, "but if it's all unprofitable volume, you're doing more work with no better result. If the price is low enough, it can get worse than if you didn't have it. If it's below variable cost, the worst thing that could happen is that the business doubles."

An alternative that is still aggressive and yet not financially reckless is the "niche" strategy: to concentrate on bidding wars for the business of large shippers whose freight fits into the company's existing operational specialties. Here, A-P-A's costs will be lower than its competitors' costs, and therefore pricing, even if still careful, will also be lower. This strategy appeals both to A-P-A's operations people, who are not being asked to overturn their systems for a new account at the expense of predictable service to old accounts, and to the marketing people, who in return for respecting limits are being given the horsepower to pursue at full speed new business that falls within the limits.

Andy Park told me in the spring of 1992, "You have to join the rate-cutting, but you have to review each one. In the last two weeks, we've been asked to bid on two huge pieces of St. Johnsbury's business. One was drums and heavy freight; the other was bulky freight, and for that we would have had to rent high-cube vans. Some of our competition would have taken both and run for it. We went after the first account and bid low there. When times are tough, you really have to be disciplined. We've turned down two huge accounts in the last three months because they didn't fit our mix. Because of this, we've remained more stable than the others. We recognize it's a gamble."

During 1991 and 1992, A-P-A paid for its gamble: its revenues and volume of freight declined slightly. During the first quarter of 1993, however, as this book goes to press, the company's revenues began again to climb, and its volume of freight rose by eight percent. Almost all the new freight has been taken over from financially unstable rivals. Shippers have become nervous about using carriers that are operating at a loss. (Their fears were realized when, in June 1993, St. Johnsbury Trucking, A-P-A's chief rival, announced that it would close.)

After several months of wooing, for example, A-P-A won the drum-and-heavy-freight account Andy referred to, and it is now A-P-A's largest customer. The freight belongs to a Philadelphia-based chemical manufacturer, Rohm and Haas. The account exemplifies A-P-A's new compromise between operations and marketing. Rohm and Haas' drums already fit the mix—A-P-A has always moved drums of chemicals—but some of the heavy freight, consisting of over-long skids of plastic sheeting, has required new procedures on the dock. (Carl Center has extensions on his hilo blades now to move the long skids, which are awkward and which don't slip easily between the carts that jounce along the dragline. The plastic sheeting is easily damaged and nothing can be piled on top of it to properly cube out. The mix has had to shift a little.)

A-P-A could pursue the Rohm and Haas account because conservative operations people are now willing to alter their patterns, within limits. But A-P-A won the account in a bidding competition, according to Clark Shaw, who was the matchmaker in this courtship, because A-P-A is after all still conservative. A-P-A defeated three of its rivals in the bidding by stressing its financial depth, its quality of service, and its sense of its own integrity as a community—values that during the 1980s dropped out of fashion not only in trucking, but throughout American industry. Rohm and Haas, Clark said, is similarly old-fashioned. It and A-P-A "are both very people-oriented," he said. "Both are involved in the quality process, are committed to integrity and honesty, and are conscious of being the best in their niche." Part of A-P-A's marketing strategy now is to seek out other companies that held firm in their sense of self in the face of the financial excesses of the Reagan years. Such companies are natural business partners.

In a sense, to pursue such customers is to turn aggressive marketing on its head. These are the customers who agree that the too-common results of aggressive marketing—extensive layoffs, operational corner cutting, poorly supported growth, and accumulating debt—are bad business. Clark said, "We have recognized that this is a shippers' market and have learned to adapt to that without sacrificing our philosophy or principles. Our marketing strategies have changed, but our philosophy of hard work, integrity, and honesty has not changed. Carriers that have had weak philosophies, or that have let their philosophies weaken under pressure of the market, have failed." This is A-P-A's strongest offense in the bidding wars, just as it was its strength in different circumstances before deregulation.

A-P-A has refused, for example, to conform to the current corporate fashion of "downsizing" to become "lean and mean"—euphemisms that paint wholesale layoffs with the panache of sports training. Like Robert Owen, who refused to lay off his textile workers during the cotton boycott of the War of 1812, Armand considers downsizing destructive. It lowers morale, and therefore productivity and service, he says, and it risks losing skilled and loyal people, who may no longer be available when the time comes to rehire. "In most instances, its better to reduce hours and spread the pain evenly." As always, he's thinking of productivity in terms of output per hour, rather than output per dollar, and he isn't willing to speed the ship by making the crew walk the plank. A-P-A's anniversary trips, its college scholarships, its cash awards for safety and productivity, its over-careful maintenance, and its purchases of first-class equipment continue. The company won't drop costs below the floor that is needed to support its sense of itself.

At length, then, the company has re-formed itself according to the lineaments of a second personality. Arthur and Armand are both moralists and communitarians, but Arthur is an inventor while Armand is a chessplayer. Bob Reichenberg, the company's regional manager for the East Coast terminals, described the contrast for me: "Armand takes well-conceived steps and never has to retreat. Arthur goes forward and back and makes mistakes. Armand seizes opportunities, Arthur makes them." (In the *Confucian Analects*, the Master says: "The cautious seldom err.")

In the spring of 1992, Armand summarized for me the strategy that A-P-A has developed under his leadership. "We are trying to steer a middle course, which is very treacherous, because steering the middle course risks losing market share. Those companies that have increased their market share by deliberate low pricing are now financially in great difficulty. Since we have become more aggressive with price and have moved off the center, we haven't lost market share significantly yet. But competitive pricing is now far more radical than it's ever been, so even taking a middle road has become extreme. This is purely a result of too great a supply of trucks and terminals and a shrinking market. In the Northeast, that shrinking is historical over twenty years and will continue. It's particularly severe because of the recession, so it'll eventually improve somewhat, but the overall decline will continue because the market of unfinished and semi-finished goods of manufacturers is in decline. There will be further fallout in trucking. There are still too many carriers. It is a tense situation for all the carriers, and the result remains to be seen. I don't see myself as particularly qualified to make the decisions we've made, but it's not scientific. It's calculated risk, it's luck. It's our gamble."

⁂

Whether trucking and other forms of transportation ought to be subject to economic regulation, and, if so, how strictly, should really be questions for technocrats schooled in the peculiar complexities of their speciality. Instead, the question has entered the arena of politics, where we prefer battle scenes to considerations of complexity. For the last fifteen years, regulation and deregulation have been flash-points of two philosophies that have been at odds since the beginning of the industrial revolution. Is the purpose of an industrial economy to promote the good of the community, even if that means imposing limits on individual enterprise? If so, then an industrial nation should function more or less as a collective. Or is the purpose of an industrial economy to facilitate the prosperity of individuals, even if that means some individuals will prosper at the expense of many others? If so, then the role of government is to referee the competition.

Opponents of transportation regulation, whose roots lie in nineteenth-century Social Darwinism, argue correctly that before 1980 the Interstate Commerce Commission was overprotective of an anachronistic system of guilds. It fostered the collectivist evils of inefficiency, overcapacity, stagnation, and corruption. Partisans of regulation, whose roots lie both in union socialism and in the progressive tradition of reform, argue rightly that the new regime of transportation laissez-faire promotes such robber-baron evils as merciless exploitation of labor, poor product quality, and neglect of public health and safety. We need to find a balance-point between protectiveness and indifference.

But technocrats can't calculate the formula, because we as a nation haven't been able to tell them where we want the balance to lie. The right point has eluded us not only in the transportation industry but in every industry and in public life. As Robert Bellah and his associates pointed out in *Habits of the Heart,* their illuminating study of American mores, published in 1985, our roots in religious nonconformism, in the political looseness of federalism, and in the frontier have schooled us in individualism and have left us with a distaste for government and a lack of enthusiasm for the public good. On the other hand, we cherish a nostalgic ideal of the close-knit small town and take pride in a heritage of commitment to civic duty. Bellah and his associates concluded: "The tension between self-reliant competitive enterprise and a sense of public solidarity . . . has been the most important unresolved problem in American history."

It is our habit to struggle for resolutions to national dilemmas on the playing field of politics, because politics is our national forum and our national game. To speak of the tension between solidarity and self-reliance is to to invite discussion in political terms, which label communitarianism as left of center and individualism as right of center. The discussion indeed belongs to politics, but only partly. The simplicity of division into left and right falsifies as much as it explains. Arthur Imperatore's insights and achievements, for example, don't lie along this muddled spectrum at all, as he himself found out when he went to Washington in 1981. He is a dissenter; he doesn't accept the premises from which most of us argue. The reason he could create a strong community, one in which individual enterprise could flourish—the reason he could find a balance point—is not that he found a political solution. His focus is elsewhere: on work. It is there that his example is of service to the rest of us.

Our accustomed experience of work is expressed in the Book of Genesis by the story of the two orchard thieves who are expelled from the idleness of paradise, and whose guarantee of a free lunch is replaced by the curse of toil. Even more than it was to the peasant farms from which that story sprang, the experience of work as a curse is endemic to the factory floors and the glass-walled offices of modern industrial society. For most people, work is a burden borne for the sake of a paycheck. For a few others, work is not a field of toil but a highschool football field, a *Nancy* brig, a place to win. Winning is the goal that laissez-faire cheerleaders have been urging upon us as we lose yardage in the global economic game, but the cheer has not been much of an inspiration, because it doesn't ring true. Most people in the working class and the middle class know that "winners" require "losers" for a victory, and that the losers may well include them. Both these models of work, winning and toiling, are forever tied to the models of boss and worker, profit and exploitation, rich and poor. They belong to the class war.

There is another model of work: the model of craft. Craft is practiced for itself, apart from its other purpose of livelihood. A craftsperson desires two kinds of quality: that of process, the working, and that of product, the work. The goals of process are competence, versatility, creativity, and perseverance; the goals of product are utility, elegance, durability, and economical use of resources. Commitment to these goals lies behind Tony DeRosa's friendliness with customers and his drive for the perfect route, behind John Occhiogrosso's tirelessness and his attention to the minutiae, behind Ronnie Parham's patience, concentration, and nerve. In the past, achieving craft goals was called mastery; in the language of corporate management, it is excellence. Arthur's genius was to create a structure that would set aside the work models of winning and toil and would, instead, inspire a zeal for craft. As he told me during our first long interview in the summer of 1990: "When people know that they're being structured and being directed, being looked to for high purpose, they bring it out of themselves willingly without even knowing it. I'm a great believer that people don't know how smart they are. I believe that very strongly. They don't know how versatile they are. To tap that is I think one of our company's great gifts."

Craft is a kind of calling. In the craft tradition, a sense of service to the public good was always part of the artisan's conception of his or her role. The work is sold, but it is also given, as a kind of offering. For the cottage weaver or the village blacksmith—for that matter, for the Neolithic village shaman—to practice a useful skill was to know that one belonged. Class hierarchy may exist and affect one's circumstances, but devotion to craft stands aside from circumstances as something more fundamentally valuable and more universally human. Teilhard de Chardin, who inspired Arthur with his understanding of the spiritual nature of work, expressed it this way: "The closeness of our union with God is in fact defined by the exact fulfilment of the least of our tasks." When Arthur determined that excellence in process and quality in product would be A-P-A's goals, the result, without his really expecting it at first, was the subsidence of the class war after the wildcat strikes against the company in the 1950s, and its gradual replacement by a craft community.

What dozens of Arthur's employees whom I interviewed wanted me to understand, above all else, was their delight in craft and their loyalty to the community of A-P-A. These were the objects of their pride, and they knew them to be the real source of their company's success. Lily Ciolino, night expediter of shipments to Canada for the North Bergen billing department, explained to me: "In my job, I need to trace shipments and help other terminals. I like working with the people. The guys I work with are all terrific. No one is ever mean or crotchety. It's all teamwork. Everyone together makes the team. No one person is important. That's what great about it. I don't mean to sound corny, but A-P-A is a family. You feel like you have a thousand brothers and sisters. That's what makes it special. That's the magic. Arthur must have bottled it, because you don't find it in many places."

Gerry Bratton, manager until 1992 of the North Reading, Massachusetts, terminal, was one of several to suggest an analogy other than the family: "It's like the Marines. You need a few good men. At the middle level of this company there's a camaraderie driven by team goals that's very strong. I don't know if after eighteen years I could do what's just quote-unquote a job."

Bob Reichenberg, the East Coast regional manager, told me: "Being in this company makes people live a notch higher on the ladder of life. A-P-A is a driven company, a driven atmosphere. You don't look to be good, you look to excel. You want higher and higher. If the company ever lacked that, it would fail, because that's its foundation. There's a very, very strong network driven by intensity. You get momentum from this, and it carries you through a fumble."

When craft replaces winning and toil, Ronnie Parham can find road driving an enjoyable thing to do, and Tony DeRosa can pursue his ambition to be happy. Jack Poor, for another example, was a dissatisfied FBI agent twenty years ago when his car ran out of gas on the road outside the Canton terminal and he walked in to ask to use the phone. The intensity of the place intrigued him. He came back to ask for a job. "I didn't much like loading trucks," he recalled, "but I saw that there was something there." Nowadays, as terminal manager, Jack sees running trucks out of Canton as a kind of intellectual game. He recalled: "Like Andy" (Andy Park, vice-president for operations and Jack's boss) "calls me one day and says, 'Why the hell did you put that thing out there?'—We'd put a trailer on the road with only 6,000 pounds on it, and Andy had seen the report.—'Wait a minute, Andy. It was styrofoam insulation panels. For a construction site.'—'Okay,' he said. 'I just don't want you to think I was sleeping.'—'Not at all, sir. I wouldn't think that.'

"It's good," Jack told me. "It keeps you sharp. You don't know when he'll call. It's like a game. I'm not gonna let him catch me. You've got to constantly want to achieve. It's tough. There's never a dull moment because you know that they care. I couldn't work for a company that didn't care. There'd be less stress, but I wouldn't have the satisfaction."

"Trucking is not Sunday school," Arthur told a radio interviewer in 1991, "but the way we do it, the way we have organized the company, the way we've ultimately won the respect of our people, it is very highly civil, very highly moral, a very highly feeling kind of company. After my brother Arnold got killed in 1975, I realized that one of the distinctions that made us different was that we actually felt love in the company. Now it's hard to convince people of that, but we have always aspired to a kind of utopian ideal to build a community, and everything we ever did was designed for that, with that in mind. It's hard to speak of this, but you're asking me direct questions. This is the truth. This is the way we lived. It is the most powerful way to live one's life, and it's the most powerful way, the most effective way, to build our kind of a business."

Marty Marino, the retired director of traffic, told me: "Arthur was tough, and he made you tough. I worked hard for him because I knew he would be a success. And it was fun. I liked a challenge. I wasn't the kind of guy to go home at 5:00 P.M., and I had the brothers' respect. I was doing the job of fifteen guys. We all worked eighteen hours a day. We slept on the desks when it snowed. It was fun. And we were the best, we were number one."

Harold Petsch, Jr., Local 617's business agent, also recalled the 1950s. "I loved the trucks. One-hundred-fifty-four-pounds bags of coffee beans, 200-pound bags of gum arabic, you had to load those things right to the roof. The work was hard but the day went fast and it was fun."

Larry Estes, with whom I rode on his pedal run to the wood-turning mills in western Maine, where he's been driving for forty years, reflected, "If I had to live my life over again, I'd do it the same way. My goal has always been to be a truck driver, and I've loved it. You have to work at being happy."

Bruce Zeman, director of purchasing, said, "It's the crazy equation of A-P-A: you got to like to work, but it's fun. Call it corny if you want. It's an atmosphere that gives people a sense of urgency at every level. It's fun to be here. For some people, in other places, working is agony." Bruce shook his head, perplexed. "That must be terrible."

These people have elevated work to its highest level, where it merges with play. Not always, surely, perhaps not even often, but enough, their work is undistracted by doubt and by conflicting desires. When Jack Poor says he comes in at 8:00 on Saturday morning to catch up on paperwork, and when he looks up at the clock, it's noon, he's describing the energizing, time-effacing absorption of children at their building blocks, and also of spiritual practitioners at their daily tasks. *"Age quod agis,* do what you're doing," the Jesuits say. The Buddhist term is mindfulness.

Entering the next century, as a national community that has continued to fragment, in a world that challenges us on grounds where we have never before met real challenge, we need to forget about winning, and to remember what we know about work. When the goal is to be the best, to build it right, to meet the standard and exceed it, work becomes craft. Then it carries its own meaning, and the paycheck ceases to be the goal, taking instead its sane place—together with dignity, security, and a sense of belonging—as one of the rewards. Such work can bring happiness to individuals and prosperity to society. Through it, in Teilhard de Chardin's words, which Arthur applied to the street-sweeper below his window during our first interview, we make our own soul, and we also collaborate in the completion of the world.

Acknowledgments
and Selected Sources

Interviews were the predominant source for this book. My greatest indebtedness is to Arthur Imperatore and Armand Pohan, for their kindness and openness in submitting to eighteen months of personal and professional questions and in allowing me completely unfettered freedom to travel anywhere in their company and to ask anyone anything. I am similarly indebted to Tony DeRosa, John Occhiogrosso, and Ronnie Parham for their generous patience and frankness. Four other A-P-A drivers—Jim Gillespie and Frank Beenick of the North Bergen terminal, Jimmy Roche of the North Reading, Massachusetts terminal, and Larry Estes of the Scarborough, Maine terminal—kindly welcomed my company and questions on their routes.

Unstinting assistance, as well as untiring answers during repeated interviews, were also granted by Burt Trebour, vice-president for labor and administration; Joe Whelan, personnel director; Bob Reichenberg, East Coast regional manager; Fred Astle, vice-president for finance; Sal Passante, director of North Bergen operations; Dan Solazzo, vice-president for sales; Andy Park, vice-president for operations; Clark Shaw, general sales manager; Sam Chominsky, North Bergen night dock operations manager; Brian Nallen, day dock operations manager; August Pagnozzi, chief industrial engineer; Pete Leota, North Bergen dispatcher; Douglas Dick, director of pricing and traffic; Dave Borngesser, director of safety; Vinny Carnavale, North Bergen city operations manager; Rich Santos, director of marketing; Ken Rice, communications manager; Diana Welch, director of Carib-

bean operations; Julian Capicchioni, maintenance superintendent; Arleen Chwatel, North Bergen billing supervisor; Lilian
Ciolino, Canadian documentation expediter; Jack Poor, Canton
terminal manager, Ron Simmons, Scarborough terminal manager; and Cliff Spear, Scarborough dispatcher. My special thanks
are due also to Maureen Saraceni, secretary to Armand Pohan,
and to Kathleen Husoskey, secretary to Arthur Imperatore.

Others at A-P-A whom I interviewed at somewhat less length
were, in North Bergen, Anna Kortrey; George Bauman, manager
of corporate accounting; Curlee Campbell, dockman; Ted Di-
Guilimi, licensing manager; Tom Downs, international manager;
Jim Dabulis, cargo claims manager; Sam De Piano, retired terminal manager; Kenny DiGrazia, yard switcher; Rich Gaggero,
general maintenance foreman; Gene Jensen, container freight
station manager; Harry Kortrey, linehaul manager; Bobby
MacDonald, city driver; Marty Marino, retired director of traffic;
John Morales, dockman; Danny Martin, chief dispatcher; Andy
Ott, Charlie Trentacosti, Steve Vegliante, and Denis Zanetti, dock
supervisors; Mike Trebour, tower supervisor and later city dispatcher; Bruce Zeman, director of purchasing; Janet Barkley, rating supervisor; and Cecilia Lombardo, Lois Hersh, Maureen
Kiszka, Mary O'Gorman, Helen Tochko, Maureen Gentile, Maureen Campbell, Maria Schiavello, and Doreen Toro, night billers.

Also, at the Canton terminal, Steve Shea and Billy Egan, dock
supervisors, and Bob Jose and Tom Wittles, dispatchers; at the
North Reading terminal, Gerry Bratton, terminal manager, and
Kevin McCauley, regional sales manager; at the Scarborough terminal, Kenny Barrows, night supervisor, Felicia Blanchard, billing clerk, Mike Brown, dockman, Mike McCready, dispatcher,
Ken Higgins, national accounts representative, and Nancy Lane,
sales representative; and at the Bangor terminal, Verne Gettig,
dockman, Red MacDonald, sales representative, Walter McLaine,
terminal manager; and Jack Nelson, night operations manager.
All of these people, without exception, were unhesitatingly frank,
friendly, helpful, and generous with their time.

Of essential help in my understanding of labor relations at
A-P-A were long interviews kindly granted by four officials of
the International Brotherhood of Teamsters: Walter Shea, Inter-

national vice-president until 1991; Bill McKernan, president of Local 617, Jersey City; Harold Petsch, Jr., business agent for Local 617; and George Cashman, president of Local 25, Boston.

Others who provided helpful information through interviews were Commissioners J. J. Simmons III and Karen B. Phillips of the Interstate Commerce Commission; Arthur Bunte, president of Trucking Management, Inc.; William M. Clifford, president of St. Johnsbury Trucking Co.; Lance Primis, president of *The New York Times* Company; Neill Darmstadter, senior traffic engineer, Allen Schaeffer, director of environmental affairs, Clyde Woodle, executive director, Trucking Research Institute, and James C. Harkins, executive director, Regional Common Carrier Conference, all of the American Trucking Associations; John McLeod, director of safety for the Motor Transportation Association of Connecticut; Trooper First Class Louis Heller of the Connecticut State Police; Larry Larned, historian for the Connecticut Department of Transportation; Arthur Adams, transportation historian; Frank Smith, president, Transportation Policy Associates; Rick Barton, president of Barton, Gingold, Eaton, and Anderson, Management Consultants, Portland, Maine; John Cavannis and Martha Casey of the Office of Mobile Sources of the United States Environmental Protection Agency; William Grant of the Hackensack Meadowlands Development Commission; and Barbara Lawrence of the New York Regional Plan Association.

Among written sources, the most important for my purpose concerned transportation deregulation and the International Brotherhood of Teamsters. Both are the subject of numerous writings, many of which are untrustworthy. On deregulation, two balanced and factual studies from academic sources are *Effects of Deregulation on Motor Carriers,* by Nicholas A. Glaskowsky Jr. of the University of Miami School of Business Administration (Westport, Connecticut: Eno Foundation for Transportation, 1990) and *Deregulation and the Decline of the Unionized Trucking Industry,* by Charles R. Perry of the Wharton School (Philadelphia, Pennsylvania: Labor Relations and Public Policy Series No. 28, Industrial Research Unit, The Wharton School, University of

Pennsylvania, 1986). Well-documented studies critical of deregulation include "Running on Empty: Trucking Deregulation and Economic Theory," by Paul Stephen Dempsey of the University of Denver College of Law (*Administrative Law Review*, Spring, 1991) and "Marketing Economies and the Results of Trucking Deregulation in the Less-Than-Truckload Sector," by James P. Rakowski of Memphis State University (*Transportation Journal*, Spring, 1988).

Three books on the Teamsters I found useful are Steven Brill's pioneering muckraker *The Teamsters*, an account of the rape of the union under Frank Fitzsimmons (New York: Simon and Schuster, 1978); James Neff's *Mobbed Up*, an exposé, based largely on FBI files, of further rapine under Jackie Presser (New York: The Atlantic Monthly Press, 1989); and Dan La Botz's *Rank and File Rebellion*, an account of the reform movement within the Teamsters led by the Teamsters for a Democratic Union (New York: Verso Books, 1990). Other helpful sources were *Teamster*, the monthly union magazine published by the Teamsters International, and Phil Primack's series on Billy McCarthy in *The Boston Herald*, June 4, 5, and 6, 1991.

Standard sources of data concerning the trucking industry are the annual *Transportation in America*, compiled by Frank A. Smith and published by the Eno Foundation; the annual *American Trucking Trends*, compiled by the Statistical Analysis Department of the American Trucking Associations; and the independent quarterly *Carrier Reports*. The American Trucking Associations' weekly *Transport Topics* is an unusually well-written and reliable trade journal, and I relied on it often. On safety issues, trade periodicals I consulted were *Commercial Carrier Journal*, *Fleet Manager*, *Fleet Owner*, and *Heavy Duty Trucking*. Notable indictments of the deterioration of trucking safety during the 1980s are "The Scandal of Killer Trucks," by Kenneth Labich, *Fortune*, March 30, 1987, and "A Trucker's Road to Safety and Sanity," by Timothy Barton, *The Wall Street Journal*, December 22, 1987.

I also consulted Gary M. LaBella's *A Glance Back: A History of the American Trucking Industry* (Washington, D.C.: American Trucking Associations, 1977); *National Air Pollutant Emission Estimates, 1940–1989* (Research Triangle Park, North Carolina: United

States Environmental Protection Agency, Office of Air Quality Planning and Standards, 1991); "Lives Upside Down to Help a World Go Round: Working Nights," by Peter T. Kilborn, *The New York Times*, May 16, 1991; and "Job Growth in the Metropolitan Region: Projections to 2015," *The New Century: Forecasts for the Tri-State Region*, Issue Number 2 (New York: The Regional Plan Association, January, 1990).

Books in which I found useful formulations of progressive corporate culture theory were *Theory Z: How American Business Can Meet the Japanese Challenge*, by William Ouchi (Reading, Mass: Addison-Wesley, 1981); *Corporate Cultures: The Rites and Rituals of Corporate Life*, by Terrence E. Deal and Allen A. Kennedy (Reading, Mass: Addison-Wesley, 1982), and *In Search of Excellence: Lessons from America's Best-Run Companies* by Thomas J. Peters and Robert H. Waterman Jr. (New York: Harper and Row, 1982). The best summary I found of Robert Owen's career was contained in *The Worldly Philosophers: The Lives, Times, and Ideas of the Great Economic Thinkers*, by Robert Heilbroner (New York: Simon and Schuster, 1953).

Articles I consulted concerning A-P-A and Arthur Imperatore were, among others, "A-P-A Makes the Short Haul Profitable," *Business Week*, October 6, 1973; "A-P-A Banks on People," by Bart Rawon, *Commercial Car Journal*, February, 1975; "Numero Uno," by Shawn Tully, *New Jersey*, January, 1981; "The Importance of Being Arthur," by Lucien Rhodes, *INC.*, April, 1982; "Ex-Aide is Charging Corruption in U.S. Agency," by Hedrick Smith, *The New York Times*, May 15, 1982; "A Volunteer Ombudsman Tells His Unhappy Story," by Barbara Crossette, *The New York Times*, May 18, 1982; "Proposed 40-Story Office Towers Would Give Weehawken Its Own Skyline," by Thomans J. Lueck, *The New York Times*, April 7, 1984; "Arthur Imperatore's Impossible Dream," by Ilene Dorf, *New Jersey Monthly*, July, 1984; "The New Emperor of the West Bank," by Jonathan Z. Larsen, *New York Magazine*, September 10, 1984; "The Newest Fashion in Urban Transportation: Ferryboats," by Mary B. W. Tabor, *The New York Times*, October 22, 1991; and "Trucker Who Rarely Backs Down," by Jon Nordheimer, *The New York Times*, May 16, 1992.

Finally, three works helped frame the conceptual basis of this book: Pierre Teilhard de Chardin's *The Divine Milieu* (New York: Harper and Row, 1960); *Habits of the Heart: Individualism and Commitment in American Life*, by Robert N. Bellah, Richard Madsen, William M. Sullivan, Ann Swidler, and Steven M. Tipton (New York: Harper and Row, 1985); and *The Confucian Analects*. The words of Father Teilhard repeated by Arthur Imperatore in the first chapter of this book appear on page 60–61 of the English version of *The Divine Milieu*. The quotations which appear in the last chapter of this book are from *Habits of the Heart*, page 256, and from Book IV, Chapters XIX, XX, and XXIII of the *Confucian Analects*. For the Confucian sayings I have modified somewhat James Legge's 1893 translation, available in a 1971 Dover Books reprint.